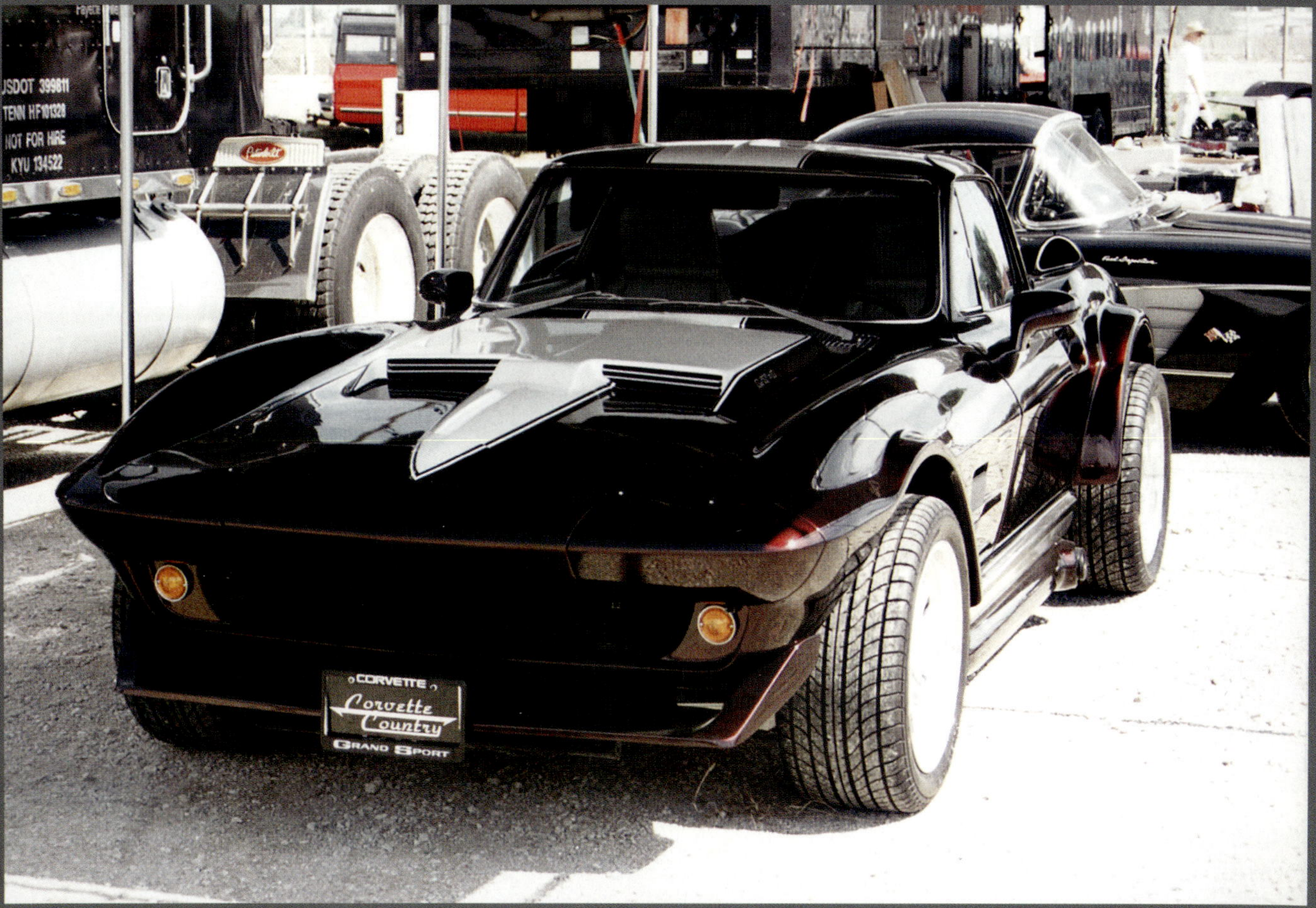

# Restify Your Muscle Car

## High-Performance Projects

Jason Scott

The Complete Street Machine Library®

# Restify Your Muscle Car
## High-Performance Projects

Printed in 2008.

Published by National Street Machine Club under license from MBI Publishing Company.

**Tom Carpenter**
*Creative Director*

**Jen Weaverling**
*Production Editor*

**Julie Cisler, Teresa Marrone**
*Book Design and Production*

**Special thanks to:** Mike Billstein, Terry Casey, Janice Cauley, Scott Parkhurst, and Mark Simpson.

1 2 3 4 5 6 7 8 9 10 / 10 09 08
©Jason Scott, 2006, 2008
ISBN: 978-1-58159-328-0

All rights reserved. No part of this publication may be reproduced, stored in an electronic retrieval system or transmitted in any form or by any means (electronic, mechanical, photocopying, recording or otherwise) without the prior written permission of the copyright owner.

### About the Author

Jason Scott has over 20 years experience overhauling muscle cars for hundreds of articles that have appeared in numerous automotive magazines, including *AutoWeek, Muscle Car Review, Chevy Action!, Mopar Muscle, Mustang Monthly, Chevy Hi-Performance, Corvette Trader,* and *Ford Trader*. His favorite restification testbed is his '69 Chevy Chevelle with its RHS 530-horsepower 427, TCI four-speed automatic, Master Power '86 Corvette four-wheel disc brakes and road-course-ready H-O Racing suspension system. He lives in Saco, Maine, with his wife, Michelle, and two children, Jenna and Cameron. Scott's other books include *Camaro Restoration Guide: 1967–1969; Muscle Car Milestones; Camaro Z-28 and Performance Specials; Original Camaro 1967–1969;* and *How To Tune & Modify Your Camaro, 1982–1998*.

**National Street Machine Club**
12301 Whitewater Drive
Minnetonka, MN 55343
www.streetmachineclub.com

# Contents

Acknowledgments . . . . . . . . . . . . . . . . . . . . . . . . . . . . . . . . . . . . . . . . . . . . . . . . . . . . . . . . . .4
Introduction . . . . . . . . . . . . . . . . . . . . . . . . . . . . . . . . . . . . . . . . . . . . . . . . . . . . . . . . . . . . . .5

**Chapter 1: Planning Your Restoration** — 12

**Chapter 2: Body Building** — 22

**Chapter 3: Interior** — 38

**Chapter 4: Long Block Assembly** — 50

**Chapter 5: Gas and Spark** — 86

**Chapter 6: Cooling and Breathing** — 106

**Chapter 7: Underhood Extras** — 120

**Chapter 8: Drivetrain** — 128

**Chapter 9: Chassis, Suspension, and Steering** — 142

**Chapter 10: Better Brakes** — 162

**Chapter 11: Electrical System** — 176

Appendix . . . . . . . . . . . . . . . . . . . . . . . . . . . . . . . . . . . . . . . . . . . . . . . . . . . . . . . . . . . . .186
Cost Estimate Worksheet . . . . . . . . . . . . . . . . . . . . . . . . . . . . . . . . . . . . . . . . . . . . . . .188
Index . . . . . . . . . . . . . . . . . . . . . . . . . . . . . . . . . . . . . . . . . . . . . . . . . . . . . . . . . . . . . . .190

# Acknowledgments

Like overhauling a car, writing a book often requires assistance from friends and others. Whether tips about how to rebuild a carburetor, or whether a particular paragraph works best before some other, it's always helpful to have someone you can turn to for advice, for guidance.

And so, while some of the information presented on the following pages is based on my own experiences, much of it—most of it, in fact—was generously shared by countless professionals from the restoration and high-performance industries. Through their hints, suggestions, and imparted wisdom, I learned about a vast variety of products and techniques that can be employed to improve high-performance vehicles during restoration.

Recognizing everyone who provided information that made its way into this book would have filled the book and left little room for me to pass on their knowledge. Still, a number of folks' contributions were invaluable and merit heartfelt and sincere thanks.

I credit my mother, Jean Scott, with my first automotive adventures. Were it not for all the Hot Wheels and Matchbox cars she gave me—which I promptly ripped the wheels off to swap them around—I might never have learned the joys of tinkering with cars.

My dad, Milt Scott, took tinkering to new heights with me at his side, working on his Volkswagens, MGs, Mazda RX-7s, and a certain midnight-blue Porsche upon which I learned improper sanding techniques. (Sorry, Dad.)

Frank Juliano and Goodwin Hannaford taught me some of the science (and art) behind performance tuning vehicles, and I likely never would have begun writing books were it not for folks in the automotive magazine business, like Earl Davis, Greg Rager, Tom Corcoran, Tom Wilson, Steve Statham, Donald Farr, Tom Shaw, and Paul Zazarine. Together—and separately—we've spent countless hours discussing our hobby and cars in general. I also need to thank Steve Siegel, another former magazine staffer, for his willingness to flog his rare collection of Hemi Mopars to test various hunches of his own or mine. Steve's cars are some of the finest examples of high-performance restorations I've seen.

I'm also pleased to count as friends, folks like John Carollo, Dave Emanuel, Rod Short, and Bill Holder, with whom I've worked closely on various high-performance, restoration-type projects.

Master restorers Greg Donahue and Roger Gibson have taken precious time out of their schedules to talk shop with me. They've restored some of the rarest and most exquisite muscle cars in existence, and their conversations yielded priceless information.

And then there are all the folks at the various restoration and performance parts companies, who generously provided information and materials for many of the projects discussed throughout this book. Myron Cottrell at Cottrell Racing Engines shed some light on the complicated workings of high-performance engines and how to improve them. Carmen Anastasio at Master Power Brakes gave me an education I'll never forget on muscle car braking systems. Ken Crocie of H-O Racing Specialties and Doug Nordin of Global West Suspension pointed out the various means to enhance stock suspension systems.

While I could go on and on thanking countless others, the above really deserved a moment in whatever spotlight I could shine their way. I hope the rest of you know you have my eternal thanks, as well.

Finally, I have to thank my son, Cameron; my daughter, Jenna; and my wife, Michelle, for their support during the many, many months that I was either locked in my office, typing as fast as my brain and my Mac would let me, or out in the shop bending wrenches like there was no tomorrow. They gave up a lot to let me produce this book, and I'm looking forward to catching up on the time I've missed with each of them.

Thanks, everyone. I couldn't have done it without you. (Again.)

—Jason Scott

# Introduction

What is a high-performance restoration? To some, the emphasis is on the words *high performance*, as exemplified by this 1968 Camaro.

## Restoration Road– How'd We Get Here?

People have been restoring cars since about 10 minutes after the first car had its first fender-bender. Of course, back then, it wasn't considered "restoring" a car—it was just repairing accident damage.

The restoration movement actually got its start when folks started rebuilding early cars. Even then, the goal often wasn't to win trophies or make money, but rather to save money by purchasing a used car and fixing it enough to keep it on the road. Of course, special vehicles—Cords, Packards, Duesenbergs, and the like—which have always attracted a following, were among the first to be sought out with the specific goal of restoring them for recreational, collectible reasons.

Those early restorations were restorations in the truest sense of the word: each part had to be painstakingly repaired and refinished, since replacement parts were scarce and often prohibitively expensive.

When a part was deemed irreparable, a restorer would seek out a repairable version. If they were lucky, such a part might be found at the local salvage yard. As time wore on, though, the salvage yards yielded fewer and fewer treasures, and restorers had to venture further and further from home to find whatever elusive part they needed. A handful of specialty salvage yards, like Bethel's Goat Farm, with its treasure-trove of Pontiac GTO parts, were especially handy ... to the few who knew about them. Car clubs were excellent ways to network with like-minded individuals, while publications like *Hemmings Motor News*, with ads for thousands of parts for vintage vehicles, often yielded just the item you needed.

The Holy Grail of many such parts pursuits was a new-old-stock (NOS) part—a replacement part from the original equipment manufacturer that had somehow never been installed on a vehicle. Such were the days before computers, when parts could linger, forgotten on dealership parts shelves until someone rediscovered them.

Though NOS parts could be expensive (especially if the seller knew what they

To some, the focus in a high-performance restoration should be on the "restoration" aspects, as with this pristine 1969 Dodge Charger 500.

had), they didn't require restoration, or at least needed only a touchup to look and work like new.

But finding NOS parts could be a formidable challenge in the days before the Internet and eBay. Such treasure hunts were as likely to end in frustration as in success. At best, they could take months of legwork, tracking down the someone who someone said someone else thought might possibly have what you were looking for.

One of those "someones" who became known as an expert on a certain model was Len Athanasiades, with his seemingly infinite knowledge of 1969 Pontiac Firebirds. As word spread of Athanasiades' F-body wisdom, he was often called upon by fellow enthusiasts for information or the whereabouts of specific parts for their restorations. Athanasiades kept those folks in mind when hunting for parts for his own Firebird, and when he tripped across a part someone else needed, he purchased it for them. Before long, this hobby turned into a full-time gig, and Athanasiades went into the restoration parts business with his new company, Year One.

By the early 1980s, with the baby-boomer generation yearning to relive the days of their youth, the popularity of muscle cars experienced resurgence, and the demand for replacement parts handily outstripped the supply of NOS parts. So began the era of the reproduction parts market. Companies like Year One, the Paddock, National Parts Depot, Original Parts Group, and others began manufacturing popular parts that had long been out of production—body panels, interior kits, chassis components, trim parts, drivetrain pieces, and more.

Almost overnight, the process of restoring a car changed dramatically. Instead of spending countless hours restoring old parts, you could phone in an order for nearly any part imaginable, pick it up, and just bolt it on. Not only was it possible to restore a car more quickly than ever, the reproduction parts industry made it possible to restore cars that would otherwise have been suitable only as parts cars.

During the 1980s and 1990s, hundreds of thousands of collectible cars were restored, most relying on reproduction parts for one aspect or another of the restoration.

## So, What's a "High-Performance" Restoration?

While restoring a car is generally understood to be the process of returning it to its former original condition, a high-performance restoration seeks to improve its performance, its appearance, or both. You're both restoring and modifying: Restifying!

Muscle cars from the 1960s and 1970s are excellent candidates for these high-performance restorations. Though top performers for their day, by today's standards, their ride quality, handling abilities, braking performance, and even power and drivability are antiquated and crude. Forty years of technological advancements have done wonders in all these areas—and others.

The art of a high-performance restoration is in updating the technology found in older cars in ways that are true to the spirit of those vehicles. In comparison to a wild street machine, a muscle car that's been given the high-performance restoration treatment wouldn't look radical; instead, it would look modern.

The paint scheme on a high-performance restoration project could feature updated hues of the original colors and perhaps some enhanced graphics or pinstripes. Under the hood—which may be replaced with a lighter fiberglass unit that includes a cold-air induction scoop—any number of enhancements could be made to improve engine performance and reliability, while the drivetrain might feature an overdrive transmission and heavy-duty rear axle assembly. Suspension modifications and brake upgrades make for better handling and stopping power, while inside, the seats might have new leather surfaces and the sound system replaced with equipment that's more capable of providing suitable cruising tunes.

A second high-performance restoration approach—and one that is very popular—involves adding equipment a vehicle wasn't originally ordered with, but that was available as an option. Radios, a gauge package, and even color change are prime examples. The end result is a vehicle that looks original, but technically isn't. It's improved to better suit your tastes. Such was the motivation for Year One's founder, Len Athanasiades when he sought to add Trans Am equipment to his standard-fare 1969 Firebird.

Beyond the parts you add to your vehicle, a high-performance restoration should include improving the durability of your vehicle and its components. This might mean taking steps to protect the paint or finish on various parts, or improving the durability of the engine so that it will provide tens or hundreds of thousands of trouble-free miles.

Ironically, with the exception of preserving the appearance, high-performance restorations really aren't that different from what people used to do with vintage vehicles years ago, before they were considered "collectible." Most people added the options they wished they had originally ordered, or they added aftermarket parts to increase performance. Whatever the case, they seldom changed their vehicle's appearance, because they were generally pretty satisfied with how the car looked. After all, style is often a deciding factor in why someone buys one vehicle versus another.

## Rules of the High-Performance Restoration Road

Technically speaking, there aren't any rules to a high-performance restoration—you can basically do whatever you want. But if you don't want people referring to your car as a "street machine" or "modified," there are a few general guidelines you can follow.

The best (and, for many, most fun) definition of high-performance restoration is demonstrated by the likes of this '69 RS/SS Camaro, which features an assortment of high-performance parts, including engine mods, paint and body upgrades, plus aftermarket wheels and tires.

**Above:** The fun part of a high-performance restoration is that the cars are generally (re-)built to be driven. And often that means being driven—hard, like this '68 Mustang . . .

**Left:** . . . or this '65 Mustang GT-350 that's doing what it was built to do—race.

Body-wise, modifications should be reserved so that the overall appearance leans more toward stock than custom. How far your car leans one way or the other, of course, is up to you. But given that most folks cherish classic cars as much for their styling as anything else, keeping things conservative is bound to make resale that much easier—should that need ever arise. Still, features such as shaved door handles with remote entry, a cold-air induction hood, optional spoilers, or oversize billet wheels with low profile tires are just some of the possibilities you might consider for your high-performance restoration.

A second guideline is to limit your modifications to those that can easily be reversed, should you, or a future owner, ever get such an urge. This usually means sticking to bolt-on changes that don't require permanent modifications to the vehicle. In general, it's a good idea to stick to modifications that can be undone in a weekend or less. Wheels and tires, performance intake manifolds, aftermarket exhaust systems, suspension upgrades, and the like are prime examples of high-performance restoration parts.

Another suggestion that may make sense for some of your high-performance restoration upgrades is to camouflage them so they appear to be stock to the uneducated eye. Suspension parts are good examples. Aftermarket shocks are usually a different color than stock shocks, but after a few coats of an appropriate-color spray paint, your high-performance shocks will look every bit as drab as stock units—at least until someone gets up close and personal with them.

Obviously, depending on your preferences, you may find yourself wanting to make more extensive changes—a paint scheme that's a bit on the wild side or a custom interior complete with a thumpin' stereo system. While such changes are relatively permanent, if done tastefully, they can be quite

# Introduction

appealing and can dramatically improve your personal satisfaction with the car or truck.

## The One Cardinal Sin of Restorations

While one popular high-performance restoration approach is adding optional equipment that wasn't originally installed on your particular vehicle, you should never claim or imply that your vehicle is a rare original. There's a simple word that describes that sort of claim: *fraud*. Many times it is the optional equipment that makes a vehicle desirable and thus more valuable. Adding that equipment to your vehicle will have the same effects; however, should someone discover that your claims of originality were false, you could open yourself up to a nasty, embarrassing, and expensive lawsuit.

This is particularly important with respect to rare options, such as dropping a Hemi engine into a Dodge Charger that was originally powered by a 318, or decking out a plain 1969 GTO in a Judge's robes. You can still make these sorts of changes, but most enthusiasts will be more at ease around you if you make every effort to point out that it's not an original Hemi car or an original Judge, but rather has that equipment because that's the way you would have ordered it originally.

## Specific... In a General Sort of Way

While this book was specifically designed to illustrate the pros, cons, and how-tos of high-performance restorations, one thing it won't do is tell you how to perform a high-performance restoration on a 1969 Plymouth GTX, or a 1960 Chevy, or even a 1958 F-series Ford pickup. There's a simple reason for this: You might not own one of these vehicles. You might own a 4-4-2, or a 'Cuda, or a Jeep, or any one of a thousand or so other cars or trucks.

As with the exterior, treating an engine to a high-performance restoration could result in a motor that looks like this bored-and-stroked, balanced and blueprinted small-block Chevy.

Meanwhile, this 426 Hemi looks completely stock. But looks can be deceiving—upgraded pistons, a hotter camshaft, ported cylinder heads, and other changes are impossible to see from the outside.

Even if specific steps to take were described and a list of parts to purchase provided, by the time this book was printed those steps and parts would likely have been superseded by newer, better steps and parts. Fortunately, it isn't necessary to know what kind of vehicle you'll be working on to dispense some invaluable information that will help you improve it. So the information you will find in the various chapters of this guidebook are intentionally a bit vague. While you won't find a finished set of instructions that you can blindly follow, you will learn what types of modifications are usually most beneficial and what features you should look for in the parts you'll buy. This advice applies to any vehicle—car or truck, foreign or domestic.

## Safety Tips

No matter what your goal is during your high-performance restoration project—a show-correct restoration, an outstanding high-performance street car, or an incredible race machine—there is one job that is imperative for each: working safely. If you don't take the time to work safely, you just might not be around—or be able—to enjoy your car when it's complete.

As every mechanic and race car crafter knows, safety often starts with how and where you work on your cars. The ideal setting is a large, well-lit shop with a concrete floor, proper fire extinguishers, a hose, and just about every tool, including air compressors, a vehicle lift system, a chassis dyno, and much, much more. But don't feel bad if your shop doesn't have half that stuff—few shops do, even the professional ones.

Still, some tools are absolutely necessary. For instance, we've all heard the horror stories of jacks that suddenly collapsed, crushing whoever was working under the car because they didn't have the car securely supported on jack stands. If you aren't careful, you could be the example others point to in the future, saying, "See what can happen if you're not careful." Besides, $100 spent at Sears on a decent pair of jack stands and a good hydraulic jack (and other needed safety equipment) could save you thousands on needless hospital bills—thousands that would be much better spent on that trick set of aluminum cylinder heads you've been wanting.

Naturally, the same warning goes for safety-wear. Tales of blindness caused by chemicals that splashed into someone's eyes, amputated fingers, crushed toes, and, yes, even plain old bashed knuckles are all based in fact. No injury is fun, and preventing injuries requires the proper apparel, so get some! Get goggles,

Interiors, too, are good targets for high-performance restorations. This one happens to be a stock-looking Mopar interior, but a number of SE-level items make for a more desirable cockpit.

gloves, face shields, welding aprons, steel-toed boots, and whatever else you need to be safe. And you don't always have to buy everything new; you might be able to borrow them or at least find suitable used safety-wear on eBay or at a local swap meet.

Of course, tools and safety-wear alone won't do the job. You have to work smartly, and you have to have the know-how to use each tool correctly. For jacks and jack stands, that means working on solid, level ground, preferably with a partner around, just in case. When working with torches or with flammable substances near heat sources such as exhaust systems, brake rotors or drums, or even electrical wires, you should always have a proper fire extinguisher *and* a hose close at hand.

Take the extra time and money to get the right tool for the job; screwdrivers are for turning screws, not prying components apart (or pushing together). Using the right tool makes the job a lot easier, and it minimizes your chance of injuring yourself or someone else or damaging your car. It can also make the difference between easily installing a new part and destroying it in the process.

Of course, it also helps to know how certain items come apart and go back together, and it's hard to beat a shop manual for that kind of insight. Likewise, it's worthwhile to pick up books that cover the specific subjects, such as tuning and rebuilding fuel-injection systems or bodywork and paint guides. Reference books, like those available from Motorbooks, an imprint of MBI Publishing Company, can be invaluable tools, maybe the most useful tool in your garage, so make sure you use them and save yourself some hassles.

Ultimately, safety boils down to common sense, and when you're working on cars, a little common sense can save your life. Play it smart and work carefully.

## So What Are You Waiting For?

At this point there's not much else to say except: Dig in!

The book was planned so you could either read it cover to cover, or jump around willy-nilly to the parts that you're most interested in.

Enjoy the book and good luck with your high-performance restoration projects. Start restifying today!

**Chapter 1**

# Planning Your Restoration

**F**ew things in the automotive hobby are as rewarding—or demanding—as restoring a muscle car. Before you begin, take stock of your goals, skills, knowledge, and budget.

Restoring a car is a long, difficult, and expensive process. It's hardly the sort of thing you should just dive into without thinking about how you're going to proceed.

Newspapers, club newsletters, and enthusiast magazines are littered with ads for abandoned restoration projects. Your car may end up in just such an ad, because the project can drag on longer than planned, show little results, and cost more than expected. In the end, you may just lose interest. The best way to avoid that is to develop a realistic plan; one that sets attainable goals for you to work toward.

Naturally, your plan should take into account your budget, what you want to achieve, the time available to you, the workspace available, the tools you have, and other factors. The goal of any good plan should be to minimize surprises, be they delays in the schedule, unforeseen expenses, changes in direction, or others. Surprises are bad news; they catch you off-guard and make you question whether what you're doing is really worthwhile, which, of course, it is.

In addition, your plan should provide a timetable so you can measure your progress. When you're sitting in the middle of your garage floor at 2:30 in the morning, surrounded by hundreds of expensive parts and a vehicle shell, it can be tough to remember that this is fun and that you're actually getting things done. A good timetable is your best defense against feeling overwhelmed.

The hardest part of developing a good plan is making yourself sit down and do it. The individual steps, which we'll cover in detail throughout the rest of this chapter, are easy and can actually be fun.

There is a worksheet in the Appendix that should help you cover most of the bases, but keep in mind they are intentionally generic so they apply to most cars and situations. Try to anticipate specific problems or requirements that you may encounter, and plan accordingly.

Start planning your restoration with the end in mind. This Road Runner's show-quality restoration has very specific needs, in terms of time, parts, processes, and attention to detail.

## What Do You Have in Mind?

Perhaps one of the most fun parts of the plan to think about—and one you've already probably considered—is what you want to do with your car or truck. What parts do you want to restore, repair, rebuild, or replace? What kinds of modifications or changes do you want to make?

You basically have three courses of action when rebuilding your vehicle: a straightforward restoration that returns the vehicle to some previous condition; a complete customization; or something in between, which is what this book is all about.

## Restoration Road

If you choose to restore your car, do yourself a favor and buy a guidebook to help you plan and execute your restoration. Many restoration guides are available for specific models, and they will help you through virtually every phase of your restoration and in dealing with nearly every part of every system.

As you read (or at least skim) through this book, pay particular attention to t he sections that focus on improving the durability of your restoration work: better finishes, tips that help you maintain parts or systems, and other such information.

Of course, you may also want to check out some of the suggested upgrades that can be virtually invisible, yet can make using and driving your classic car or truck much more enjoyable.

Assuming you at least lean toward a majority of restoration (that is, restored or reproduction) parts, you should expect your restoration project to be expensive.

# Planning Your Restoration

The specifics will vary widely, depending on the particular vehicle you'll be restoring, what parts need to be bought or refurbished, and how much of the work you can do yourself.

You should also prepare yourself for the harsh reality that you're likely to spend twice as much restoring your vehicle as it will be worth when you're finished. If you spend $20,000 restoring a nice 1968 Dodge Charger, you would be foolish to expect it to fetch much more than $10,000 if you choose to sell it shortly after completion. (Naturally, the specific options and condition of the vehicle have a great bearing on final value. A 440 Magnum will naturally be worth more than one powered by "just" a 383.)

## Custom Creations

The term *customize* means different things to different people. To some, it's as simple as adding aftermarket wheels, while to others it's fabricating a tube-frame chassis, chopping the top, or gutting the interior and replacing it with artful aluminum panels or unique upholstery. Or all of the above ... and then some.

There really aren't any rules to customizing cars or trucks. Whatever you want is whatever you should do. Your only limitations are your finances, your skills, and your imagination.

Given that freedom, it's hard to expect any book to provide much specific guidance. But that doesn't mean you won't find anything of value in the remaining pages. In fact, the only thing that associates the information in the rest of this book with a high-performance restoration rather than an all-out custom is that most of the described modifications and equipment are intended to be invisible, to appear mostly stock. While a stock or nearly stock appearance isn't of much importance to a custom street machine, the information is still sound and worth considering for your vehicle's buildup.

As with restorations, economics aren't really in favor of custom street machines. The biggest problem is that everyone's tastes are different, so the changes you make may not be desirable to anyone else. You'll have a harder time finding a buyer, let alone one who's willing to pay what you've spent on the car. Fortunately, custom parts typically cost less than comparable resto parts, and the vehicle you'll be starting with can be a cheap, plain-Jane model. That helps, especially if you don't have any intention of selling the vehicle.

## High-Performance Restorations

A vehicle that's been treated to a high-performance restoration is a customized vehicle, but mildly so. The Golden Rule of high-performance restorations is that any modifications should more or less preserve a vehicle's stock appearance. Outside of that, almost anything is fair game. Stock appearance is generally acceptable to most enthusiasts, if only because it gives them a sound foundation on which to do their own customizing or high-performance restoration work.

Expense-wise, bolt-on performance parts are more plentiful and less expensive than most resto parts, so you'll save a few dollars on materials, and you shouldn't encounter any extravagant bills for custom fabrication work. Plus, many parts can be refinished instead of replaced, which is obviously less expensive than buying new parts.

In the end, the car should turn heads wherever it goes, and when it comes time to sell, you shouldn't have any trouble attracting interested

Building a stock-class drag racer, like this '69 GTO, will obviously focus less on detailing and a bit more on durability and performance.

**Left:** While this former SCCA Trans-Am racing '68 Camaro looks great, its restoration concentrated much more on performance. After all, road racing can be very hazardous to a car's sheet metal.

**Above:** An interesting application of the high-performance restoration concept is creating a "clone," like this replica of a '65 Shelby GT-350 Mustang. The owner couldn't afford the real thing, but was able to build an excellent, exact replica. The car was ultimately sold and made a perfect vintage-series road racer—all the fun, but without the risk of destroying a super-rare, real GT-350 in a wreck.

buyers. Anyone who's yearning for a restored *whatever* will see your car as mostly restored, needing only the removal of a few aftermarket performance parts, which can be replaced with restoration-correct items. Meanwhile, anyone looking for a more custom ride will see your car as a great starting point, needing only a few more performance parts. And you'll probably attract a number of buyers who will be satisfied with the vehicle as is.

High-performance restorations also tend to be more flexible in terms of timetables. Assuming you're planning to drive the car when it's completed, there's really nothing to prevent you from driving it while it's a work in progress. For example, if you get the engine and drivetrain completed, you can start driving the car before the body and interior have been worked on. And you can even drive the car as you're rebuilding the interior—so what if you rip out the headliner and have to drive the car while you wait for the new one to arrive? Or perhaps you'll replace the brakes some weekend but have to wait to install new suspension parts. Your new brakes will work just fine without the new suspension parts, so you could drive the car indefinitely until you get around to bolting on the new stabilizer bars, springs, and bushings.

Depending on the changes you're planning to make, you might be able to use used parts purchased from salvage yards for pennies per pound. Interchange manuals can help you locate suitable replacement parts, including stabilizer bars, control arms, seats, consoles, brake system components, tilt-equipped steering columns, and more.

## How Far Do You Want to Go?

One of the hardest decisions you may have to make is how much, or how little, you want to rebuild during your high-performance restoration. It helps to plan this in advance because it allows you to budget your time and money. You can also schedule what projects should be tackled in what order, to minimize expenses and downtime and maximize the quality of your restoration.

Things can get very expensive in a hurry if you first decide to build the car one way, then change your mind and have to redo work that you've already done. For example, if you rebuilt your engine using some modestly upgraded parts, such as a better cam and headers, but then decide you want a fully custom street machine with a race-ready stroker motor, you'll either be rebuilding the engine again, or replacing it entirely. Either way, one thing is sure: you will spend a lot more money than you originally planned.

Some of the work you choose to do may depend on the vehicle you're working on. A car or truck that's in good condition, such as an older restoration or an excellent original, might allow you to focus on the areas that you wish to improve or upgrade. But if you're starting with an unrestored vehicle, you'll obviously have much more work to perform as you repair or replace worn-out or damaged parts.

Of course, it's also possible that your plans may result in completely overhauling a vehicle that's in excellent shape. You need to decide what parts you want to replace, whether they need it or not. For instance, you may choose to overhaul the engine, equipping it with a

# Planning Your Restoration

**Above:** Naturally, your plan has to take into account the condition of the car you'll be working on. Someone else's abandoned "project car," like this '62 Corvette, can be an especially difficult restoration project.

**Right:** Likewise, obviously rough cars, like this rusty Mustang (Rustang?) convertible are like black holes, sucking up vast quantities of time and money.

hotter camshaft, better cylinder heads, a new intake, and headers. Or you might decide to only bolt on the headers for now. Likewise, the body may be in fine shape, but perhaps you want a new suspension system and upgraded wheels and tires. With a high-performance restoration, what you upgrade is largely up to you, but what you choose to work on will have a huge impact on how much your restoration will cost, how long it will take, what tools and skills will be needed, how much space you need to work in, and more.

Another convenience of high-performance restorations is that you can choose to work on your project in stages as time, money, or other resources allow. If you keep your vehicle roadworthy (which includes keeping it safe), you can spread projects out over a number of months or years.

Unrestored cars may require more extensive work, but even then you have choices. For example, the chassis on most cars (even unrestored ones) is usually in good enough condition that it doesn't require extensive repair. Assuming that's true for your vehicle, you may not need to restore its frame, subframe, or unibody structure. You could, instead, focus your efforts and resources on improving the body, interior, and drivetrain. Such a restoration is typically referred to as a cosmetic restoration. On the other hand, if you're extremely detail oriented you may prefer to go the extra mile and fully restore the chassis structure before tackling anything else.

Ultimately, how much of your car or truck you choose to restore is up to you, but defining some goals and plans at the outset can make things easier, less costly, and quicker.

## How Much Can You Afford to Spend?

Whatever your plans, and whatever condition your vehicle is in when you start out, any changes you make will normally depend on your finances. Since few of us have the luxury of endless supplies of disposable income, it pays (if you'll pardon the pun) to figure a budget for your buildup project. The worksheet included in the Appendix can help you plan your budget, but only if you're honest with yourself when you fill it out. It's up to you to stick to your budget once you've established it.

About now, you're probably rolling your eyes and thinking something along

**Below:** A complete, solid "driver," like this '69 Chevelle, makes for a far easier—and less costly—starting point.

**Right:** Restoring original race cars, like this altered '64 Mercury Comet, can present unique challenges, given the many modifications and custom parts.

the lines of: I've got better—and more fun—things to do than waste my time planning a budget. I'll grant that planning a budget isn't exactly exciting, but it's vitally important, because your budget will often dictate some hard decisions. For example, ideally, you might want to rebuild your engine while you're having the body and paint work done. And that's a great plan, unless your budget limits you to doing one or the other. Obviously, knowing this ahead of time can save you some head- and heartaches.

But more than that, knowing what you can afford to do and when you can do it helps you plan a schedule. If you can't have the bodywork done while your engine is being machined, you may be able to spend time beneath the car cleaning, repairing, and detailing the underbody, which doesn't depend on the bodywork being done. Likewise, you could choose that time to work on the interior, replace a few suspension parts, or tackle any number of other tasks.

A budget helps you avoid overspending, too, because you won't be as likely to endlessly dish out money for parts that you weren't planning on buying, nor will you be as likely to spend more for parts than you know you should. It's easy to lose track of how much you're spending, but a budget helps you stay focused, so you don't end up short of funds when bigger, more important tasks need to be paid for.

Some say the best way to determine your budget is to ask yourself one simple question: How much money do I have? Unfortunately, things aren't really that simple. First, your project is probably going to cost far more money than you have available, and that means you basically have three choices: one, you can plan different phases of your project to coincide with times when you predict you'll have extra money (say, after you get a tax refund, if you're lucky enough to get one); two, you can simply plan to save your money until you have more; or three, you can look into getting a loan.

Unfortunately, most lending institutions don't see car restorations as viable investments, so you'll probably have to get a personal loan or take out a second mortgage. The trouble with personal loans is that they're often small—a few thousand dollars or so—and probably won't be enough to finance your entire project.

Saving until you have more money is a terrific idea, but it requires patience and—let's be honest—that's not any fun. If you wanted to wait a few years to start working on your vehicle, you wouldn't be reading this book now.

So that leaves option one: working on your car in phases as money permits—a perfectly acceptable and common way to handle things. It simply means you have to think about which projects to handle when and be willing to spread your project over several months or a few years. In these cases, it often helps to create what accountants would call a cash flow analysis, or a timeline of when you think you'll have enough money to handle the various projects you have planned.

As you plan your budget, be sure you obey the two important criteria: be honest and be conservative.

Honesty is important because it's easy to say, "Well, I'm sure I can find someone who'll do X for me for Y dollars," when you know perfectly well that your odds of having that happen are somewhere between slim and none.

Being conservative means that even if you know you can get a certain part for a certain price, or find someone to provide a specific service for a specific price, estimate high. Between now and when you need the part or service, its price can change. If you aim high and the price remains the same, then you'll be ahead of the game dollar-wise. But if the price goes up and you haven't built in an

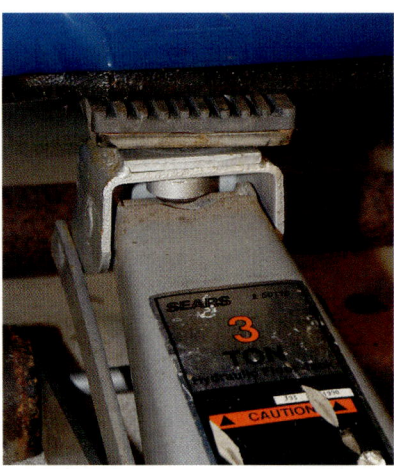

**Left:** Working safely is critical, and the right tools are essential. A heavy-duty floor jack is invaluable. You can even make it "paint friendly" by using a rubber-covered jack pad, like this one from the Eastwood Company.

**Above:** Floor jacks are for lifting, *not* for supporting cars. Never work under a car unless it's properly supported on appropriately rated jack stands. Again, you can make them finish-friendly by simply laying a rag or an old kitchen sponge atop them.

# Planning Your Restoration 19

Restorations require lots of tools—both basic and specialized, like hoists, engine stands, compressors, and more. But you don't always have to own them if you can borrow or rent them.

A camera is an invaluable tool. It lets you take "before" shots that may provide critical insight into how things are supposed to look when you get around to reassembling them days or months later. A digital camera is especially handy, because you can take tons of shots at no expense, and you can refer to them instantly. Plus the photos help document all the hard work you're doing, for posterity.

allowance to compensate, then you'll be over budget in no time.

## How Handy Are You?

This should be obvious, but just in case it's not, restoring a car requires lots of hands-on work, much of which often requires special skills and equipment. If you lack the skills to do the work or you don't have the right tools, not only will it be harder for you to restore your car, but it's more likely you'll be disappointed with the results.

Of course, assuming you're willing to learn as you go, there really isn't any part of your restoration project that you can't tackle on your own. You just need to be willing to take a little longer and possibly settle for imperfect results. Such projects are also the ideal times to learn from friends who have performed the work before on their own projects.

It's rare that any one individual possesses all the skills needed to handle every part of a restoration, and it's important to recognize and surrender to your own limitations. It's usually much wiser and less costly in the long run to let professionals handle the highly visible parts of your restoration—namely, the bodywork and paint job—because mistakes made here may be very noticeable and even more costly to repair. So if you're comfortable with rebuilding your engine but get a little queasy at the thought of upholstery, then tackle the engine yourself and hire someone to do the interior.

Skills alone won't get the work done, however. You also need the right tools for the job, and restoring an entire car or truck will involve working on many parts or systems that require specialty tools. Bodywork in particular uses a number of hand, air, and power tools like panel nibblers, body files, welders, spray guns, and others. Engine builders use torque wrenches, ring compressors, dial indicators, and other tools. Buying all the tools you need probably isn't feasible, especially if you only need them once. You can rent certain tools—engine hoists and stands, transmission jacks—but many specialty tools aren't even popular enough for rental centers to carry. You can borrow them from friends, but some are so esoteric that few people are likely to own them. That brings you back to buying the tools yourself or leaving those jobs to a professional.

Two other resources you will need, even if you are handy and do have the right tools, are the time to do the work yourself and the space in which to do it.

## Got Any Plans for the Next Few Months?

Are you the sort of person who has trouble making and, more important, *keeping* commitments? If so, you might want to consider a different hobby. Cars take time and require a sizable chunk of time and attention to restore and maintain. If you don't want to spend endless hours on your back on a creeper beneath your car, then this just isn't the right hobby for you.

If you're planning to do all or part of the work yourself, you have to carefully examine your social calendar for the next year or so and figure out if you really have the time to devote to your car. If you're willing to give up several dinners a week (or at least settle for fast food eaten with greasy hands), then that's a

Beyond the idea and the car, you'll need a space in which to do the work. Few folks have this extensive a shop, with its lifts and generous space. Smaller spaces—even just a driveway—can work fine, but may require additional time to rearrange things for certain jobs or to wait on the weather.

step in the right direction. Likewise, you can't mind missing several months of your family's life.

When you're thinking about how much time you'll be able to spend on your car, it's likely that once you subtract all your daily and weekly obligations from your calendar—working, sleeping, eating, family time, mowing the lawn, and so on—you'll find you have a lot less time than you imagined. But even if you can only devote three or four hours per week (especially if it's in one large block, such as a Saturday afternoon), you will still make some progress.

One of the keys to feeling good about working with limited time is to tackle smaller projects that can be completed in a short time, and save larger projects for periods when you'll have more time. For example, if you try to tackle rebuilding your engine as a project, it's likely to take many, many weeks if you can only work four hours at a time—it would be almost impossible not to get discouraged. However, if you decide to replace your front suspension one weekend, that's doable. Then, the following weekend you could do the rear suspension, or you might even be able to squeeze both ends into one weekend's resto time, for an even more immediate payoff.

Perhaps the hardest part of managing your resto time is keeping interruptions and delays to a minimum. Kids, spouses, neighbors, and even friends can rob you of your precious restoration time. If you can manage to politely keep others from interrupting you, you should find that you'll be much more productive. Or an alternative is to get them involved in the process; draft them for projects they can handle.

## Space: The Final Frontier

The amount of space you need for working on your car varies, depending on the project (or projects) you're working on, how much you will be doing yourself, and, of course, how much space you have available.

Not only will you need space to work on your car, you also need space to store your new and used parts, which can take up lots of space when they aren't neatly assembled into a car.

It often helps to think of what you'll be doing in and around the car, as you think of how much space you should have. Interior work will likely require at least one and maybe both doors to open fully. So, in addition to a 6- to 7-foot vehicle width, you will need an additional 3 feet or so on each side, for a total of about 13 feet. But even that may not be enough, because 3 feet is a pretty cramped space if you're moving around tool chests, floor jacks, and other equipment that you don't want to hit your car with.

You don't want to try restoring a car without an enclosed workshop or garage of some sort, if only because you will be at the mercy of Mother Nature whenever

## Planning Your Restoration

you want to work. Of course, if it happens to be a beautiful day out, you can always roll your car or truck outside for some fresh air and sunshine.

Ideally, for a full ground-up restoration, you should have at *least* a spacious two-car garage (about 24 feet square or larger) to dedicate to your project. If you don't have a two-car garage, then you won't be able to dedicate that much space. And even if you do have a two-car garage, other factors might prevent you from monopolizing the garage.

In the real world, you can make do with a cramped one-car garage. You will just have to be careful, and projects will probably take a few minutes longer as you shuffle things around to make space for equipment or access to the vehicle.

The more space you can take over, however, the better off you will be, because you won't have to continually pack up at the end of the day. If you happen to be in the middle of a large project, you can simply leave things where they lay, then pick up where you left off the next day. While it may seem like a small inconvenience to put things away at the end of a job—and get them out again the next time you return to work—that time can quickly add up. If it only takes you 15 minutes to put things away, and another 15 to get them back out, that's 30 minutes out of your already limited work time. Multiply that by a couple of weekends and you're talking several hours of lost time—time that could have been spent working on parts rather than carrying them around.

If you can leave your projects in mid-step, you'll need to prevent others from accidentally disrupting your parts. This is especially important if you happen to lay parts out in a specific order, such as their assembly sequence. Spreading the word that your work area is strictly off-limits can prevent costly accidents or mistakes later on.

One intriguing solution for finding cheap extra work space is using a temporary shelter, such as a Cover-It garage. They're available in several sizes (as well as custom sizes), including a 24-foot-by-24-foot two-car model, and they're inexpensive (a one-car size typically sells for less that $700) compared to building another garage. The steel-pole framework is covered by a heavy-duty plastic-like fabric that's both water- and windproof. It assembles quickly and easily with the help of a friend or two, and it doesn't require any special permits, since they aren't permanent structures. They can be erected over a concrete or paved surface, or you can build an inexpensive wooden floor. Install a propane heater to combat cooler weather, run electrical cords for lights, shop tools, and maybe a radio, and you have a nearly perfect dedicated shop for not a lot of money. When your resto project is finished, you can store your vehicle in it or dismantle and store the garage until you get another project car.

**Below:** You also shouldn't start a restoration without a set of shop manuals for your vehicle. They show you the right way to take things apart and, more importantly, to put them back together.

**Right:** Catalogs, magazines, and books (like this one) are also good to have around. And your favorite Internet search site, like Google or Yahoo!, is a quick way to find good, free advice plus just about any part you could want or need.

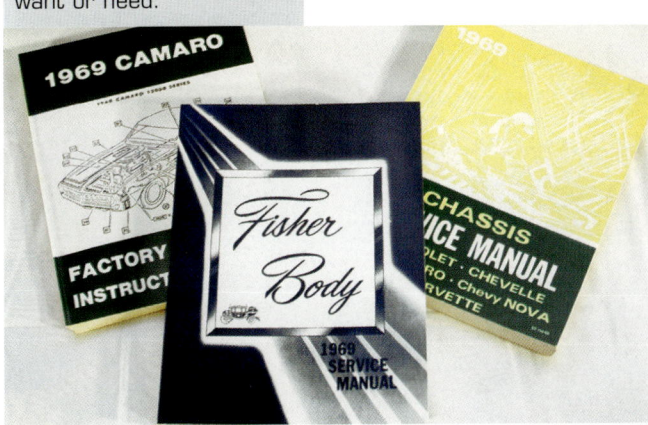

# Chapter 2
# Body Building

The paint and bodywork of your completed project will say more about it than any other aspect. Even if you choose not to perform this work yourself, understanding the labor and technologies involved will better prepare you for your project.

If there is one area where vintage vehicles excel, it is body design. In fact, for most enthusiasts, the sole purpose for owning a particular vehicle is because they like its looks.

Given the high-performance restoration Golden Rule of maintaining a mostly stock appearance, you might wonder what can possibly be done to the body to improve it, without violating that guiding rule. The answer, of course, is quite a bit.

## Paint

For most restorers, the top upgrade is to improve their vehicle's paint.

Factory paint is generally designed to provide a durable, good-looking finish that car buyers will be happy with for many years; and, for the most part, the factory finish usually fulfills those goals. But for enthusiasts, it leaves a bit to be desired.

As good as the original paint was, it was rarely ever perfect, and it didn't last forever. Refinishing your vehicle is a great way to rid the car of any blemishes, thin areas, flaws (such as runs, orange peel, or sags), or simply to improve its luster.

## Paint Types

To many, paint is paint. But nothing could be further from the truth. In reality, there are several different types of paint, and each has its particular set of advantages and disadvantages. It's good to know a bit about the different types of paint available, though, in the end, the choice of materials isn't always as important as choosing who sprays it on; a painter skilled at working with a certain type of paint can make it look as good as any other.

## Lacquers

In the 1950s and 1960s, the high technology for original-equipment finishes was lacquer paint. It was easily applied and lasted like nails. While lacquer paints are still available and offer similar advantages, they are hardly state of the art, nor are they the same as the lacquers of old. In fact, not only have the formulas for lacquer paints changed since the 1960s, but formulas for lacquers are always different between factory finishes

While this may look like a beautifully restored '65 Shelby GT-350, it's really a plain-Jane Mustang that's been treated to a number of "high-performance restoration" body modifications, like the Shelby fiberglass hood and R-model front valance. The wheelwells have also been subtly flared for clearance and appearance.

and refinishing blends, even if the paints are supplied by the same maker. Since factory paints are oven cured, the paint is chemically different than paints used in repair centers and custom paint shops, where vehicles are air dried. So even if you want to use the same paint that your car originally left the factory with, you can't, and couldn't—unless you spent several million dollars on a factory-style paint facility—completely disassemble your vehicle, and duplicate the production painting process.

One of the biggest problems with lacquer-based paint is that it is costly, both for you and for body shops. Because lacquer paints have so many environmentally unfriendly elements (specifically the solvents that help thin the paint for application, then evaporate when the paint dries), body shops have to be extra careful with them. That translates into extra equipment and procedures to keep the process as "green" as possible. All that care adds up to extra costs for you.

But you can't blame environmentalists for lacquer's high costs; it has always cost more than other paints, such as enamels. The reason in the old days was that lacquers required more work after the paint was sprayed. Because lacquers "drop" as the paint dries (picture the colored pigments in the paint like rocks sinking in a pond), lacquer finishes look dull after they dry and require wet sanding or buffing to yield a high-luster finish. The problem is, some lacquers don't set for several days, or even months! That means waiting for the paint to set to finish the job, at which point a body man would get to

This Corvette's body has been upgraded with a number of Grand Sport-inspired panels, along with custom paint and steamroller-sized wheels and tires.

spend quality time buffing—perhaps several times, with different polishes—to achieve the desired results. All that time costs money, so lacquer finishes are traditionally more expensive.

Beyond the cost of applying a finish, lacquers are easily damaged by contaminants. Bird droppings, bug splatter, acid or alkaline rain, gasoline, and other substances can literally soak into a lacquer finish, permanently damaging it.

## Enamels

The original alternative to lacquer paints is enamel-based paints. Unlike lacquers, enamels go on in fewer, thicker coats that dry relatively slowly. These two characteristics make the paint unsuitable for production use, and they require advanced skills to apply. Enamels have the advantage of drying with a ready-to-go finish and require little, if any, buffing (other than to remove any contaminants that may have landed in the still-wet paint as it dried), and that means a lower cost.

In addition, quality enamel paints also leave a durable finish that better resists damage from contaminants, because the molecules of enamel paints chemically bond to each other during drying. Two-part enamels require a hardener to cure, and they're very durable. Plus, the hardener causes them to dry faster, which has long been a drawback of enamels.

Some say that two-part enamels are hard to repair, but that's no longer the case. Early two-part enamels were harder to repair, but modern two-part enamels are as easy to work with as any other paint. The drawback of two-part enamels, though, is price. They can easily cost twice that of traditional enamels.

## Waterborne Paints

Modern OE automotive finishes are waterborne, meaning that they do not use caustic solvents to make them sprayable; instead, they use water. The main benefit is that waterborne paints are more environmentally friendly because they dry as the water separating pigment particles evaporates. Overspray, which is typically recaptured, doesn't harm the environment. Waterborne paints even have health benefits for painters because of the lack of harmful vapors (though you still need a quality respirator to avoid coating your lungs with color pigments).

In addition to the health and environmental benefits, waterborne paint, which is basically latex paint, can yield remarkably lustrous finishes, especially for vibrant colors. As the water evaporates, the pigment particles fuse together, forming a glossy, cohesive, plastic-like shell that protects well against contaminants and natural elements, including harsh sunlight that fades other paints.

Waterborne paints aren't all rosy and sweet—they require special equipment and processes to apply properly, and that can increase the costs of working with them. But more and more paint shops have the ability to work with waterborne paints; and they could be an excellent choice for your vehicle.

## Primers

Because primers are completely covered by color coats, many people wrongly assume that the primer used has no effect on the finished paint job. In fact, different primers can dramatically alter the appearance and durability of a finish.

Durability-wise, primers are needed because automotive paints won't adhere well to bare metal. Primers serve as the foundation for subsequent layers of paint. One superior type of primer is what is known as an etching primer. Etching primers chemically bond with the sheet metal, helping to prevent flaking later on.

Primers also have to provide a suitable bonding surface for the paints that will be applied over them. Again, certain

## VIRTUAL PAINT JOBS

Paint jobs take a lot of hard work, a lot of time, and usually a lot of money to do well. So it's a bad thing if you discover that the paint job you had in mind just doesn't look as good as you thought it would.

One way you can save yourself from such horrors is to preview what your car will look like using your personal computer.

Simply load a digitized picture of your car (you can use a digital camera, you can scan a traditional photograph, or most photo developers can put an image on disk for you for a minimal cost) into almost any computer painting program (Adobe's Photoshop is the industry standard, but much less expensive packages can do a good job). Then, select a color that approximates the color you want and digitally repaint your car.

You can try adding stripes, painting the bumpers, de-chroming the car, using two-tone paint schemes, and more.

One fun way to kill time is to experiment planning different colors for your muscle car's bodywork using your PC. Whether you scan in a line-art sketch and digitally "paint" it or use a free online tool like American Racing Equipment's website, you can quickly get an idea how your car will look in different hues.

If your painting program uses "layers" (think of them as sheets of transparent plastic you can lay over your images), you can make different changes on different layers and quickly compare different looks, without actually altering the original image.

If all this sounds too complicated, American Racing Equipment's website (www.americanracing.com) features a "Wheel Visualization" feature that allows you to select your vehicle (or one close to it) and start clicking on wheels to see what looks good. One of the handier features is the ability to digitally "paint" your vehicle any color you wish. Granted, you can only paint it a single, solid color but it's still good enough to get an idea of what things will look like. And it's as simple as clicking a button.

---

primers are better at this task, but the ultimate choice depends on the paint being applied over them.

When it comes to improving your finish's appearance, primers can smooth the finish *and* alter the vibrancy of colors.

Sanding primers are generally thicker to help fill in minor imperfections in a panel's surface, plus they work better for block sanding to smooth a panel. The smoother a panel is, the smoother the final paint looks. This is especially critical on dark colors, which tend to magnify even the slightest irregularity in a panel's surface.

Primers can also be tinted to more closely match (or even contrast with) the color coats that will be applied over them to subtly shift the paint's color. Generally speaking, light-colored primers make a color more brilliant or vibrant. Primers that are similar in color to the final paint tend to make the color look richer and deeper. Alternatively, as a way to fine-tune a finish color, you could theoretically use a primer that contrasts with the paint color for differing effects. For example, a dark gray or blackish primer used under a red paint would make the paint appear slightly darker.

## Base Coat/Clear Coat Systems

Until the 1980s, mass-produced vehicles typically featured single-layer finishes with color coats that were directly exposed to the elements. Then someone got the idea to spray a few coats of a clear paint over the color coats, and somehow those crude, old single-layer finishes just weren't good enough anymore.

In the beginning, base coat/clear coat finishes were used because they tended to make a finish look deeper. It also gave the paint a fresh, wet look that enthusiasts like.

# Body Building

Then a funny thing happened: people discovered that clear coat finishes didn't just *look* good, they *lasted* well, too. The clear coat (which is actually several coats) makes it easy to repair minor finish imperfections or damage without altering the appearance of the paint, since the color coat is untouched during the repair. The clear coat also worked like suntan lotion for a vehicle's paint, blocking harmful ultraviolet light rays from reaching and discoloring the color coats.

One common misconception of base coat/clear coat finishes is that they result in more paint being applied to the vehicle; this isn't necessarily so. While a traditional single-layer (color only) finish might have had five light coats of color applied to get even but thorough coverage, a base coat/clear coat finish might consist of only three coats of color plus two coats of clear, for the same total number of coats. Of course, you can ask your custom painter to apply additional coats of either the base color or the clear, as long as you're willing to pay for the extra paint and labor.

## Color Your World

While power is probably the first thing that comes to mind when you think about vintage high-performance vehicles, colorful could easily be a close second. Many cars from the 1950s, 1960s, and 1970s were painted in vivid yellows, oranges, greens, purples, teals, and other colors that helped define the era. A car like Pontiac's GTO Judge relied upon its orange-colored Carousel Red paint to attract attention, as did Ford with its Grabber colors, and the Mopar gang with its unique palette.

But there are two inescapable problems that any enthusiast faces when it comes to paint colors: First, your car might not have been painted one of those flashy colors that you like so much; second, you may not like those flashy colors, even if your vehicle is painted with one.

Fortunately, you're considering performing a high-performance restoration, and that means you can modify the vehicle to suit your tastes—not just those of the person who originally ordered it. After all, your car's color could've been picked by a dealership salesperson ordering vehicles for inventory.

One option is to change to an alternate color that the vehicle was originally available in. Your particular car may have been painted Burnished Brown, but you may prefer Daytona Yellow. So have it repainted Daytona Yellow; the car will still look stock, until someone checks the trim tag codes.

If you don't care for any of the colors that were originally available for your vehicle, you can "order off the menu" by picking a color that was available on a different model, a different car line, or a different year. Or, of course, you can pick a custom color.

Ironically, many manufacturers made it possible to special order nonstock colors—or even no color—when ordering a new vehicle. Chevy's Camaro Z/28 was frequently ordered with Corvette-only colors and was given either no paint code on the trim tag or given the special code "—" or the word "SPEC" (for special). Many racers preferred their cars to come through without any paint (since the cars were going to have to be worked on, then custom painted) so the factory happily supplied a vehicle finished in primer only.

Perhaps the most famous examples of creative paint options were the Grabber colors available for 1970 Mustangs. Designer Larry Shinoda was charged with revitalizing the Mustang but had to work within a number of limitations, not the least of which was that colors had to be from "approved" hues. While he didn't have time or money to conduct studies to get new colors approved, Shinoda cleverly realized that Ford had a rainbow of colors that had been "approved" for use ... for other Ford models. The Grabber colors were actually approved choices for fleet vehicles like municipal vehicles or fire trucks.

A basically stock-but-updated body is the hallmark of a high-performance restoration. This '69 Chevelle has been lowered slightly, has been painted a modern hue that's reminiscent of Le Mans Blue, and had numerous emblems removed and their mounting holes filled for a cleaner look.

You should consider two things when contemplating a color change, however: one is that the only good color change is a thorough color change that covers all visible traces of the original color, including in the doorjambs, under the trunk lid, inside the engine compartment, in the cowl area, and elsewhere. Two, whatever you choose for an exterior color, it should complement your interior, whether it's stock or modified.

## Paint Schemes

The automotive world would be a pretty boring place if cars were always single, solid colors. Fortunately, it's not— nor has it been since about the days of Ford's Model T, which was available "in any color you want ... as long as it's black."

During the 1950s, chrome trim was everywhere, in the 1960s stripes became all the rage, and by the 1970s the trend was toward de-chroming vehicles and applying monochromatic finishes. Depending on your individual tastes, you might want to apply one of these looks— or one from another generation, or maybe something completely custom— to your car or truck.

## Copious Chrome

Massive chromed bumpers, plated emblems, and polished trim are the hallmarks of 1950s vehicles, but if you happen to own a vehicle from the 1960s or 1970s, you can easily add such distinctive treatments to your vehicle for a flashy appearance.

Almost any metal part that's small enough to be dunked in a large bathtub-sized chemical bath can be chrome plated. Plastic parts, such as some emblems or body pieces like spoilers or hood scoops, can be given a chrome-like finish that's similar to that applied to plastic model kit parts, but generally of higher quality and with greater durability.

Chrysler was serious about aerodynamics in the 1960s. The 1969 Dodge Charger 500 was their first "aero warrior" and featured a flush-mounted Coronet grille instead of the Charger's usual recessed grille that caught lots of air.

### PRICELESS PAINT—ALMOST (HOW TO GET A GOOD, CHEAP PAINT JOB)

A good paint job doesn't have to cost you a fortune. In fact, there are several ways to get inexpensive paint jobs—even as low as $1,000—that you'll still be proud to show off. Many people have made deals with their paint/body men to promote their shops (often with as little effort as just displaying the shop's business cards at shows) in exchange for a reduced charge.

A more likely route is to have an inexpensive paint shop, such as Maaco, do the paint work. The key to keeping the costs down and getting good results is to do the prep and bodywork yourself. If you're lucky enough that your vehicle doesn't need any bodywork other than sanding and repainting, then this is a pretty easy route. You just remove all the trim, lights, and so on, then all they have to do is paint it. And in most cases, those types of shops can paint well (Lord knows they have lots of practice!); it's usually their prep work that gets rushed and therefore leaves something to be desired.

This same approach can lower your bill at a custom painter's shop—you do as much of the disassembly, prep work, bodywork, and reassembly as you can, leaving them basically just the paint work to charge you for.

Naturally, if you have a friend who's a painter (of cars, not houses), you can barter your services for your friend's services. You could rebuild the friend's engine, if he or she will paint your car. That's often an effective method.

These are just a few ways, and there are undoubtedly others. It's not so unrealistic to get an excellent, cheap paint job. You just have to be ready to do a little work yourself.

No matter what route you take to get an inexpensive paint job, make sure you go to a reputable shop. If you're not sure about how to choose a shop, check out the sidebar on that very subject elsewhere in this chapter.

How and where you apply the additional chrome is your choice. The possibilities will vary from car to car, and even with the particular color of your vehicle. White and black vehicles, for example, don't highlight extra chrome the way bright colors do.

## Super Stripes

Chevrolet is often credited with starting the striping frenzy, though the first Mustangs were available with striping just above their rocker panels, and Carroll Shelby's GT 350 Mustang had its bumper-to-bumper twin racing stripes. Many European GT race cars, such as Ferraris, had asymmetric stripes running the length of their sleek bodies.

Of course, there are countless styles of stripes that you can apply to your vehicle. The broad, full-length Chevy Super Sport style stripes are popular additions, but so are simple pinstripes along the sides.

Pontiac fans might recall the somewhat elaborate stripe scheme applied by the folks at Royal Oak Pontiac to some Royal Bobcat 1969 GTOs. It consisted of a broad stripe that accentuated the GTO's hood bulge and scoops, plus it ran along the lower body, swept up at the front end, then ran rearward as a broad pinstripe along the top of the fender and door, until it ended mid-door with a Royal Pontiac decal.

Ford applied the aforementioned rocker striping to a number of vehicles, plus there were the Mustang C stripes. Bumble-bee stripes were used on the rear of certain Mopars and the front of Chevy's Camaro, and Buick integrated the deck lid spoiler on its GSX models with a bold stripe that ran along both sides of the cars, then swept up and across the spoiler. Then there was Pontiac's Judge stripe scheme—in either the long 1969 style or the eyebrow stripes of 1970–1971. And who could forget the unique striping and decals of the AMC SC/Rambler?

The key is, in a high-performance resto spirit, the stripes should be easily mistaken for stock, since they're not easily removed. That pretty much precludes wild, custom striping jobs that are more appropriate for street or show machines.

Your options are hardly limited. In addition to the vast assortment of stripe schemes you can copy, you can also mix and match two or more stripe schemes, apply them in matching or contrasting colors, or apply them in some color that the factory never envisioned.

On the other hand, removing stripes could also be considered a high-performance restoration enhancement. "Stripe delete" options were available on many vehicles that featured stripes as standard equipment or received stripes with a specific option package.

## Two-Tone Paint

Automakers have long offered two-tone paint schemes, which typically featured the horizontal surfaces of a vehicle's body painted in one color, while the vertical surfaces were another. In many cases, the extra-cost paint job was quite attractive, though that depended on the colors used, the body style, and your preference.

It's easy enough to apply a two-tone paint scheme to your vehicle, using either factory-offered colors or specifying your own custom choices. In addition, you could alter the paint scheme by applying one color to only the lower beltline area, or some other design. Again, because reversing this change would require repainting the vehicle, a high-performance restoration paint scheme should be based on factory-available schemes. But that doesn't mean you couldn't come up with your own two-tone paint treatment that combined styling cues from two or more factory schemes.

## Monochromatic

Pontiac's rubber-nosed 1968 GTO was produced with a monochromatic paint scheme and had minimal bright trim. The

A number of muscle cars, like this '69 Camaro, were available with body-colored front bumpers. For the Camaro, the VE3 "endura" bumper was a rubber-like material, but you can paint your steel bumpers (as was done on the Olds Rallye-350 Cutlass) or replace them with fiberglass versions for a weight savings.

rubber nose was painted body color, rather than chromed (as on its lower-cost Le Mans sibling), and the look was stunning. The front end had a unified appearance that few disliked (except for the early paint problems Pontiac experienced).

Chevrolet followed suit in 1969 with the optional body-colored Endura rubber front bumper for the Camaro, and Pontiac's Firebird made a similar move, though it retained a center chrome grille surround.

The year 1970, however, brought what many enthusiasts consider to be the best executed monochromatic appearance from an auto manufacturer in the form of Oldsmobile's screaming yellow Rallye 350 Cutlass.

Unlike previous GM efforts, the Rallye 350 featured body color front and rear bumpers, and many standard Cutlass trim pieces were toned down or simply left off. The tasteful contrasting striping and "RALLYE 350" graphics made the car that much more appealing.

The monochromatic look generally transfers quite well to vehicles of almost any era, though certain vehicles and colors do not lend themselves to this treatment.

But for vehicles like Dodge's 1970 Charger, the Plymouth Super Bee, the Ford Mustang, and many others, painting the bumpers (at least the front one) the body color is an easy change, and it can be cheaper than having the bumper rechromed.

### The Flat Look

The opposite of the monochromatic look is painting certain body panels in a sharply contrasting color, such as flat black. Ford popularized this technique

## HOW TO CHOOSE A BODY OR PAINT SHOP

Finding a good body shop is like finding a needle in a haystack. Lots of shops can do the job and do it exceptionally well. Lots of shops can complete work on time. For some reason, few can do both. When you find one that can, you've struck gold. Of course, that's easier said than done, but we've learned a few things over the years that might help make finding that elusive "good body shop" just a bit easier.

### Ask Around

Car shows are like fashion shows. When you go to shows—and you should go to as many as you can before and during your restoration process—think of them as auditions for body shops. Find the cars that look good to you, and ask the owner who did the body and paint work and how the experience went. If they were happy with their body shop, they'll be proud to tell you about it. If not, you can bet they'll tell you that too.

### Check References

Okay, this sounds silly, but you really *should* check out a body shop's references. Check with the Better Business Bureau for any complaints against them. Ask for customers' names and phone numbers so you can talk with them and see their cars. Take a quick "shop tour"; it doesn't need to be spotless, but it should at least be organized.

### Consider Your Options

Always check with several body shops for estimates. Most shops will have comparable rates, so don't expect a lot of variation between estimates. If you find someone who's considerably higher or lower than the average, be suspicious. Low rates may mean shoddy work (though not always), while high rates rarely translate into a commensurably better job (though sometimes they do). In short, don't shop on price alone.

### Ask Questions

Never take anything for granted. If you're unsure about something, don't assume they'll do what you think is right. Ask about it. Whether you want to check out your options in terms of body repair, paint materials, or even paint processes, ask. And don't just ask one source—ask several at different shops, so you get a range of experience and opinions.

**Left:** Not long after the Charger 500 hit the track, Dodge added an 18-inch wedge-like nose cone to slice the air on NASCAR's high-banked superspeedways. They even named the car after one of the tracks: the Charger Daytona. A Charger Daytona was the first stock car to exceed 200 miles per hour!

**Right:** Out back, Chrysler gave the Charger 500, Charger Daytona, and the Plymouth Superbird flush-mounted rear windows for a fluid, fastback-like shape.

Some emblems, like this awe-inspiring "Hemi" badge, are highly desirable. But many folks choose to remove their emblems and fill the mounting holes prior to painting, for a clean look.

on several Mustang models, and Chrysler chose the look for Plymouth's Six-Pack lift-off fiberglass hood.

Flat black is also an excellent color for many body accessories, such as the deck lid and lower valence spoilers like the ones on Ford's Boss 302 Mustang, and shaker-style hood scoops found on some Chrysler models. Interestingly, flat black works exceptionally well with lighter colors—white, yellow, or pastel-like colors (such as Ford's Grabber Green, Grabber Orange, or even Grabber Blue)—because the high contrast makes those brighter hues really pop.

At the same time, flat black can work equally well with darker colors—blues, grays, blacks—but in a more subtle manner.

Of course, any color can be sprayed in a flat finish, which can make for interesting combinations. For example, flat maroon stripes or accessories on a glossy red car would be a variation of the monochromatic look. Or flat creme-colored stripes on the same car might look good, too.

## All the Trimmings

Whether you're treating your vehicle to a monochromatic paint scheme or not, you might find it appealing to alter your vehicle's trim.

Most manufacturers applied chrome-plated emblems and bright aluminum or stainless-steel trim to vehicles with reckless abandon in the 1950s, 1960s, and 1970s.

But blacked-out or painted trim—including roof drip rail moldings, wheel arch moldings, emblems, grilles, grille surrounds, headlight surrounds, and other items—can be subtle, yet make a dramatic difference in your vehicle's appearance.

Painting roof drip rail moldings or other trim parts with the body color won't call attention to them. On the other hand, depending on the color of your vehicle, you might want to make them flat black, to contrast with a bright yellow paint job the way the buffed aluminum contrasted with red paint.

Blacked-out grilles were almost standard fare for performance appearance packages, like Chevy's Super Sport models, and they tend to make a nice change for nearly any vehicle. For vehicles that were originally equipped with a chrome grille, spraying it with an appropriate shade of gray (say, light or dark argent) could provide a hard-to-put-your-finger-on difference that really sets your car apart.

On the other hand, you might choose to just remove some of your vehicle's original trim. Replacing the door handles with electric door latch releases gives a nice, clean look. Likewise, removing emblems and thick, lower beltline and wheel arch moldings can simplify the car's appearance even further.

Another high-performance restoration change related to emblems is to make them easily removable to facilitate cleaning (or even replacement, should they become damaged or need repairs). Many emblems had mounting posts that stuck through holes in the body. Sheet-metal speed nuts were typically affixed to the posts on the back side of the body panel, and the installation was considered permanent, since removing the speed nut generally destroyed the soft plastic or die-cast posts.

There are a number of more modern ways of retaining emblems these days, including tube nuts—some of which use a rubber washer to seal out moisture—that

**Left:** Perhaps the most common body upgrade is to bolt on a high-performance hood. Chevy's ZL2 "cowl-induction" hood is perhaps the most copied hood style ever and was a popular option on the 1969 Camaro, on which it debuted.

**Right:** Hood pins have secured race car hoods for nearly half a century, and they're a popular—and simple—high-performance restoration upgrade for fiberglass or steel hoods.

allow you to simply press your emblem on, then pop it back off for cleaning.

Some folks have also had luck drilling small holes through the mounting posts, then using small cotter pins or clips to retain the emblem. Of course, with such a mounting system, in order to remove the emblem you would have to have access to the back of the panel to which it is attached, and that's not always possible.

Another thought is to replace bulky emblems with graphics that are either paint or decals. Many vehicles were later equipped with decals instead of emblems, and those decals can easily be retrofitted onto your older model. Camaros, Mustangs, GTOs, and scores of others are prime candidates for decal graphics.

If later-model decals aren't available for your vehicle, you can have them painted directly on the body, or you can have custom decals made by a local printing or sign-making company.

## Body

One way that automakers often differentiated high-performance models from less special models was by using distinctive body panels or body accessories, such as spoilers, flares, and scoops.

You can do the same thing with your vehicle; however, you are likely to have many more choices available now than the factory envisioned 30 or more years ago.

Ruling out radical custom bodywork, which isn't necessary or suitable for a stock-looking, high-performance restoration, there are essentially just two ways to modify your vehicle's body: to change body panels or to add or remove body accessories.

## Replacement Panels

There are a number of reasons why you might need to install replacement body panels on your vehicle. The most obvious is that your original or existing panels might be damaged or rusted. But even if your panels are in excellent condition, panel replacement might make sense based on how your vehicle will be used or what look you want to achieve.

Automakers often outfitted high-performance models with special hoods to distinguish them from the run-of-the-mill models. Those hoods are easily fitted to same- or similar-year models that didn't feature that hood. In many cases, performance models became readily identifiable by their scoops, including the dual-scooped GTO hoods, shaker-style Ford hoods, the cowl-induction Z/28 hood, the flip-up air grabber Mopar scoops, and others.

Given that most of these hoods appeared during the 1960s, however, when performance was paramount, appearance was sometimes a secondary concern to the performance-enhancement benefits of some body accessories. Most of the aforementioned hoods featured functional ducts or scoops (and sometimes both!) to funnel air to the induction system to increase engine power. The Big Four manufacturers each deployed at least one version of a cold-air induction system on their vehicles.

Today many of these production hoods are available from aftermarket body panel suppliers, along with many designs that were not originally available. In addition, some aftermarket companies have adapted popular hood designs for one vehicle to others that

When mounting painted panels, use plastic washers under the fasteners to prevent chipping the paint. Plastic washers can be sourced from autobody refinishing suppliers, or you can make some by cutting up milk jugs.

# Body Building

Fiberglass (or other composite) panels have long been used to reduce weight. Lightweight hoods, deck lids, door skins, fenders—even complete bodies—are available to replace damaged steel or to shave pounds for racing. This US Body Source fiberglass hood for a third-generation Chevy Nova features an L-88 Corvette-style cold air induction scoop.

Reproduction nose cones are available for Chargers and Plymouth Road Runners. This fiberglass one is from Janak Reproductions. *Janak Reproductions photo*

were never so equipped. The shining example of this is the legendary RPO ZL2 cowl-induction hood that was optional on the 1969 Camaro Z/28. Although the design was originally used only on the 1969 Z/28, over the years, aftermarket companies have grafted the scoop onto hoods for Chevelles, Novas, and even Mustangs.

A third reason for replacing panels is to reduce weight, because (as any racer will tell you) reducing weight is as good as adding power. That makes lightweight panels performance enhancements of another sort.

When it comes to reducing the weight of your body, there are essentially three methods: fiberglass panels, aluminum panels, or thinned sheet-metal panels.

Fiberglass is by far the most common material for high-performance body panels, including hoods, deck lids, fenders, door skins, bumpers, bumper brackets, and even complete body shells! From a manufacturing standpoint, fiberglass is cost-effective to manufacture, plus it makes possible the designs that would be difficult or impossible to produce in stamped sheet metal.

High-quality panels, once prepared and painted, can be indistinguishable from stock panels, yet can weigh considerably less. Fiberglass hoods, for example, typically weigh around 30 pounds, which compares quite favorably to a stock hood that would weigh well over 100 pounds, with hefty hinges, springs, and latch assemblies. And while the ultimate weight savings is realized by retaining the hood using hood pins, most aftermarket panel manufacturers offer reinforced versions for use with hinges (with special, lightweight springs) and traditional latch assemblies.

Although automakers frequently turned to fiberglass for various body panels, there were special projects for which fiberglass wasn't always an option. As most enthusiasts know, the automakers sometimes built limited runs of cars that were specially prepared for use in factory experimental classes. Some of the more popular examples included Ford's Thunderbolts and early 1960s lightweight Pontiacs.

In these instances, the rules for the racing classes often precluded using fiberglass body components. When that was the case, the factories sometimes produced acid-dipped sheetmetal panels, which were considerably thinner than standard panels. A panel that was half as thick would weigh half as much.

Another alternative was to stamp the panels out of aluminum, which is considerably lighter than the steel normally used to produce body panels. Super Duty Pontiacs are, perhaps, the most notable example, though Ford also experimented with aluminum body panels for some FX cars. Such panels are occasionally available in used condition, but you're not likely to find, let alone *afford*, those exotic panels.

Modern aftermarket fiberglass panels tend to be of excellent quality. As always though, you should shop around and try to see the panels in person before you buy them—or at least get a satisfaction guarantee so that you can return them if they don't fit properly or are otherwise unacceptable.

## Body Shells

Aftermarket body shells are available in both factory-style steel and lightweight fiberglass.

Bare body shells typically feature a hefty price tag and need a great deal of time and effort to work with—you are, after all, literally starting from scratch. But all that time and money gets you something pretty unique: a brand new classic car.

If you happen to use a fiberglass body shell, you'll get a couple additional benefits—namely a body that is considerably lighter than a steel body, and one that won't ever rust. Just be aware that while fiberglass body shells are available for a number of vehicles, some, like Mustangs and Camaros, require a tube-frame chassis to set them on because the fiberglass shell can't serve as the unitized or semi-unitized structure of a steel body

**Left:** Rear spoilers were popular options for many muscle cars. This '70 Road Runner features a pedestal-mounted "Go Wing."

**Right:** Camaros are often credited with popularizing deck lid spoilers, like this one that was part of the RPO D80 package (which also included the front "auxiliary valance" air dam).

shell. So that adds to the expense and complexity of your buildup, and moves your car quite a distance from stock.

## Accessory Body Components

Another way that automakers dress up high-performance models and improve performance is by using accessory body components.

Some of the components, such as hideaway headlight doors, are sophisticated mechanical systems that are model and year specific, and thus can't be grafted onto just any vehicle. Though, if you have a donor car, you could swap them to a same- or similar-year vehicle without too much trouble. Such systems were popular options on Pontiac GTOs and Chevrolet Camaros, and were standard on Dodge Chargers, Mercury Cougars, Chevrolets Corvettes, and a handful of additional vehicles.

Other equipment, like the Endura rubber bumpers (also used on GTOs and Camaros, and later Corvettes), were merely a way of adding a subtle improvement to the vehicle's appearance. Of course, the rubber bumpers also tended to resist denting, which helped minimize damage in minor parking lot collisions. They also made for some great television ads. Unfortunately, the parts generally needed to be repainted after even minor encounters, because the bumper material was more flexible than the paint applied to it, despite the addition of flex agents to the paint. Although these rubber bumpers were only available for a few specific models, it is possible to purchase fiberglass bumpers for a number of popular vehicles, at least allowing for a weight savings and a monochromatic paint scheme, although they're actually far more fragile than steel bumpers. It is possible, incidentally, to have fiberglass bumpers chrome-plated in the same manner that plastic components are plated, though it is unlikely a fiberglass part with such a finish would be mistaken for a chromed steel bumper.

The most radical of body appendages were certainly the similar-but-different nose cones of the winged warriors: the Dodge Charger Daytona and Plymouth SuperBird. These massive snouts were bolted to the front of the vehicles and added nearly 18 inches to the length of the cars but rewarded them with a bullet-shaped proboscis that literally sliced through the air and dramatically lowered the drag coefficient of each vehicle.

The vast majority of accessory body panels, however, were merely bolt-on parts that could be affixed to any vehicle with relative ease.

## Spoilers and Air Dams

Rear spoilers are always popular picks, both because they provide visual upgrades and because of their potential performance improvements that result from redirecting airflow around and over the vehicle. In many cases, rear spoilers can be easily mounted to vehicles for which they weren't originally intended.

Some cars—like Camaros, Chargers, and this '69 GTO—were available with a hidden headlight option, which can make for an attractive upgrade if one's available for your car.

# Body Building

Of course, the ultimate rear spoilers were the two-foot-tall wings found on Chryslers "wing cars"—the Dodge Charger Daytona and Plymouth Superbird, like this reproduction unit from Janak Reproductions. *Janak Reproductions photo*

**Left:** Another worthwhile modification for many cars is to add an air dam or front spoiler, like the one adapted to this '63 Chevy II. Done right, an air dam will not only look good, but will prevent air from getting under your car, making it handle better.

**Right:** A number of GM muscle cars were originally available with a hood-mounted tach. Though not terribly practical in the rain or at night, a reproduction model could be just the thing for your car's hood.

The key aspects to check when contemplating installation of a spoiler (either aftermarket or factory designed) are the width and, perhaps, the angle of the spoiler. While the reason for checking the width should be obvious—the spoiler might be too narrow or too wide for your vehicle—the angle of the spoiler is typically dependent on the angle of the deck lid, unless the spoiler is adjustable. In most cases, the spoiler's surface should be horizontal or kicked up in the rear. (Here's an interesting tidbit: according to the late Larry Shinoda, designer of the Boss 302 and Boss 428 Mustangs, all the Boss 302 spoilers that sloped downward toward the rear were installed improperly at the factory—they should have been adjusted to slope upward at the rear.)

Front spoilers, which are often called chin spoilers or air dams, are often specific to a given vehicle design, though some generic aftermarket units are available, and certain factory-style spoilers are generic enough that they could be adapted to other vehicles.

## Brake Ducts and Scoops

A number of scoops were used by automakers and aftermarket tuners (like Carroll Shelby or Baldwin-Motion's Joel Rosen) to use the air flowing around a vehicle to help force-feed cold air into the engine, or to cool various components, including brakes, rear ends, or even the occupants of a vehicle. Ducts were also grafted into fenders of vehicles such as Firebirds, Camaros, and Corvettes to aid in cooling the engine compartment.

## Hood Tachs

Another performance enhancement was the short-lived hood-mounted tachometer. Typically housed in a reverse-facing scoop, hood-mounted tachometers were popularized by Pontiac on its GTO and Firebird models, and on Buick's GSX, and were intended to put the tachometer in the driver's line of sight to minimize the need for a driver to look away from the road (or track) to keep an eye on engine speeds. Some experimental models even included rpm-triggered shift lights. Reproduction units are available today and can be easily grafted onto almost any vehicle, though they do require cutting a sizable hole in your hood (another good reason for an aftermarket fiberglass hood).

Interestingly, Pontiac used a hollowed-out hood tach shell as a rear-facing cowl-induction scoop for a concept car it dubbed the ET (for Elapsed Time), which was to be a stripped-down GTO designed to compete head-to-head with Plymouth's Road Runner. Fortunately (or unfortunately, depending on your perspective) the ET was deemed too barren, so equipment was added back onto it, and the project name was changed to the Judge. The cowl-induction scoop was killed along with the ET.

## Roof Modifications

Few people give much thought to their vehicle's roof, but there are actually a few possible modifications.

Vinyl roofs were popular options and aftermarket add-ons. Some people believed they were classy. Some people thought they made the car look like a convertible with the top up. In any event, they were generally considered to

be attractive, and they were installed on millions of vehicles.

Vinyl tops came in several styles: full, which had material stretching from drip-rail to drip-rail and covered the A-, B- (if equipped), and C-pillars; partial, which left some body color visible on each side of the roof and didn't cover the A-pillars; or landau, which was popularized by Chevy's Monte Carlo and covered approximately just the rear one-third of the roof (the C-pillars and the section of roof between them).

Vinyl tops were and are available in a number of colors and textures. Note, however, that lighter colors can become stained over time when exposed to contaminants or the elements.

In addition to vinyl roofs, some people opted to simply have their vehicle's roof painted a different color from the remainder of the body. Chevrolet offered such an option on the 1969 Camaro. The result gave the appearance of a vinyl roof but with a glossier look. Still, it was somewhat odd, and proved to be unpopular.

### LEXAN = LIGHT-WEIGHT WINDOWS

Drag racers have been using Lexan for their cars' windows for years, because the plastic material is significantly lighter than traditional automotive glass.

While Lexan is perfectly suitable for race-only or show-only modified vehicles, Lexan should never be run on the street because it gets so pitted from sand and road debris that it's difficult to see through it, especially when bright lights shine across it, creating a blinding glare.

In addition, Lexan is not as safe as DOT-approved automotive glass. Flying debris—just a small rock—can crash right through a Lexan window, potentially hitting the driver and causing him or her to lose control of the vehicle.

Last, it deserves mentioning that it is possible to have an aftermarket sunroof installed. However, these rarely result in a factory look (factory sunroofs typically had a sliding glass panel plus a sliding shield to block light from coming through the sunroof) and often resulted in leaks and a weaker body structure.

## Window Upgrades

Few people give much thought to their vehicle's windows, unless they are broken or, in the case of power side windows, malfunctioning. But you can upgrade your vehicle's windows and enjoy your vehicle more.

The most obvious change is to replace standard windows with tinted windows, or to at least tint the installed windows. In spite of the extra expense, there are two good reasons to replace aged windows. First, windows (and windshields especially) are often pitted, scratched, or cracked, so installing new windows will yield better vision with reduced glare. But if the first reason isn't compelling enough, the second reason may be that many states have laws that strictly forbid tinting windows to any shade darker than what was originally available from the factory.

Another change would be to convert manual windows to power windows. If power windows were optional for your vehicle, it would be easiest to find a donor vehicle from which you can pirate the necessary components. Alternatively, you can usually purchase the parts from a restoration parts supplier. You might consider attempting to retrofit a late-model power window motor to older systems because of the increased speed; however, such upgrades are typically custom processes.

Some aftermarket companies produce power window kits for customized hot rods. Such kits are often designed to be somewhat universal, so they can be adapted to almost any vehicle and thus might provide an alternative method of upgrading to power windows. There are two types: one that uses the existing mechanism and drives the original manual crank pin, and one that's a true, custom, weld-in setup.

Lexan windows, like those used in race cars, are a possibility, too. However,

Though hardly exciting, new weatherstripping will look good, plus will cut down on wind noise and rattles.

they don't really look like glass, and you had better check with your state's department of motor vehicles to see whether Lexan windows are street legal where you live. (Lexan windshields generally are not legal; however, some states allow side or rear windows to be made of Lexan.)

## All the Trimmings II

The final body modifications we'll cover for high-performance restorations involve alterations to trim components.

Many vehicles left the factory with an abundance of bright moldings, emblems, and other body hardware. You have the option of adding optional trim to base models, removing excess trim or changing its finish such as by painting the components, or replacing emblems with decals or painted graphics.

In addition to moldings and emblems, though, all vehicles feature at least one outside rearview mirror. A quick and easy upgrade is to install a passenger side mirror, if your vehicle isn't so equipped. A better upgrade is to install remote-controlled mirrors in place of manually adjustable units. Remote mirrors were often factory options, but if they weren't available on your vehicle, you could always retrofit a later-model remote-controlled mirror. Be aware, however, that early remote-controlled mirrors were cable-activated and thus more difficult to adapt than newer electric mirrors.

Finally, there's the antenna, which isn't really a body component at all but a part of your vehicle's audio system. Some vehicles didn't clutter their clean body lines with an antenna, but instead used antenna leads that were integrated into the windshield. Such systems are difficult to adapt to vehicles that weren't equipped with them from the factory, mainly because window designs are typically specific to a certain body design. However, aftermarket hidden antennas, like those available from Dakota Digital, are installed in concealed locations in your vehicle and require no external aerial, yet still provide excellent reception.

Assuming you're stuck using an antenna, though, you can choose between using a manual antenna or an electric unit. Manual antennas are simple and will virtually last forever (unless someone snaps the mast off). Many late-model antennas are designed with a fixed base and a removable mast, however, so broken antennas are an easy, cheap fix.

Electric antennas are high-tech and provide your vehicle with a less-cluttered look when the antenna isn't needed. Unfortunately, since nearly all power antenna systems use plastic gears, it's only a matter a time before the gears break or wear, and the unit quits working. Depending on how and where the unit is mounted, replacement may be difficult.

Speaking of mounting locations, though most antennas are generally mounted to a front fender, some vehicles featured rear-mounted antennas, and there's nothing that says you can't choose to mount your antenna in either location or on a different side than it was originally mounted. It's also easier to access a power antenna unit from inside the trunk if it needs service.

Of course, a high-tech solution to the age-old antenna problem is a hidden antenna, which is really nothing more than a coiled-up antenna that's stuffed inside a little black box you can conceal beneath your car's sheet metal, rather than on top of it.

If you're going to race your car and want to give your sponsors (or companies that donated services) due credit, you can apply stickers to sheet magnets available from sign makers, then just trim to the size of the sticker and apply it to your car. The same can be done with static-cling vinyl for fiberglass or composite panels.

# Chapter 3
# INTERIOR

**W**hen rebuilding your muscle car, don't overlook its interior. After all, it is where you will (should) be spending a great deal of your free time once the project is complete. Altering the interior to your needs will make time spent driving your car much more enjoyable.

If you plan to drive your high-performance car or truck, you'll be sitting in the seats, holding the steering wheel, looking at the gauges, listening to the radio, and just looking around. In short, you'll probably have more contact with your car's interior than any other parts of it. So doesn't it make sense to make it an enjoyable place to be?

For some people, enjoyable may mean restored to 100 percent original condition. If that's what you like, that's what you should do with your interior. But if you would prefer a few changes to your interior, that's precisely what a high-performance restoration is all about: personalizing your car to suit your tastes without significantly altering the overall look that you fell in love with in the first place.

## What Should Be Changed?

A vehicle's interior is so visible that you might be wondering just what kind of changes you can make that won't destroy the car's stock appearance. Surprisingly, there are quite a few subtle changes you can make that most enthusiasts will never notice, but that will dramatically increase your satisfaction with your car.

Of course, deciding what *you* should change is really up to you. You need to assess what aspects of your vehicle's interior you are unsatisfied with.

For some, the seats may be uncomfortable. Or maybe the upholstery just isn't to their liking. Others will be more concerned with upgrading the audio system. Weekend racers may need to add safer seat belts and more gauges to keep a close eye on their car's vital signs. It's a personal decision, so you need to determine just what it is that you want changed.

The following information will outline some of the possibilities and perhaps give you a few ideas about how to carry out some of the changes.

## Seats

Inch for inch and pound for pound, there's no part on your vehicle that you spend more time in contact with than the seats.

During that time, you've probably either learned how to get comfortable

If you drive your muscle car regularly, you'll spend more time looking at its interior than its exterior, so making the car as comfortable and exciting as possible is important.

in your vehicle's seats or come to the conclusion you never will. If you're lucky, you might have actually realized what it is about your seats that you don't like; maybe the cushions aren't firm enough or the seat back angle is too laid back.

Based on that information, you should be able to decide whether restoring your seats will make you happy, whether you need to change your stock seats slightly, or whether you need different seats to be happy.

## Fixing What You've Got

With all the time you spend in your seats, sliding in and out of them, wrenching around to fish money or your wallet out of your pockets, and forgetting about that screwdriver in your pocket before you sit down, it's a wonder your seats have held up as well as they have.

Now that you're restoring your vehicle, though, you have no excuse (except perhaps a lack of money) for not fixing your faded, cracked, or otherwise damaged seats. Reproduction seat covers are available from a number of restoration parts suppliers, as are various trim pieces for seats, including seat backs, headrests, knobs, bezels, and even new foam seat cushions; pretty much everything but the actual seat frame—and even those are available for some cars.

Of course, one of the subtle changes you might make is to change the color of your seats, either to match a new paint color or just for change's sake. Changing seat color is rarely as simple as just

# Interior

Replacing old muscle car seats with newer, more supportive, more adjustable seats is a popular upgrade. One option is to pirate seats from a newer car, like these late-model Camaro seats.

changing the color of the cover, however. You may also have to change headrests, plastic trim panels, or seat backs that won't match. To complete the color change, you would either need to order replacement parts or get vinyl dyes (which are usually applied like a spray paint) to change the color. Note that the dyes typically work best when changing a light color to a dark color.

Another change you may want to consider is upgrading the seat cover material. It's hard to beat the durability of the vinyl that most muscle car seats were covered with, but, as anyone who's ever sat on a sun-baked vinyl seat can tell you, that hot vinyl sometimes leaves a bit to be desired. By contrast, modern-day base seats are usually covered in cloth materials because they don't get scorchingly hot in the summer or bitingly cold in the winter. The cloth also remains flexible in all temperatures, which helps prevent cracking or tearing.

Some older vehicles use eye-catching fabric inserts in otherwise vinyl seats. The famous houndstooth Camaro seats were available in three color combinations—black and white, black and orange, and black and yellow—to match or contrast with different exterior paints.

Cloth fabrics look good, and if professionally installed to closely match the original stitching patterns, the changeover could easily be one of those "hmmm ... something's different here, but I can't quite put my finger on it" sort of changes.

Unfortunately, cloth seat covers can be stained relatively easily and are more difficult to clean. (Vinyl can usually be cleaned with Formula 409 or some other household cleaner.) Instead, cloth seat covers require special cleaners and usually some fast action on your part to keep stains from setting. Still, if you're careful—and who isn't with a car they've spent hundreds or thousands of hours restoring?—the risk of staining your vehicle's cloth seats should be minimal.

If you don't like cloth fabrics, or feel they would be too noticeable as nonoriginal, there is always leather. Custom leather upholstery usually costs more than cloth, but it will look much more like the stock vinyl. Two benefits of leather are the rich feel, and the fact that you'll stick like glue to it if you wear the right clothing (such as a leather jacket). On the other hand, leather will still suffer from essentially the same problems vinyl faces: it gets hot in the summer and cold in the winter, it doesn't stretch very well, it punctures rather easily, and it cracks as it dries out. It's hardly a low-maintenance upholstery material, but it can look great and feel even better.

A good upholsterer should also be able to fashion new seat cushions from firmer foam if that's a concern, or even slightly alter the contour of the seat to provide better support. Your upholsterer may know of other possibilities, as well, so be sure to take a few minutes to discuss things with him or her.

## Musical Chairs

The best way to improve some seats, however, is to replace them.

When it comes to replacement seats, you have three options: install seats that were optionally available when your vehicle was new, retrofit later-model seats to your vehicle, or install aftermarket seats.

Upgrading your stock seats to optional seats may be an attractive option if your vehicle was originally equipped with a bench seat, but you want the more sporting buckets. Or you may want to swap out your stock buckets for a bench seat to save weight or get that bare-bones racer look.

Don't forget about the back seat, either. Many vehicles—particularly

GT-style sports models like the Mustang and Camaro—were available with folding rear seats to increase cargo space. Replacing a nonfolding seat with a folding version is a straightforward swap. Similarly, certain limited-production options offered to homologate a vehicle for competition use were shipped from the factory without a rear seat, to save weight and to discourage buyers from driving their race-bred vehicles on the street. These vehicles typically featured a fully carpeted floorpan in the back to hide the otherwise unfinished look of the steel floorpan.

As auto manufacturers gradually realized that seats need to do more than just provide a place for you to plant your posterior, the manufacturers realized that vintage seats just weren't up to the task—not even the optional deluxe versions. Good seats need to be comfortable to sit in for short trips *and* long ones, and they need to help keep you in place behind the wheel so you can stay in control of your vehicle. So cars started shipping with seats that featured infinitely adjustable seat backs, bottom cushion angles, thigh and lumbar supports, and other features allowing you to dial in the perfect seating position for you—or adjust it after you've been sitting a while, to prevent fatigue. Retrofitting these new OEM seats into older vehicles presents only modest challenges to modify mounting brackets.

Some modern seats offer additional creature comforts, like heating coils to keep your backside warmer in the winter, or even massage features, which are the ultimate for long-distance hauls. Others, like certain Recaro seats offered in Pontiac's mid-1980s Fiero, feature speakers in the headrests to help you get lost in your favorite music as you cruise along. Obviously, these may present additional installation challenges, due to the electronics and any motors or apparatus that also need to be installed as part of the unit.

Aftermarket seats—especially those from manufacturers like Recaro, Sparco, Momo, or Corbeau—are usually designed for performance-driving enthusiasts, so they adjust to suit your body shape and size. They also feature side supports to hold you in place when racing through corners. As a bonus, they typically shave precious weight from your vehicle, compared to stock seats. In fact, many of the high-end OEM seats are actually made by these aftermarket suppliers, but the aftermarket versions typically feature more universal mounting configurations and optional adapters to simplify installation.

Racing-style seats are also a possibility. Though they would be hard to pass off as original (given that they are generally just thin, lightweight shells with a thin vinyl or cloth cover and only minimal padding), if you intend to race your car a lot, or if you prefer the race car seat feel, they may be just the thing for you.

The best thing about seats is that they're fairly easy to remove and replace (usually four bolts are all that secure them), so you could always bolt in the race seats when you're heading

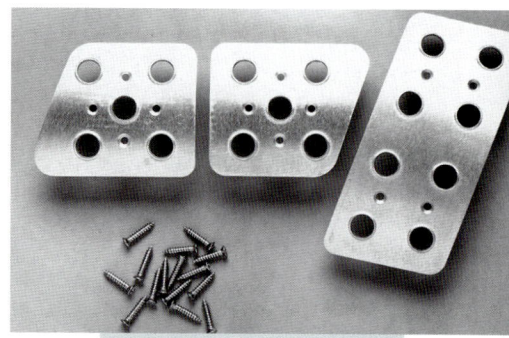

Aluminum pedal pads are an excellent, subtle upgrade for your interior plus make fancy footwork easier to master.

**Left:** Aftermarket performance seats, like this Procar model, are lightweight, offer excellent support, and even have channels through which you can route multipoint seatbelt harnesses.

**Right:** Racing seats forego adjustability to save weight. This is a Procar model. *Procar photo*

# Interior 43

A high-performance car needs high-performance seatbelt harnesses like this 5-point, quick-release set from Autopower. *Autopower photo*

## Seatbelts

Few people think about their vehicle's seatbelts. That's understandable for vehicles manufactured prior to 1967, since few vehicles prior to then actually had seatbelts, at least not as standard equipment. Today, of course, we know the value of wearing seatbelts. They can save your life in an accident. With that in mind, it makes sense to have seatbelts and ensure that they're in safe condition.

For vehicles that have seatbelts, you can either purchase new reproduction belts or have your original belts restored. This should be considered a mandatory restoration step for any vehicle, because the stitching on your 30-year-old seatbelts can't possibly be as strong as it once was.

If your vehicle wasn't originally equipped with seatbelts, you should install some. If belts were optionally available for your vehicle, that would be one option; or you could choose to install aftermarket belts.

Early seatbelt systems usually used separate lap and shoulder belts. Although effective, they were hardly convenient or accommodating, given their fixed, nonretractable mountings. Later-model belts integrate the lap and shoulder belts into one harness, with a single buckle, and usually included a retractor to keep the belts snug, but to the track, then reinstall your street seats for cruising or stock/restored seats for shows.

still allow you mobility—unless or until an accident causes the belt to hold fast to prevent you from flailing about. These systems can often be retrofitted to older vehicles.

Finally, you can install racing-style multipoint safety harnesses. A four- or five-point harness may even be required by racing sanctioning bodies if you race your car.

When mounting any seatbelts, use bolts rated for safety-belt use, not just standard bolts. Also, it's a good idea to reinforce the mounting points of the belts to prevent the bolt from pulling through in an accident. A quarter-inch steel plate about the size of a pack of cigarettes is generally sufficient, though a larger plate would obviously provide additional security.

## Door Panels

Your vehicle's door panels and other interior pieces can also be upgraded to make your interior more comfortable, more attractive, more durable, or lighter weight. Aside from simply replacing weary stock panels with fresh reproductions, you could replace your stock panels as part of an interior color-change project. Another option is to re-cover your stock panels with a different material, such as upgrading from vinyl to leather, or possibly switching to a cloth covering.

Your options may depend on the design of your doors and interior, but in general, you're talking about re-covering your original door panels with different material or using the stock material but in a different color.

All-out custom machines might look appropriate with aluminum door panels, but they are a radical appearance change and aren't really in keeping with a high-performance restoration. They also result in a fairly loud interior, which may not be appealing if you drive your vehicle regularly; however, sound deadener applied to the rear of the replacement panel can do wonders to keep down the noise.

## Headliner

If you're changing your interior's color, you may need to change your headliner, as well. Reproduction headliners are available for all the popular vehicles from the 1950s, 1960s, and 1970s and usually in all the popular colors.

If you don't like the material the original headliner was made with, it's also possible for an upholstery shop to replace your headliner with a custom fabric, though this obviously involves more effort (and money). Depending on your headliner's condition and what material it's made of, you may be able to get away with re-dyeing it.

## Carpets

Surprisingly, there are a handful of ways to upgrade your vehicle's floor coverings. According to various restoration parts suppliers, the most popular restoration task is replacing a worn-out carpet with a new reproduction one, and that job (which may or may not be so simple, depending on your vehicle) can dramatically affect the appearance of your car's interior.

If you're considering replacing your carpet, but you're changing the paint or interior color, using a replacement carpet in an appropriate color is a terrific way to make a stock-appearing change.

You may have noticed that modern automotive carpets don't look the same as most vintage ones. If you find yourself preferring modern cut-pile carpets over the old-style looped-pile carpets, it may be possible for an upholsterer to custom install the modern carpeting. Be aware that factory and reproduction carpets are molded to fit the contours of a vehicle's floor pan. A custom installation may not fit as snugly.

When you're replacing your carpet, it's the perfect time to either remove or replace some or all of your sound deadener. In the old days, sound deadener was thick, heavy tarpaper-like material. Today, that same material is available, but so are high-tech replacements like Dynamat, which features a dense, rubber-like material to deaden sound with an aluminized top layer that serves as a heat barrier. Despite the improved sound-deadening qualities, high-tech barriers can actually reduce weight, compared to the stock felt-like paper. Also unlike stock sound deadener, aftermarket sound deadeners often feature an adhesive-coated face to mold them and hold them to the surfaces to which they're applied, which makes them ideal for vertical panels and even hanging surfaces like the underside of the roof, hood, or deck lid.

Of course, if weight is a big concern—and road noise isn't—you could always remove some or all of the sound deadener. The weight reduction can be a significant advantage for racing, but be prepared to hear and feel every pebble that strikes the underside of your floor pan. Heat from the engine and exhaust will also be more noticeable.

A number of special performance models from the 1960s came equipped with rubber floor mats instead of carpets. As simple as that sounds, successfully reproducing the bare race car look does require an impeccably prepared floor pan ... and a very high tolerance for road noise.

## Dash Pads

Most dash pads are molded, padded vinyl, so there's not much you can do with them, short of changing the color to match an interior color change. Color changes can be accomplished by installing a reproduction pad molded in a different color or by re-dyeing your current pad.

If your pad isn't in bad shape but has a small cut or two, you may be able to get away with restoring it with an inexpensive vinyl dashboard repair kit from someplace like the Eastwood Company.

## Steering Wheels

One of the casualties of the automotive industry's switch to air bag–equipped steering wheels is the loss of factory-optional steering wheels (though there's technically no reason they couldn't offer more than one steering wheel, the cost tends to be prohibitive).

In the old days, however, steering wheels were one of the many ways buyers could personalize their vehicles' interior. Instead of a standard steering wheel, a buyer might have had the choice of several different styles available, or the buyer could pick up a custom wheel at the local auto parts place.

So-called "sport" steering wheels were common options, or were usually included with most high-performance

A smaller-diameter, leather-wrapped aftermarket steering wheel like this LeCarra model will compensate for "light" steering feel, plus will improve your grip on the wheel itself. *LeCarra photo*

# Interior 45

One of the more important updates you can make to your interior is adding aftermarket gauges to keep tabs on your high-performance engine. A full complement of gauges should be considered essential, including tachometer, oil pressure, oil temperature, coolant temp, fuel pressure, and volt meter. These gauges are from VDO. *VDO photo*

packages. In addition, real or simulated wood steering wheels were some of the most attractive wheels to ever be installed in cars—even if they weren't particularly well-suited to performance driving, given their slippery feel.

If you're considering upgrading your steering wheel, it is usually easy to swap your wheel for another from the same manufacturer. For example, Mustang steering wheels will usually fit any Ford or Mercury, while a wheel from one GM vehicle will usually fit any other GM vehicle. This means that many late-model, non–air bag wheels will fit your vehicle, which greatly expands your options.

Aftermarket steering wheels are available in a dizzying array of styles to fit nearly any non–air bag-equipped vehicle. You can choose between reproduction-style wooden wheels, leather-wrapped racing-style wheels, or a host of other specialty-type wheels.

It's worth keeping in mind that changing a steering wheel is more than just an aesthetic change. A replacement wheel can not only enhance your ability to grip it, but can also improve the overall feel of how your vehicle handles. A smaller-diameter steering wheel increases the steering effort needed to turn the front wheels and also magnifies feedback from the wheels. A larger-diameter wheel will have the opposite effect. Thus, a new steering wheel can be an important tuning aid, to compensate for poor factory steering systems: if your steering feels too light, swap to a smaller-diameter steering wheel; or if the steering feels too heavy, a larger-diameter steering wheel may help. Unfortunately, since factory steering wheels from the 1950s, 1960s, and early 1970s were rather large in the first place, your only real choice for reducing heavy steering effort may be to change the steering gearbox—perhaps with an aftermarket rack-and-pinion unit to further improve performance.

## Steering Columns

Conventional wisdom might have you thinking, "Oh, c'mon ... there's nothing 'high-performance' about steering columns!" And there probably isn't anything special about your stock one—it merely connects the steering wheel to the steering box.

But steering columns with tilt and telescoping abilities allow you to fine-tune your driving position and therefore can play a significant role in how well you can control your vehicle.

Tilt columns weren't terribly common in the good ol' days, though they were available on some models, primarily as a luxury option. They became noticeably more popular in the 1970s, which should make them fairly easy to find at salvage yards, in inexpensive parts cars, or on eBay.

Telescoping columns, which allow you to alter the fore/aft location of the steering wheel at the flip of a lever, are a rarity even today, though they've been common in Corvettes since the mid-1960s. Again, the benefit is being able to tailor the layout of your car's controls to best fit your needs. The ability to move the steering wheel an inch or so closer or farther away can make a dramatic difference in how you feel behind the wheel.

If you're not able to retrofit a column from a later-model vehicle to your classic one, a number of aftermarket choices exist from companies like Ididit or other vendors of street rod parts. Many can even be painted to match your interior, allowing them to blend right in.

## Consoles

There isn't much that can be said about floor-mounted consoles, other than that you can add one if you don't have one already, or remove one if you do.

Consoles were common options for vehicles with bucket seats, though they were not always included with bucket seat packages. In fact, many stripped-down race vehicles purposely didn't use consoles to minimize cost, complexity, and weight.

If you're contemplating adding a console to your vehicle, you can go with a console that was originally available for your make, model, and year vehicle, or you might adapt a console from an older or newer model vehicle. Aftermarket consoles are also available, though these may be harder to pass off as stock equipment.

Finally, the console may have an impact on the shifter you can use, or the shifter you choose may preclude certain console designs, unless you make modifications.

## Instrument Panels

No high-performance vehicle is complete without a full complement of gauges to inform the driver about the vehicle's vital signs. Fortunately, most performance packages of the 1960s and 1970s included an assortment of instruments, such as tachometer, oil pressure, water temperature, and volt or ammeter. Clocks were usually separate options from the gauge package and may or may not have been available with the gauge package.

If your vehicle doesn't have the usual gauges, you can add them in a couple of ways. The cleanest installation is to get your hands on a factory gauge cluster

Gauge face colors and even typefaces can also contribute significantly to your interior's appearance. These are VDO gauges. *VDO photo*

and swap it for your standard cluster. Note that doing so may require different sending units and possibly even a different wiring harness.

While factory instrument clusters may make for the cleanest installation, they're not necessarily ideal. Aftermarket instruments are typically more accurate and often react more quickly, which could be especially important for engine rpm and fuel or oil pressures.

Blending a factory cluster with aftermarket gauges is one alternative. However, such installations are hardly simple because aftermarket gauges are rarely the same size as factory gauges, which means you'll need to craft some sort of adapter or bezel. Also, many factory gauges combined several gauges into a single pod—such as the old Tic-Toc-Tach, which combined a clock and tachometer—maybe one gauge pod that housed oil pressure, ammeter and fuel level gauges. Few aftermarket instruments incorporate multiple gauges in one unit. But, it is possible to adapt aftermarket gauges to factory instrument panels if you work carefully.

A number of options exist to mount gauges, including custom instrument panels, auxiliary gauge consoles, or specialty mounts like the A-pillar gauge pod being positioned here.

# Interior 47

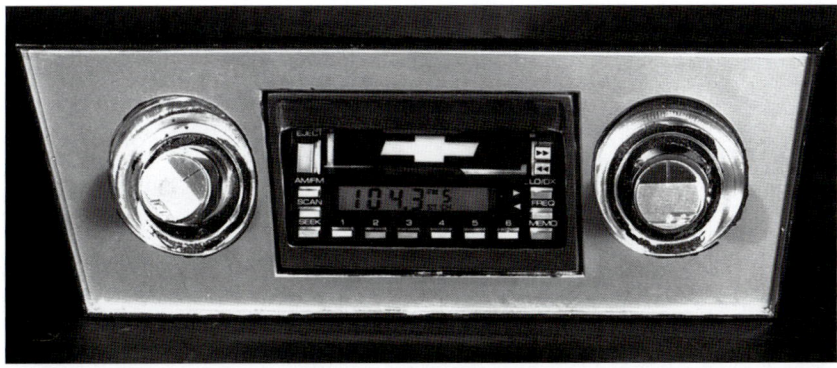

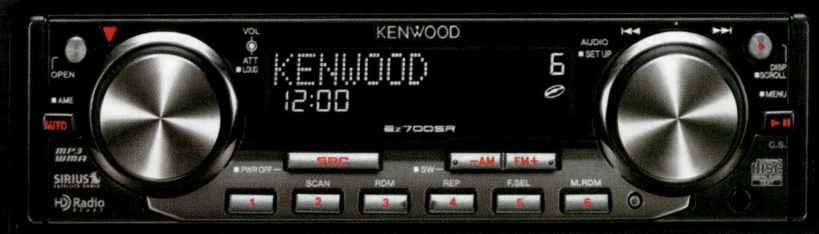

**Top:** Most muscle cars came with AM radios. Custom Autosound offers AM/FM replacements with cassette decks and CD changers. The systems fit in the stock location and, on first glance, even look like vintage radios.

**Above:** If you can't do without good tunes, a number of audio equipment manufacturers, like Kenwood, offer excellent "head units" that will substantially improve your car's audio performance. *Kenwood photo*

Because of the benefits of aftermarket gauges, it may be beneficial to mount some somewhere in your vehicle, even if you're not trying to replace your factory gauges. While it's easy enough to mount auxiliary gauges under the dash with a mounting bezel available from any auto parts store, it hardly looks original, and they're tough to see when driving, which limits their usefulness.

One way to hide the aftermarket gauges is to mount the under-dash bezel on a hinge, to allow you to flip the gauges out of sight when showing the vehicle. Some vehicles have better options, though. For example, Shelby Mustangs mounted auxiliary gauges in a unique hump that fit into the dash pad dip between the left and ride sides of the dash. This gauge pod has been reproduced and can be used to mount gauges. If you're handy with fiberglass, you could create your own gauge pod in a similar fashion.

Another way to conceal them is to steal a page from aftermarket stereos and simply mount them somewhere in your instrument panel but fashion an attractive cover to hide them when you don't want them visible. Of course, this depends on how much space is available in your instrument panel and where it's located. One spot that's often available is the glove compartment, which conveniently features its own cover.

Unfortunately, few glove compartments are in direct line of sight for the driver, which generally makes the glove box a poor place for gauges.

The factories realized that line-of-sight placement of gauges was important, even back in the 1960s. One solution that came from that concept was the hood tach, which was offered on a variety of Pontiac and Buick models, among others. Today, reproduction hood tachs are available and can be adapted to nearly any vehicle.

If your vehicle happens to have a rear-facing hood scoop, such as Chevy's cowl induction scoop, you may be able to mount gauges in the end of the scoop, where they won't detract from your vehicle's appearance, yet are still easily visible from the driver's seat.

Some aftermarket gauge pods are available to mount gauges to the A-pillar. These pods are generally designed for late-model vehicles like Mustangs and Camaros or sport compacts, but they can often be adapted to older vehicles with minimal effort.

Perhaps the ultimate in instrumentation is a heads-up display (HUD). Originally found in multimillion dollar fighter jets, heads-up displays project speed, rpm, or other data against the inside surface of the windshield, resulting in a reflection that appears to float several feet in front of the car—squarely in the driver's line of sight. Apart from F-14 Tomcats, HUDs have been installed in a number of land-based vehicles, including late-model Corvettes plus Olds Cutlass and Pontiac Grand Prix models from the 1980s and 1990s. Unfortunately, those systems are typically tightly integrated with the car's engine control module, making them difficult (if not impossible) to retrofit to low-tech vintage vehicles.

However, aftermarket companies like Défi and SportVue have HUD systems that can be adapted to a variety of vehicles to let you watch your car's instruments while you watch the road.

## Audio Equipment

Stock equipment from the 1950s through the 1970s generally consisted of an AM radio and a single speaker, mounted high in the instrument panel. AM/FM radios were high-tech options, and an eight-track player was cutting

**Left:** Most CD changers, like Kenwood's 10-disc unit here, mount in the trunk but give you plenty of tune capacity and a convenient remote control. *Kenwood photo*

**Right:** Factory speaker systems often consisted of only a single in-dash speaker. Aftermarket speakers, like these Kenwood units, are available in a variety of sizes so you can mount tweeters, midrange, and woofers throughout the car for rich sound in any frequency. *Kenwood photo*

edge for the day. As for speakers, if you were lucky, there may have been an optional one in the rear package tray.

If your car's original radio is an AM-only unit, you could take the same route as many muscle car owners back in the day: add an FM converter. Such adapters were a quick, easy way to add FM functionality to your car. Most folks mounted the converter to the bottom of their instrument panel, but stealthy glove box–mounted installations were also popular. While you're not likely to find a new FM converter, they're frequently available on eBay or in *Hemmings Motor News* for just a few dollars.

The next rung on the upgrade ladder is to install the top-of-the-line audio options that were originally offered for your vehicle. Unfortunately, eight-tracks and monaural sound still leave a bit to be desired.

Companies like Custom Auto Sound make modern AM/FM/cassette stereo systems and CD-changer controllers that are direct replacements for vintage radios, fitting in the stock dash openings without modifications. Many of the stereos even use stock radio knobs for a stealthy appearance.

Those systems will greatly improve your car's audio capabilities without drawing any unwanted attention to themselves.

But if you're interested in taking advantage of the latest car audio technology—remote controls, satellite radio reception, multi-disc CD players, 1000-plus megawatt amps, and iPod connectivity—it's possible to make it almost as much fun to spend time in your car with the engine *off* as with it on.

Obviously, you can replace your stock radio with a high-tech head unit from one of a number of audio component suppliers, such as Blaupunkt, JVC, or Kenwood. While the overall dimensions of today's high-end receivers are generally no bigger than radios of yore, they don't typically feature knobs, which means they won't generally fit the hole in your original dash. This presents two options: enlarge the opening in your original dash or get a replacement dash that you don't mind hacking up, in order to keep your original dash pristine.

Another option for installing a new receiver is leave your stock radio in place—and maybe even functional through the stock speaker, for show purposes—but to conceal your new system. Since instrument panels in most muscle cars were cavernous compared to today's vehicles, and there should be

Boost the power output of your high-performance stereo with an amplifier. Most are mounted in the trunk, as well. This unit is from Kenwood. *Kenwood photo*

plenty of space to tuck components out of the way once you fabricate mounting brackets. If you're concerned about a high-tech head unit sticking out of your dash, you may be able to fashion a cover that blends with your dash to conceal the stereo. Or you could try mounting it in the glove box. Or, you could make the unit removable when not in use, leaving only the wiring harness to conceal.

There's usually plenty of space for other gear elsewhere in the car. Space beneath seats can be used for amplifiers, while speakers can be placed in the kick panels, under the dash, under the package tray, and in the door panels. Or there's always the trunk, which is often the location of choice for killer bass woofers and related gear.

Last, whether you subscribe to the "less is more" theory or not, consider locating or fabricating a radio delete panel and simply remove the stock radio. Radio deletes were available for a number of vehicles in the 1950s, 1960s, and 1970s and today are considered a sign of a true race-bred machine.

## Video Equipment

In-car video systems can add the ultimate creature comfort to your classic car—full-color video right from your favorite seat. Such systems come in a variety of screen sizes and typically either extend from the stereo head-unit or are a separate unit that's designed to be mounted to the roof. The systems often tie into your stereo system for audio capabilities to simplify installation and (hopefully) maximize quality.

## Heating, Ventilation, and Air Conditioning Systems

There are three ways to upgrade your HVAC system: remove it to duplicate a heater delete option; upgrade it with original options such as a rear window defogger (if one was available for your vehicle); and finally, add a modern air conditioning system, such as one available from Vintage Air.

If your vehicle originally had air conditioning, you may want to consider converting it to modern 134A refrigerant from the R12 refrigerant it originally operated on. This change requires a number of new components; however, many companies produce upgrade kits for the restoration and auto repair markets. The parts are designed to be direct replacements and should look close to correct for your vehicle.

## Roll Cages

A final interior modification is to consider installing a roll cage. Obviously, large steel tubes running around your interior aren't going to look stock; however, they may look right at home if the vehicle you're creating is supposed to resemble a vintage race car. Or the General Lee.

If you race your vehicle and it goes fast enough, the race-sanctioning body may require that your car have a roll cage for safety's sake.

It may be possible to install your roll cage so it can be removed and reinstalled as necessary. In fact, some roll cages are designed that way. To improve rear-seat access, some roll cages have removable bars or braces.

If you're forced to install a permanent roll cage, you can camouflage it by either painting it or covering the bars to match your interior. While they won't be invisible, they will blend in better and be less noticeable.

A performance meter, like this Vericom system, can give you a way to gauge your car's power and performance, which can be an invaluable tuning and setup aid.

# Chapter 4
# Long Block Assembly

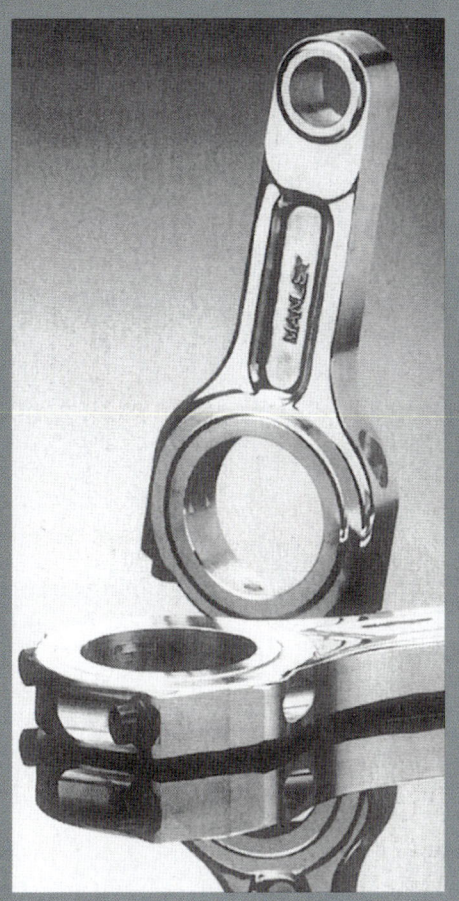
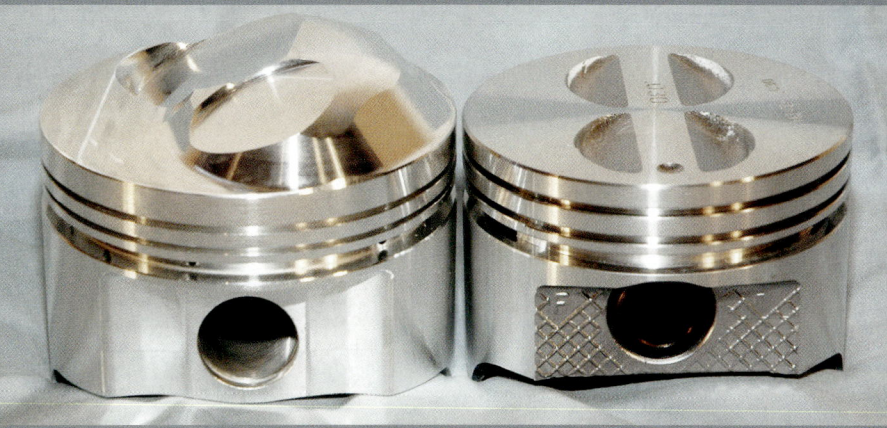

**B**uilding the long block for your muscle car requires careful planning, attention to detail and precision machine work. Getting these features right will ensure a long, trouble-free life for your engine.

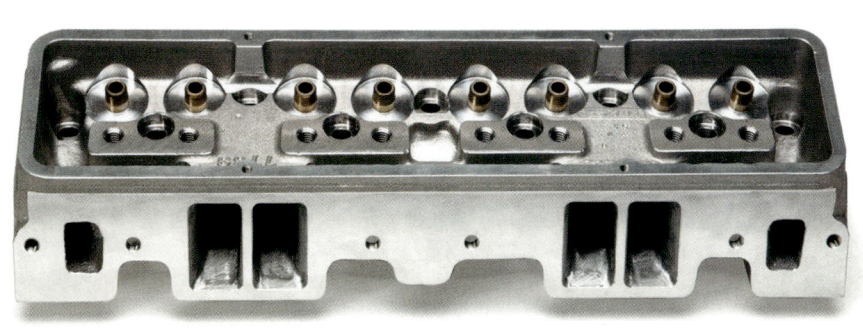

One of the most exciting and most popular parts of any restoration is rebuilding the engine. For many enthusiasts, the engine defines the vehicle's character, its personality, and its purpose. The heart of any engine is the long block, which consists of the block and crank, along with the heads and valvetrain.

Part of what makes an engine so much fun to work on is that there are so many different changes and upgrades you can make, and few of them have little—if any—impact on the engine's appearance. You can double your engine's power output but leave it looking dead-stock.

Even if certain performance parts do change the look of your engine, you can often artfully conceal their presence with just a little creative painting and wire routing. Parts that can't be hidden are generally bolt-on pieces anyway, so if you ever change your mind and want the engine to look stock again, you can swap things back in a jiffy.

The possibilities are endless when it comes to overhauling your engine during a high-performance restoration. A common goal is to simply freshen up a tired engine to restore stock-like performance. Of course, it's at least as popular to enhance the engine with aftermarket performance parts for more power and durability. To illustrate the extremes, you could detune the engine to deliver improved fuel economy and reliability, or build a race-ready stroker motor for high-stakes competition. The choice is up to you—and your finances.

## The Art of Deception

Engines are, perhaps, the easiest aspect of your vehicle to give the high-performance restoration treatment, since most of the parts that you might consider changing to improve performance are normally internal parts and thus unseen, anyway. An engine with forged-aluminum, high-compression pistons or a hot camshaft looks no different than one with cast rods, cast pistons, and a mild cam.

While the rule of thumb for high-performance restorations calls for retaining a generally stock appearance, some car owners prefer to stretch that rule when it comes to engines. After all, an engine isn't generally visible once the hood is closed, so the car will still look stock even if the engine sports a polished, high-rise intake and a set of headers. In fact, it's common to see cars at shows that feature engines dressed up with chrome accessories, aluminum cylinder heads, or other modifications, yet are otherwise completely stock. And more often than not, even modified engines are fairly easy to return to a stock appearance by swapping the stock parts back on.

Speaking of swaps, engine swaps are common upgrades among high-performance restorers. Given that many vintage vehicles came with a variety of engines—from economical four- or six-cylinders to more powerful small block V-8s or high-performance big blocks—you have the ability to select and build the most appropriate engine for your needs and your tastes, then make things appear as stock (or not) as you choose.

In other words, while your particular vehicle may have putt-putted off the factory's assembly line with a thrifty six-cylinder, feel free to upgrade to your favorite small-block. Or if the mood strikes you, go ahead and stuff in a big-block. It's up to you. In fact, a really good high-performance restoration might feature an engine that wasn't even available when the vehicle was built—such as a 1957 Chevy Bel Air with a

The long-block assembly is basically the block, the heads, and all the internal parts—crank, rods, pistons, cam, etc. Since these parts are more difficult to change once the engine is installed in the car, it's worth spending some time (and money) to get them the way you want them *before* installing it.

big-block Chevy V-8 (which wasn't available until 1965). The trick here, from a high-performance resto standpoint, is to make the installation look as if it's something that *could* have rolled off the production line.

Another exciting possibility stems from the availability of most engine families in a range of displacements and power levels. For example, the small-block Chevy V-8 was available in displacements ranging from a tiny 265 cubic inches all the way up to 400 inches. And with aftermarket parts, it's possible to build mega-inch small-blocks of more than 460 cubic inches! The beautiful thing about this is that a 265-inch small block looks the same as a 460-inch small block, so no one would even notice—until you stepped on the throttle and rocketed away.

## Decide What You Want

The first step when rebuilding your engine is to decide how you want to use it. How you answer that question will determine, to some extent, what parts you should use, as well as what machining operations and modifications should be performed.

All driving falls into a few basic categories; we'll focus on the performance-oriented uses most vintage vehicles are subjected to, namely high-performance street driving, drag racing, and show use. Obviously, your vehicle won't be seeing just one of these uses. You may do some weekend drag racing with your high-performance street car, or you may show your full-time drag racer. You need to figure out what you'll be doing with the car 80 to 90 percent of the time and build the engine to handle those situations best.

A high-performance street engine rarely develops anywhere near peak power. In fact, it spends most of its time loafing along in the lower end of the rpm scale, making enough power to scoot you along within what we hope are legal limits. The hard part of building an engine for this use is making it survive a variety of operating conditions: extreme temperatures (both hot and cold), light loads to heavy loads, light throttle to full throttle, lots of short trips, stop-and-go driving, plus hours on end at highway speeds. A street engine has to be ready for just about anything, including weekend trips to the drag strip or leisurely cruises through the countryside. In this case, it pays to think first of durability: this engine should be rock-solid reliable and last for many years and hundreds of thousands of miles. The key to achieving this is to select heavy-duty parts and avoid trick modifications that sacrifice reliability for power.

Most vintage muscle car engines fall into the high-performance street category, and their components should serve you well, once they've been restored.

Drag-racing engines, on the other hand, only have to survive for short, but extremely intense, bursts. Even if a drag engine is rebuilt once per season, it will log only a handful of miles compared to a street engine. Here, the primary goal is producing power with enough durability to hold together through full-throttle, high-rpm/high-load

While there's nothing wrong with merely rebuilding your engine to stock specs—especially if it's rare, like this mighty Street Hemi—engines are one of those assemblies where you can have your cake and eat it, too: you can beef up your engine's internals, yet keep its stock outward appearance.

power shifts. Because of the extreme engine speeds and loads, you need a bottom end that's strong, yet lightweight, so that the engine can accelerate quickly and efficiently. But since the engine only needs to last a dozen or so seconds for any given pass, it's pretty reasonable to expect lightweight parts to survive long enough to reach the lights at the big end.

If you're building a show car, you want the engine to look its best. In this case, performance is a secondary concern. In fact, you can create a fabulous show engine that consistently wins Best Engine trophies but is internally stock. For show purposes, your only real concern is the engine's outward appearance, and you have a lot of options. If you expect that your show car will not be driven—and true show cars can't be, or you risk damaging expensive and time-consuming finish work—then save yourself a hefty sum of money by *not* spending a fortune on costly internal parts. Rebuild the internals to stock form, then focus on making the most of the engine's appearance.

Another novel high-performance resto route is to dress up your engine in vintage (or at least vintage-looking) parts, like vintage valve covers, air cleaner lids, breather caps, and more. Using actual vintage parts is likely to increase the difficulty and expense a bit, since you'll actually have to find them. Fortunately, many reproduction parts suppliers carry reproduction parts patterned after vintage pieces. Or there's always eBay.

## Determining Your Budget

Once you've figured out what you want, you need to think about whether or not you can afford it: how much money can you spend on your rebuild? While certain stock parts aren't suited for high-performance use and will need to be replaced to ensure your engine's survival, most stock parts can live quite happily under conditions that the factory never anticipated, but only if they are carefully selected, inspected, and prepared. You'll have to buy certain parts to improve power—a new camshaft, new pistons, or a long-stroke crankshaft, for example—but spending money isn't the key to making power. The time and thought you put into selecting and preparing parts is.

If you're on a tight budget, you may find that it makes sense to plan your entire engine buildup in stages to maximize performance (however you define it: power, reliability, economy, and so on).

One common sequence begins with building a rock-solid short-block assembly that will serve as the foundation for whatever power you have planned for later. Getting the block, crank, rods, pistons, and other bottom end parts in shape first means you won't have to re-rebuild the short block later. In fact, depending on your particular vehicle, once your bulletproof short block is dropped between the fenders, you may never have to

**Top:** Updating your engine's appearance can also improve it. While this race-prepped 530-horse, 427-inch big-block Chevy could have been painted the traditional Chevy Engine Orange, an aluminum-like finish should brighten the engine bay and add a touch of class, too.

**Above:** Another great idea is to drop in a modern powerplant, like this Corvette ZR-1 LT5 V-8. Find a donor car and you can retrofit the engine, transmission and controls, giving your classic ride a reliable, exciting powertrain.

# Long Block Assembly

remove it again. Instead, you will install other performance parts—cylinder heads, intake manifolds, camshafts—on the short block as it sits in the car.

Naturally, despite the need to be thrifty, you will want to ensure that your engine will run as well as possible, so it's wise to earmark a certain chunk of your budget to refurbish the cylinder heads, ensure the ignition and fuel delivery systems are up to snuff, and, of course, replace or repair any worn or questionable parts, such as water pumps and alternators.

Later, when you have more money, you can swap the heads, cam, or intake to increase power, confident that your short block will handle the added stresses.

## Get Down to Business

Once you've determined what you want your engine to do, and you know your budget, you can start selecting, acquiring, preparing, and assembling parts.

Although it doesn't work in all cases, for many engine builders it helps to break down your engine project into smaller projects, keeping in mind that every system interacts with each other, thus they need to work in harmony. Sections on each system will be covered in more detail, but the following few paragraphs will give you a quick overview of the major systems.

The *short-block assembly* is the foundation of your engine and needs to be designed and built to withstand whatever power level you envision for the engine.

Your *cylinder heads* largely determine the airflow characteristics of your engine, and since engines are essentially nothing more than air pumps, they represent some of the best places to make (or lose) power.

The *camshaft* and *valvetrain* control valve events: when they open, how quickly, how far, and for how long. As a result, the cam and valvetrain components control how much air flows through your engine and ultimately determine power production.

## Short-Block Assembly

Engines wear out. It's inevitable. If your engine has any appreciable mileage on it, it's probably time for a rebuild. Unfortunately, time isn't kind to engines, either, so even if your engine has low mileage, you should still plan to rebuild it. (The notable exception would be an all-original vehicle where preservation is a more important goal.)

When it comes to wear, your engine's short-block assembly—its cylinder block, crankshaft, connecting rods, pistons, and bearings—wear most, because they are subject to the highest loads in the engine.

Since power is determined by the force exerted on the pistons, they, the connecting rods and the crankshaft, must all be up to the task of harnessing that power and sending it along to the transmission. Naturally, the block must be capable of keeping everything together in the process.

For show engines or mild-performance street engines, merely freshening things up inside may be suitable. New bearings, rings, and gaskets could be all you'll need, and machine work on existing parts may be minimal, as well. But for high-performance street use, and especially for racing use, it's crucial that the bottom end of your engine be strengthened.

Of course, the specific components you need to replace or modify will depend on how you'll use your engine. As you read about each short-block

Swap meets are a great place to find engines that can be rebuilt. A word of caution on late-model EFI engines though: remember that you'll need the necessary electronic control systems to make it hum.

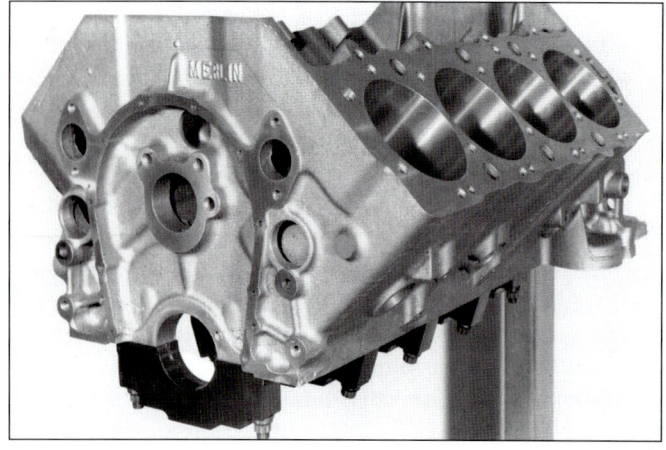

**Left:** If your original engine block isn't good enough to reuse—or maybe just isn't big enough—you can always look at aftermarket blocks, like this race-ready Donovan small-block Chevy that's capable of being bored and stroked to big-block proportions. *Donovan Engineering photo*

**Right:** High-performance engines have high-performance bottom ends, like the four-bolt main bottom end of this aluminum Donovan block. *Donovan Engineering photo*

component, pay attention to the recommendations for the different engine uses (show, high-performance street, or drag racing). This will help you discover what work and expenses you should be considering.

## Engine Block

The engine block (also called a cylinder case) is the single largest part of your engine, and everything else either bolts to it or is fitted within it. It's the foundation of your engine, so you need to select it carefully.

### Selection

If you are rebuilding your engine, the odds are pretty good that you've decided to reuse the existing engine block. But you don't have to, and in some cases it may make sense to get a different block, even if you aren't planning to alter displacement. Not all engine blocks (even those of the same basic design) are equal. Blocks cast in certain years may be stronger, or they may have different bell-housing bolt patterns that may make selecting a transmission more difficult. Likewise, some may be of a low-performance design with two-bolt main bearing caps, while other high-performance blocks have four-bolt main bearing caps.

Reusing the block you already have is generally the most economical route. Fortunately, most production blocks are suitable for high-performance use. With careful preparation plus a few well-chosen improvements, production blocks can even survive racing.

If your engine plans call for outrageous power levels or extreme operating conditions, you might want to think about using an aftermarket engine block. They are available for a number of GM, Ford, and Mopar engine families, among others.

The main benefits of aftermarket blocks are increased strength, more flexibility in terms of displacements (usually the result of taller deck heights and the ability to accommodate a longer-stroke crankshaft), and sometimes lighter weight, if the block is aluminum instead of iron.

You will also need to choose between a new block and a seasoned one—one that already has several thousand miles on it. This may be the most important decision to make, though for most people the smartest choice is the only realistic choice: a used block. That may sound contrary to what you may have expected, but used blocks have gone through the heating and cooling cycles of normal use countless times, which settles the block and de-stresses it. You don't want a block that's been overheated, however; this can warp the block permanently. Likewise, don't use any block that has suffered a catastrophic failure. Piston failure, a broken rod, camshaft, or crankshaft, or other major malady may have damaged the block beyond repair. Be careful before shelling out money for a used block of unknown or suspicious origins.

Whatever block you wind up considering—even if it's your original block—it's vital that you inspect it. As a minimum, you should have the block cleaned and magnafluxed to check for cracks; measure the cylinder bores for taper and roundness; check for gouges or a ridge at the top of the cylinders; check the deck surfaces for flatness; and have the main bearing bores checked for roundness, size, and alignment. If you're building an all-out race engine, you should verify tappet (that is, lifter) bore placement, check for core shift that might have occurred during casting, and verify a host of other dimensions. (For more on such topics, pick up a copy of a rebuilding guide for your particular engine.)

**Recommendations**

Compared to some of the decisions that you'll make, deciding on an engine block is a pretty easy choice. Sure, you still should consider how the vehicle will be used, what your budget is, and a few other factors, but your choices are limited to two options: a stock production block or an aftermarket block.

Again, show vehicles—whether in restored or modified classes—should be much less concerned about performance potential than with appearance. For modified classes, looking like a high-performance engine is good enough; it doesn't need to be a real race engine to look the part.

For applications where the engines will be driven (and probably driven hard), the quality of the block and its suitability for performance use are far more important.

If your goal is a superbly restored original vehicle, you'll need to use an original production block, as long as one is available. Beyond that, as any purist can tell you, the block should be dated within a reasonably short distance (less than two months is a good rule of thumb) prior to the vehicle's assembly date. Furthermore, on vehicles that were so coded (like most GM cars and trucks) the block should feature the original VIN stamping, which identifies the engine as belonging to a particular vehicle with the matching VIN sequence.

If you're less concerned with your vehicle being all original, yet want it to *look* original on the show field, you might consider rebuilding a less common engine for it. A good example would be Pontiac's overhead cam Sprint six-cylinder, which was available in Firebirds and other models during the late 1960s. It's both a capable and visually appealing engine, and one you hardly see at shows.

For restored show classes, originality is key. The engine block needs to look

## TWO BOLTS OR FOUR?

One of the biggest selling points for many enthusiasts is whether an engine block is two-bolt or four-bolt, referring to the number of fasteners that retain each of the three main bearing caps (main caps 2, 3, and 4). Four-bolt blocks are generally stronger than two-bolt blocks; however, it has been shown time and again that two-bolt blocks can retain the crankshaft in engines that produce as much as 500 horsepower, especially if crank speeds rarely exceed 5,500 to 6,000 rpm for any length of time. The automakers knew this and didn't waste time or money equipping production passenger car engines with four-bolt mains unless the engine was intended for high-performance or racing use. Chevy's top-performance small- and big-block V-8s were often outfitted with four-bolt mains, as were Ford's top engines like the Boss 302 and 429 engines (some of which even had *six* bolts securing their main caps). Chrysler's Hemi was a shining example of an engine that begged for and had four-bolt mains.

Of course, high crank speeds aren't the only condition where four-bolt mains are beneficial. Since the extra bolts stiffen the block, they are desirable for heavily stressed engines in trucks. When subjected to the pains of towing heavy trailers or hauling hefty loads, the block can actually bend and twist as it strains to overcome the vehicle's resistance to moving.

But factory four-bolt mains aren't necessarily the hot setup.

In fact, if you're building an engine for frequent competition use, you would be smarter to hunt for a two-bolt main engine block, because they can be modified to accept four-bolt main caps that are stronger than the factory's. Factory four-bolt blocks typically use four parallel bolts; each runs vertically into the block. But with a two-bolt block, you can have it machined to accept four-bolt main bearing caps that feature "splayed," or angled, outer bolts, which make the engine assembly much stronger. Note, however, that not all machine shops are capable of performing the needed processes to install splayed-bolt main caps. Check with local machine shops if this process appeals to you.

correct, which means it should be painted the proper color. If you've ever seen how the factories typically painted engines back in the 1960s and 1970s (the mostly complete engine assemblies would swing into a paint booth on a conveyor system, and a painter would douse them in color in under 30 seconds) then you know it doesn't take much effort to improve on the factory's paint, which often featured both runs and bare spots. Several light coats of a high-temperature spray paint in the correct color will give you thick, even coverage that will last a long time and look good doing it.

On the other hand, if you're building a car to compete in modified show classes, it's in your best interest to make things as interesting and attractive as possible in order to compete with others who have done the same to their vehicles.

Big blocks have a little more visual pizzazz, which is generally attributed to their extra bulk. A tastefully decked-out big block is a safe bet for show purposes, and you can generally attach any number of aftermarket performance parts to one, including exotic induction systems such as superchargers.

Then again, though they're hardly rare on show fields, a well-thought-out, high-performance small-block is plenty exciting. Don't feel bad if that's what you're working with, whether by choice or by economic need. All things being equal, it still costs less to build a small block than a big block.

Beyond stock engine blocks, you have the option of using an aftermarket engine block, which adds a certain race-inspired mystique to any vehicle. Chrysler's Hemi is tremendous, but a Keith Black Hemi is even more exciting because of its exotic nature, as are blocks from Rodeck, Bill Mitchell Racing Products, GM Performance Parts, Ford SVO, and others. Aside from the reputations these blocks have, they also provide other advantages for show vehicles, including unique appearances, exotic materials, and of course the ability to be built into large-displacement, high-horsepower performance engines.

For high-performance street use, the specific engine block you run isn't nearly as critical as the components with which you fill it, so long as the block you

An engine dyno, like this Land & Sea DynoMite system, is the ultimate way to break in and tune your engine, since you can easily access and alter almost anything on the engine. *Land & Sea photo*

use is sound. For bragging rights, it would be nice to have a high-tech aftermarket block like an aluminum Bow Tie Chevy small block, but that's hardly necessary or cost effective. A production block will usually do, as long as it passes the dimensional and crack-inspection tests. Depending on the power level you want and the engine speeds you expect to run, a block with four-bolt mains may be a wise investment, if your engine was offered that way. Below 400 horsepower and 5,500 rpm, there's generally little need for the heavy-duty main bearing cap designs; but if your engine will be making more than 400 horsepower or spinning higher than 5,500 rpm regularly, a stronger block will keep the crankshaft more securely located and prevent block distortion. Fortunately, a number of engines came from the factory with four-bolt (or even *six* bolts for some big-block Fords) main caps.

Because the block's function is far more critical for driving situations, you should ensure that it is accurately machined to provide flat sealing surfaces, defect-free bores, and accurate dimensions and alignments.

# Long Block Assembly

**Left:** Your high-performance engine's "bottom end"—the crank, connecting rods, pistons, and bearings—need to be top quality to survive demanding driving. There are lots of options, from rebuilding your stock parts to upgrading to high-quality parts as in this Lunati kit. *Lunati photo*

**Right:** After inserting high-quality bearings in your block's main bearing saddles, setting the crank in is pretty straightforward. But it pays to carefully check bearing clearances (either by mic'ing or using Plastigauge) and checking end play. You should also install high-quality aftermarket main bearing bolts or studs to retain the main bearing caps.

Race engines demand a strong block, but, interestingly enough, that doesn't always mean a factory four-bolt main block is desirable. In many engines, factory four-bolt setups—though stronger than factory two-bolt setups—are considerably weaker than an aftermarket four-bolt main system that uses splayed outer bolts and stronger caps. This is the case with Chevy V-8s, in particular.

An aftermarket block is really the hot setup for the track, however. In addition to stronger, four-bolt mains, aftermarket blocks usually feature strengthening in key locations, superior metal alloys, plus more precise manufacturing tolerances. In addition, if the rules for your racing class permit it, you can build a mega-inch engine that simply wouldn't be possible with stock blocks.

## Crankshaft

The crankshaft harnesses the forces pushing the pistons downward in the bores and converts it to rotary motion that is transmitted to the rear-axle assembly to turn the tires. In short, the crankshaft is the most essential component of a reciprocating engine assembly; it's what keeps things reciprocating.

The crankshaft throws are under high loads, so the crankshaft must be in excellent condition; the slightest defect can lead to disastrous results, like an expensive engine in pieces. But this doesn't mean you always need the most exotic crankshaft, you just need one that's well matched to your driving conditions and one that's properly prepared.

### Different Types

Factory production crankshafts have served countless drivers well for years and years, in both stock and modified engines, even under racing conditions. There are two basic types of crankshafts: cast iron or forged steel. Forged cranks are stronger, but they're also significantly more expensive, if you don't already have one. They can be identified by a wide (roughly 3/8 inch) parting line on the unmachined portions of the crank throws (cast-iron cranks have a narrow parting line).

When properly machined and balanced, cast-iron cranks are perfectly suitable for high-performance use, as long as crank speeds are kept below 6,000 rpm.

Aftermarket crankshafts are available in both cast iron and forged steel. The advantages of aftermarket cranks are their availability in nearly any stroke length you desire. This is the key to building a large-displacement stroker motor.

### Selection

A crankshaft should be crack free and straight, meaning the throws are properly indexed to each other and the crank isn't bent, which would prevent it from spinning freely in an engine. A competent machine shop can magnuflux inspect the crank for surface cracks, and even sonic test it for internal problems. A machine shop can also verify that the throws are properly indexed. As for straightness, you can check that on your own simply by laying the crank in oiled bearing shells set in the block's main bearing saddles,

## ENGINE-SWAPPING PITFALLS

Swapping a small-displacement or weak engine for a larger engine better suited to high-performance or racing use is a common upgrade.

Unfortunately, engine swaps rarely go as smoothly as they seem like they should, even if the engine you're swapping in was originally available in your vehicle's make, model, and year.

If you're doing a "custom" installation, such as a Chrysler 426 Hemi into a Model T Ford, you're going to encounter all sorts of challenges, the likes of which this book couldn't possibly begin to solve for you.

You can avoid a number of snags if you prepare for them in advance.

**Engine mounts** are the most common problem. If your year, make, and model was available with the engine you're installing, then you can buy factory parts for the job, which may be simple mounting brackets or a different K-frame front crossmember. You can also purchase solid racing-style engine mount brackets or fabricate your own.

**Transmission mounts** can be a problem, too. If the transmission was originally available in your vehicle, you may only require a transmission crossmember or mount designed for it. If your new tranny wasn't available, you may be able to adapt a mount from a vehicle the transmission *was* available in, or you'll have to craft your own mount or crossmember.

**Wiring harnesses** for your old engine may not connect to all the electrical and ignition components on your new engine. Some components may be mounted in different locations. If you have changed ignition and accessory components, you can purchase a reproduction wiring harness for that combination. Otherwise, you can modify your existing harness or create a new one.

**Hood clearance** can become a problem if your new engine is taller than your old one. There are a few different ways to tackle this problem. One is to install a hood scoop or a hood that has a scoop built in. You could also decrease the height of your engine by using shorter engine mounts, a shorter air cleaner assembly, or even a shorter intake manifold.

**Driveshaft length** may need to be altered to suit your new engine or transmission installation. You may be able to find a factory driveshaft that is the necessary length. If not, you could always buy an aftermarket driveshaft. If your driveshaft is too long, you can have it shortened by a driveline specialty shop or a competent machinist.

**Firewall clearance** is sometimes a problem if your new engine is either bigger than your current one or is mounted farther back. This is especially a problem on engines equipped with rear-mounted distributors, like most GM vehicles. About the only choices you have are to mount the engine farther forward or to "clearance" the firewall by pounding it back. Note that reshaping the firewall could cause problems with heating systems, windshield wipers, and so on.

**Throttle linkage** or cable assemblies are generally specific to the engine to which they attach. If you change your engine—or even just your carburetor—there's a good chance you'll need to change your throttle linkage or cable. Reproductions of factory parts are available, or you could purchase linkage for use in street rods or race cars and adapt that to your vehicle.

**Automatic transmission** kickdown cable or linkage assemblies may also need to be changed. Factory components should be available, some aftermarket systems are available, or you can create your own custom kickdown system by fabricating parts and combining them with factory pieces.

**Manual transmission** clutch linkage could be a problem if your vehicle or engine wasn't originally designed for a manual transmission. If your vehicle wasn't designed for mechanical linkage, you can adapt a late-model hydraulic clutch system to your vehicle or fabricate your own mechanical linkage based on factory systems and a few pieces you'll have to create or modify.

A new manual transmission shifter may also require a hole in the floorpan in a different location, which could affect floor-mounted consoles.

**Pulley system alignment** also pose a problem if you run your old power-steering pump, alternator, or other engine "accessory" with your new engine. Locating original pulleys with the proper offsets can be difficult; however, you should be able to purchase aftermarket pulleys or reproductions that make putting together a complete system much easier. In addition, shimming some of the pulleys or brackets can fine-tune their alignment.

# Long Block Assembly

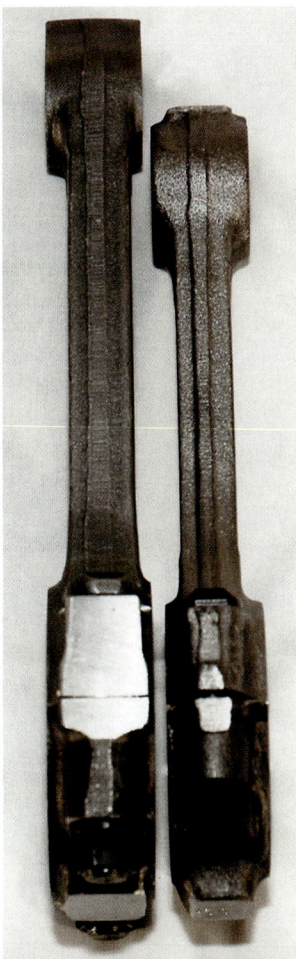

**Above:** Here you can see the rod beam "seam." When the seam is heavily stressed, like during racing-type use, forces can converge there, causing a crack or outright failure. Grinding the seam smooth and polishing the beam removes the "stress riser." The remainder of the rod should be deburred for the same reason.

**Right:** These are both stock rods—a Pontiac Super Duty rod on the left, and a Chevy small-block rod. Both can be rebuilt—including smoothing the rod beams, deburring, and stress relieving them, and fitting them with high-quality aftermarket rod bolts—and can serve you well in mild- to medium-performance engines.

then spinning it slowly with a dial indicator on each main journal. Excessive movement by one or more journals typically indicates the crank is bent (or at least that a journal is out-of-round).

Beyond those basic requirements, you might desire a crankshaft that is of a particular material—cast iron or forged steel, for example—or of a particular stroke length. You may also want a particular snout diameter (machined to accept either a small- or a big-block harmonic damper) or even a crank with lightweight hollow rod journals for quicker acceleration.

Naturally, whatever crank you're looking for must also fit your engine block in terms of the rear main seal design: either two piece or one piece.

If you've got the choice between using a forged crank and a cast one, the forged is preferable; however, if you lack the funds for a forged crank, don't feel like you're settling for inferior equipment. It's highly unlikely you'll ever suffer a crankshaft-related engine—other parts are far more likely to fail first.

## Connecting Rods

Connecting rods link the pistons to the crankshaft. It sounds like a simple job, but it's actually incredibly demanding. A connecting rod must endure unimaginable forces that continually stretch and then compress the rod during each revolution. As the rod pushes the piston up the bore, there are compression forces caused by the resistance of the piston and the speed with which the crank is thrusting the rod upward. As the piston reaches top dead center, the piston attempts to keep rising, but the rod must yank it back down as the crankshaft swings downward. This causes the rod to stretch. As the piston reaches bottom dead center, the opposite happens. The piston tries to keep dropping, but the rod starts pushing it back up, causing the rod to compress. Of course, the combustion forces also compress the rod. This process repeats thousands of times per minute and is especially punishing at high rpm, where the stretching and compressing forces are amplified.

Factory stock rods are excellent low-performance items and work well in mild high-performance applications without much special attention. Extra work can prepare stock rods for severe service; stock rods have successfully been used in 9,000-rpm drag-racing engines—and lived to tell about it. Of course, they did receive some special attention from the engine builder before doing so.

But stock rods aren't ideal performance pieces. Compared to most aftermarket rods, stock rods are heavy, which slows down engine acceleration and therefore slows vehicle acceleration. Stock rods aren't made from the choicest materials. Forged steel rods, such as the renowned Pink rods from the Z/28 302 and LT-1 350, are available through GM dealers' parts departments and are good choices, but they're expensive and somewhat heavy. Stock rods—whether made of cast, powdered metal, or forged construction—are not machined to precise tolerances. While the specified length for Chevy 305 and 350 V-8 rods is 5.700 inches, mass-production tolerances allow for the length to be a few thousandths of an inch longer or shorter, so it's possible to have one rod that's 5.702 inches long and another that's 5.698 inches in the same engine. The difference may not sound like much, but it can significantly affect engine operation, because the cylinder with the shorter rod will have less compression than the other cylinders, while the long rod will push the piston farther into the chamber, raising the compression in that cylinder. Different compression in each cylinder can cause an imbalance that shortens engine life.

Aftermarket rods are produced in far smaller quantities for enthusiasts who know their value and are willing to pay for it. Typically, even inexpensive aftermarket connecting rods will feature specific design improvements over stock rods, such as larger, stronger rod bolts or even capscrew-style bolts that allow manufacturers to greatly improve the strength of the big end of the rod. They can also be made of superior metal alloys and can be treated to machining processes that are either too costly or time consuming for mass-produced rods.

Aftermarket rods can usually be specified in different lengths, which can greatly affect engine performance by altering rod angularity and piston velocities. Longer rods tend to help an engine develop more power because the rod spends less time trying to push sideways and thus more time pushing the piston up or pulling it down as the crank continues its rotation. Longer rods also allow pistons to stay at TDC longer. This keeps the air/fuel mixture compressed longer and aids combustion because the mixture burns more completely. Shorter rods, however, can allow quicker engine acceleration, but give up some power to do so.

Not all connecting rods are made of iron (or steel), though. Aluminum rods are available for most engines and can greatly reduce reciprocating mass and increase horsepower. Aluminum rods aren't suitable for street engines, however, because of the significant expansion rates of aluminum, and they fatigue faster. Professional drag racers love aluminum connecting rods, and aluminum connecting rod manufacturers love professional drag racers because the racers often replace their rods after a few runs down the strip.

If you're planning to build some serious horsepower and torque with your engine, then you should invest in a set of forged steel aftermarket rods. Stock cast-iron rods will work just fine for moderate high-performance engines, but the money you'll spend to prepare them will nearly equal the cost of a set of ready-to-use aftermarket forged rods. (The same could also be said of reusing powdered metal rods.)

For the record, buying connecting rods at a swap meet is a risky proposition. There are a number of defects that are undetectable to the naked eye that could mean a particular rod or set of rods is unusable. The rods could be bent or twisted, stretched, have ovoid-shaped journals (at either end), or they could be cracked. Even if the set you get isn't damaged beyond repair, you'll usually have to rebuild them, and it probably would have been smarter and cheaper to have ordered a new set of aftermarket rods.

Whatever rods you work with, inspect them carefully for weak areas. Not all rods are machined identically, and some are definitely superior to others. For instance, pay particular attention to the sides of the rod at the small end; it's fairly common for

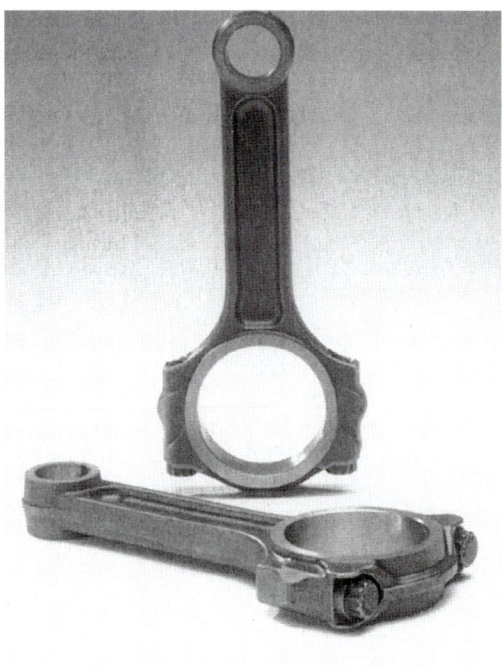
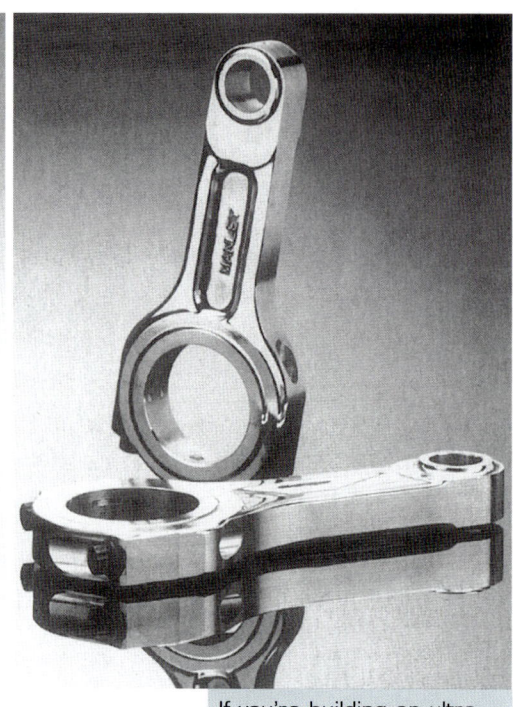

If you're building an ultra-performance engine, you should strongly consider aftermarket rods, like this Lunati Pro Billet piece. Aftermarket rods typically feature better materials, no-compromise production methods, and superior designs that make them far better suited to surviving severe operating conditions. *Lunati photo*

During any high-performance engine rebuild, you should carefully measure all components. Here, we're checking the size of a rod's "big end" with a vernier caliper to ensure it's within specifications.

## CRATE MOTORS

Each of the major manufacturers offer ready-to-go performance engines through their parts channels. The engines have come to be known as "crate motors," because they're shipped in wooden crates.

Many crate motors are excellent bargains, offering 350 or more *net* horsepower, right out of the box. Although a price tag of around $3,000 may not sound like a bargain, by the time you add up a pile of aftermarket performance parts, a bunch of costly machine work, and your time, you'll find it's often less expensive than the piecemeal approach, and you'll get a factory warranty to boot.

---

the small end bore to be machined off-center, resulting in one side being thinner than the other. That thin side may be unreliable. The same can be true of the big end. Also, if the rods have been rebuilt once or twice before, they may have insufficient material left in the rod cap, thus compromising strength.

You also need to be leery of rods that have anything but the faintest signs of rust on them. Rust attacks the metal, causing pits, and those pits weaken the rod. While sandblasting the rods may remove the rust, it won't remove the pits and may actually make them worse.

### Pistons and Wrist Pins

Pistons have the difficult duty of compressing the air/fuel mixture, then standing up to the intense heat and pressure that result from that mixture burning after ignition. The pistons may even have to endure detonation, which can be extremely damaging; and they have to do this thousands of times per minute! It's a cruel existence.

Pistons come in three basic flavors: cast aluminum, hypereutectic (high silica content), and forged aluminum. Cast pistons are strictly low-performance items. They aren't suited to high performance, and they won't withstand sustained high rpm (over 5,500 rpm); but they are very stable, in terms of size, and they run very quietly. Most production engines used cast pistons because they were reliable and far less expensive than forged pistons.

Hypereutectic pistons are sort of a middle ground between cast and forged pistons. Made of an aluminum alloy with high silica content, they essentially combine the advantages of cast aluminum (stable size, reliable, cost-effective) with increased strength, which had always been the big advantage of forged pistons. In recent years, many auto manufacturers have used hypereutectic pistons in a number of production and over-the-counter engine assemblies, because they're essentially a best-of-both-worlds solution.

Forged aluminum pistons have long been the choice for high-performance and racing engines, mainly because of their strength. They still hold a significant advantage in this regard over pistons made by other processes, but forged aluminum pistons are expensive, and because they expand a great deal when subjected to heat, they must be installed with fat clearances that allow the piston to move around in the bore when cold. Because of this, they are rather noisy (the noise typically fades as the pistons heat up), and they can wear faster. But forged pistons can still handle higher temperatures, higher loads, and higher engine speeds, so they are still the top choice for racing use.

The wrist pins (also called piston pins) connect pistons to the connecting rod, and raise another aspect of piston design worth thinking about: the pin type. Some pistons use pressed-in wrist pins and some use floating wrist pins. Pressed-in pins may be pressed into the piston but left floating in the rod's small end, or they may be floating in the piston but pressed into the rod's small end. Floating pins float in both the piston and rod and are typically only used in professional competition engines. For most applications, pins that press into the piston but float in the rod are the best choice. Pins that float in the piston require that the pin bores be machined to receive spiral snap-ring locks to keep the pin from sliding out of the piston and contacting the cylinder wall.

### Selection

In most cases, when rebuilding an engine you're probably going to use aftermarket pistons, because they're available in different compression ratios, different overbore sizes, and they

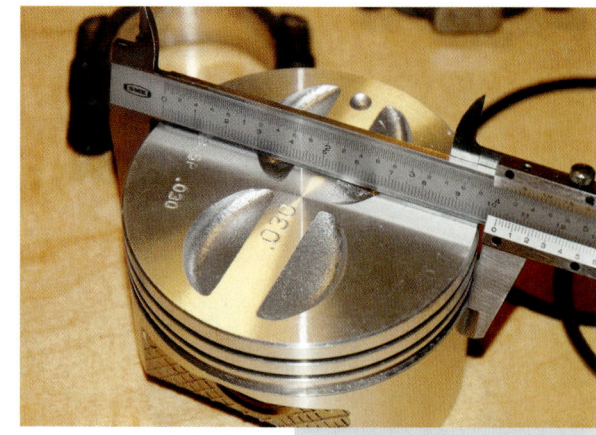

**Left:** These two aftermarket pistons illustrate the difference between a "domed" (or "pop-up") piston on the left and a "flat-top" piston on the right. Domed pistons provide higher compression, which can yield more power, but also can be problematic with pump gas, because they cause detonation. Flat tops also allow for uninterrupted flame-front travel through the combustion chamber.

**Right:** While aftermarket pistons are usually consistently sized, as with everything else, pistons should be measured and matched to the best-sized cylinder to ensure proper clearances. Ideally, your cylinders should be bored and honed to fit your piston-and-ring package to ensure ideal clearances for how you'll use your engine.

typically cost less than factory parts. If you're reading this book, chances are pretty good you're more interested in the strength of forged pistons than the value of cast or hypereutectic pistons. Whatever material you choose, you should pay particular attention to the weight of the pistons you're buying. Factory pistons are heavier than necessary to minimize the chance of failure, but the extra material also slows engine acceleration. You'll also need to be concerned with compression ratio, which requires taking into account the combustion chamber volume of your cylinder heads, the thickness of the head gaskets, the camshaft profile, the fuel you'll be running, and even the engine design itself. Few engines that are forced to run on pump gas (92–93 octane) will react well to compression ratios over 9.5:1. Higher compression ratios will cause the engine to detonate under all but the lightest loads, potentially destroying the engine with every knock and ping.

A final word on piston design: when possible, it's best to use a flat-top or even dished piston, because pop-up piston domes can interfere with the travel of the flame front during the combustion process.

Selecting piston pins is often easy: pistons typically include an appropriate pin. Of course, most piston manufacturers will happily sell you (or substitute) the specific pins you want. High-strength piston pins are available, as are lightweight piston pins. High-strength pins are a good idea, even if they weigh a few more grams than a standard pin. Lightweight pins should only be considered for competition engines that will have them frequently replaced.

### Machining and Preparation

Just like any other engine component, pistons and pins need to be prepared properly if they're going to last. Used pistons should be thoroughly cleaned, including the ring grooves, which will require a ring groove cleaner that scrapes carbon buildup and other deposits from the grooves. All pistons should be checked for cracks by having them magnafluxed, then deburred to remove any potential hot spots. Finally, piston and pin assemblies should be balanced to match the heavier assemblies to the lightest assembly's weight. If you're really into competition use, you may want to consider shedding a few grams (unless your pistons are lightweight units to begin with) for quicker engine—and ultimately vehicle—acceleration.

## Piston Rings

Pistons don't completely fill the cylinder bore because they need some clearance to allow for expansion and an oil film to lubricate the cylinder walls. Of course, if this clearance gap wasn't filled, the engine would develop little compression, therefore hardly make any power. Plus, it would burn oil, and the oil would quickly become contaminated by gasoline.

Preventing all of that is up to the piston rings. Piston rings are little more than seals that fit in grooves on the piston and help seal the piston to the cylinder walls. Most engines use three rings per piston. The top ring is the compression ring; it helps prevent the

# Long Block Assembly

Test fitting pistons to measure gaps is a simple but important step.

There are lots of ways to install rings on your pistons—but only one is correct: using a piston ring expander, as shown here. Like most parts, a variety of ring designs and materials are available. For most street engines, simple moly-faced rings are suitable. Zero-gap rings will further lock in cylinder pressures.

compressed air/fuel mixture from blowing out of the cylinders, and it ensures that the rapid expansion of gases caused by combustion isn't lost in the same manner. The second ring helps further limit any pressure losses. The lowest ring groove is occupied by the oil control ring package, which keeps the oil out of the combustion chamber.

Most piston rings don't make a perfect seal because of the ring end gap, the point where the two ring ends come together. Because the rings expand as they get hot, they must have a slight gap that allows the rings to expand without breaking. Rings are generally sized to fit a particular bore diameter (such as 4.030 inches, for a 0.030-inch overbored, 5.7-liter Chevy). You'll need to verify that the ring gaps are correct before assembly. If you desire a specific gap, order rings that are slightly oversized so you can file one end of the ring to achieve that specific end gap.

## Selection

There are three things to be concerned with when selecting piston rings: the ring material, including any coatings that may be applied; the ring sizing and end gaps; and the oil control ring package.

In the old days, the top two rings were typically just plain iron, but performance top rings are now typically moly faced or plasma coated to improve their sealing and wear properties. Second rings still are typically plain iron, while the oil control package usually consists of steel upper and lower scraper rings, plus a steel expansion ring between the two.

As we covered in the previous section, piston rings require a gap to allow for expansion when the rings heat up; however, the larger the gap, the more compression you'll lose, so end gap is a critical setting. Certain piston ring designs provide a zero gap by having the ring ends overlap, sort of like tongue-and-groove boards, rather than butt against each other. Zero gap rings are the ultimate in cylinder sealing because they virtually eliminate blowby, thereby maximizing power.

Oil control packages are available in a special low-tension design to reduce friction, but this design can result in excessive oil consumption and unsightly puffs of blue smoke from the tailpipe because excess oil gets past the rings. Just watch stock 5.0-liter Mustangs; they use low-tension oil control rings and almost always "puff the blues" when accelerating or starting up.

Whenever you rebuild an engine, aftermarket piston rings are the most logical choice of the variety of materials, sizes, cost, and availability.

## Machining and Preparation

The critical element of piston rings is the end gaps. The correct measurements are typically provided with the set of rings, or they can be customized to your needs and the engine's application. An excessively large gap will allow too much cylinder pressure to blow through. Too tight a gap might result in a broken ring if the ring expands so much as it heats that the ring ends press against each other. You measure the gap by squaring each ring about an inch into its respective bore (an inverted piston usually works well for this), then measuring the gap with a feeler gauge. If the gap is still too large, your only option may be to purchase oversized rings and file the gap to fit. To do so, you'll need a ring filer (a special, small grinding wheel). Remember to only grind one end of the ring (to leave the other square) and only grind a little bit at a time.

Beyond measuring and correcting ring end gaps, piston rings need little work to prepare them for use; however, it should be noted that the only correct way to install piston rings on pistons is with a set of piston ring expansion pliers (a satisfactory set will cost you about $10 at any Sears tool center). You'll also need a ring compressor to squeeze the rings into the piston ring grooves for insertion into the cylinder bores. Several types of ring compressors are available: the band type, the pliers type, and the cone type, which is widely used by professional engine builders because it's easy to use and seldom breaks rings.

## Main, Rod, and Cam Bearings

Bearings basically minimize wear between two metal parts. Oil between the bearing surface and the surface of the moving part, such as a crankshaft journal, is responsible for reducing friction. One important—and often overlooked—role of the bearings is to trap and absorb small contaminants, like bits of metal or dirt, and prevent them from touching the crankshaft's journals, which would damage the fragile journal surface.

The bearing surfaces are relatively soft, so particles can actually imbed into the surface and get stuck there—hopefully, safely beneath the thin film of oil, out of reach of the crankshaft or camshaft journals.

Beyond those two functions, bearings do little more than provide the proper clearance for oil to flow through, but that's a critical job. Too much clearance and oil pressure will drop, and the part (such as the crankshaft) may move excessively, leading to rapid wear. Too little clearance and oil may not be able to flow through, increasing friction and wear. This usually causes the bearing to burn up and eventually spin loose in its bore, or the engine may seize.

### Selection

When purchasing bearings, buy them to match any machine work that may have been done to the crankshaft. For example, if the crank was turned 0.010 inch undersize on the main and rod journals, get main and rod bearings that are designed for that change.

Bearings aren't terribly expensive, so spend the few extra dollars for quality bearings from a reputable company, like Clevite-77.

### Machining

There isn't any machine work to be performed on bearing shells; however, you may wish to *very lightly* deburr the bearings with a ScotchBrite pad. You don't want to remove any of the bearings' surface coating, just any high spots.

It's also in your best interest to match bearings to specific crank journals and block bores for the best fit. To do this, measure each crank journal, main and rod journal, and upper and lower bearing half with a micrometer and record the figures on a sheet of paper. With your ideal clearance in mind, subtract the journal diameter from its corresponding bore's inside diameter to determine the overall gap. Then choose bearing halves that, when subtracted from that figure, most closely

---

## OLD-MODEL CAR, MEET LATE-MODEL ENGINE

One of the more interesting trends is the installation of high-tech, late-model engines into vintage vehicles. When done well, the combinations can be outstanding: the classic looks of your favorite vintage vehicle, with the power, economy, and reliability of a modern powertrain (you'll often have to use a modern transmission, too, to best complement the engine).

Such swaps present unique problems, including the need for a high-pressure fuel system, retrofitting an electronic control module to manage the powertrain, and other subtle changes. But in the end, who could argue with the appeal of a 1969 Camaro powered by a modern LS7 Gen III small-block, or a 4.6-liter-powered 1966 Mustang fastback, or maybe even a Viper V-10-powered 1970 Charger?

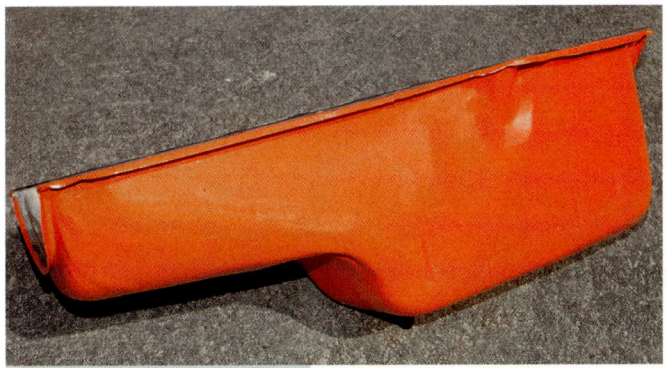
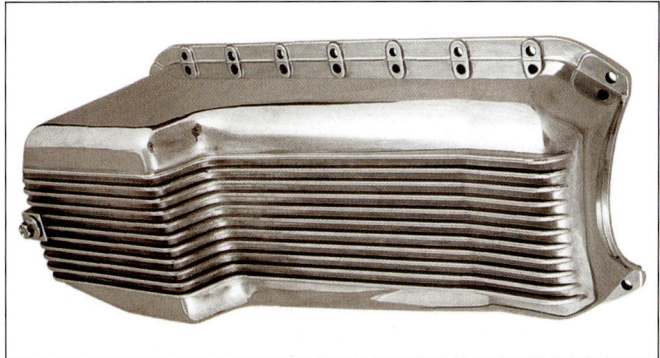

**Left:** Oil pans present additional opportunities for improvement. This Corvette pan has a larger (longer) sump, so it holds more oil, which keeps the oil cooler. The catch is that oversized pans don't fit in all vehicles.

**Right:** Another option is this Trans Dapt–finned aluminum pan. Though stock capacity, the aluminum dissipates heat much better than steel, so your oil stays cooler. Plus, the thicker aluminum construction helps deaden unwanted sound. It looks pretty cool, too. *Trans Dapt photo*

approximate the desired clearance. Confused? Here's the formula:

(bore diameter − journal diameter) − (upper bearing half thickness + lower half thickness) = clearance.

An easier method is to simply trial-assemble the engine, and check clearances with PlastiGauge, thin strings of crushable plastic that you place on the journal prior to torquing the cap in place. Then you remove the cap and measure the thickness of the squished plastic with the provided gauge (usually on the wrapper) to determine the clearance. If gaps aren't within tolerances, you can try swapping bearings from one journal bore to another and remeasure.

A special note on cam bearings is in order, because they are tougher to install than main and rod bearings: They have to be pressed into their journal bores. Cam bearings are fragile, and unless you have the proper tools for the job, you're likely to ruin a few bearings in the process. Machine shops charge little for this service, so it's easier—and possibly cheaper—to let them install them. That way if they ruin one, they'll have to replace it, not you.

## Oil System

Most people assume your engine's oil system is only responsible for lubricating the engine, but the oil actually has five critical duties: it cleans the engine by picking up dirt or other particles and depositing them in the oil filter; it cools the engine by absorbing heat and dissipating it to the air flowing around the oil pan (or oil cooler if you have one); it seals the piston rings to the cylinder walls, thereby helping maximize compression; it protects metal components from corrosion and rust; and it lubricates to prevent wear between parts. With all that to do, it's clear why a high-performance engine needs a high-performance oil system.

### Oil Pan and Pickup

The most visible part of any oil system (unless you have a horrendous oil leak) is the oil pan. Stock oil pans for most engines are made of stamped steel and will typically hold 4 quarts of "liquid gold," plus the filter holds another 1/2 quart. Stock pans also tend to feature simple baffles designed to keep oil trapped in the deepest part of the pan, the sump (though the baffle does little to keep the oil pump pickup submerged in oil).

A variety of aftermarket oil pans provide both increased oil volume and better baffling to prevent the oil pump from sucking air. In addition, an aluminum oil pan dissipates heat better and tends to muffle sounds better, quieting the engine.

If your vehicle has a low ride height, make sure when selecting an oil pan that the sump area won't accidentally contact the ground. This could tear open the pan, spilling oil everywhere, causing the engine to starve for oil and possibly seize—not to mention letting dirt, rocks, and other things inside your engine that could cause unspeakable damage.

Your oil pan choice typically dictates the oil pump pickup and screen assembly you need to use because the pickup's location and height depend on the shape of the pan. In general, the pickup should be between 0.25 and 0.375 inch from the bottom of the pan, with its location within the sump determined by the type of driving the engine will endure. Drag racing engines should have the pickup at the rear of the pan because that's where the oil will go under acceleration. Circle track engines usually have the pickup on the right side of the pan, and street engines usually have the pickup in the middle of the pan because they have to contend with a variety of driving conditions.

**Oil Pump**

The stock-type oil pump draws the oil from the oil pan through a pickup tube with a coarse filter screen to prevent large debris from being ingested. The pump then sends the oil to the oil filter and then off to the rest of the engine through passages called galleries.

Pumps usually featured steel gears inside a cast-iron housing. The size of the gears determines the volume of oil the pump can move in a given period of time. Oil pressure is determined by a number of factors, including a bypass spring mounted in the oil pump cover or block. Other factors that influence oil pressure are the oil filter and the sizes of the oil galleries within the engine. The old rule of thumb is that you want 10 pounds of oil pressure for every 1,000 rpm, so an engine running at 5,000 rpm should have 50 psi of oil pressure.

Another type of oiling system, known as a dry sump system, uses a crank-driven oil pump and scavenge system. As the crankshaft spins, it turns a belt that spins the shaft of an external oil pump. One or more chambers of the pump actually pump oil into the engine, while one or more scavenge chambers suck oil from a small oil pan that essentially has no sump. An external, remote oil reservoir tank and cooler are plumbed in to ensure the system has plenty of cool oil to circulate. Dry sump systems are able to provide a more constant supply of oil to the engine, especially at high rpm, and they reduce windage problems because of the scavenge stages of the pump. Dry sump systems are considerably more complex and expensive than stock wet sump systems, however, and their benefits are minimal in street-bound applications.

**Windage Trays and Scrapers**

Oil that isn't in the oil pan sump can't be drawn in by the oil pump, and therefore won't do the engine much good. Additionally, because oil has weight, excess oil on parts like the crankshaft can slow the crank's rotation down.

Windage trays and crankshaft scrapers are designed to alleviate these problems. The windage tray mounts to special extended main bearing bolts and acts like a baffle to prevent oil from sloshing up onto the crankshaft as you race around or hit the brakes. A crank scraper, on the other hand, actually skims oil off the crankshaft counterweights as it rotates.

Windage trays and crankshaft scrapers aren't generally used in production engines, nor are they necessary, but they do provide minute benefits if you are compelled to free up every last horsepower trapped within your engine.

**Oil Coolers**

Oil flows through the engine and absorbs heat, and when it gets hot, it thins out, decreasing its ability to clean, seal, and lubricate the engine. This is especially critical for engines that will be operated for extended lengths of time, such as those used in road racing and even street driving.

An oil cooler can considerably improve your oil's ability to do its jobs. Factory-installed oil-to-water (actually it was engine coolant) coolers were available at various times, as part of various option packages. The factory coolers used an adapter that mounted between the oil filter and the engine block. Coolant from the radiator flowed through the adapter, cooling the oil. It's a simple system, and it works; but it does have its problems.

First, the oil is only in the adapter for a short time, which means there isn't much time for the oil to transfer its heat to the coolant through the adapter. Second, if your engine begins to run hot, the oil is allowed to heat up. Third, if the oil was running cool on its own, the coolant will actually heat it up. It is worth noting, however, that factory oil-to-air

Oil pumps and their related components are not all created equal. If you're upgrading your engine's performance, upgrade the performance of its oil system with a high-volume pump. You'll also need to ensure your oil pickup height is set properly for your application. And a heavy-duty oil pump driveshaft should be considered an essential.

# Long Block Assembly

Once your engine's built, you need to treat it right. Synthetic oil, like Mobil 1, reduces friction, withstands heat better, and doesn't break down as quickly as conventional oil. Nearly every top race team uses synthetic oil, too, which oughta tell you something.

coolers are available on most fleet vehicles (police cars) and trucks with tow packages.

Most aftermarket oil coolers are oil-to-air coolers. An adapter is installed between the oil filter and the block, but this adapter routes the oil through a hose to a miniature radiator that should be mounted in an area that gets decent airflow. As with the cooling system radiator, the oil cooler radiator absorbs heat from the oil as the oil flows through tubes in the radiator. That heat is then transferred to a series of fins between the tubes, and ultimately dissipated to the air flowing through the cooler. The cooled oil then flows back to the adapter through another hose and back into the engine. Some coolers are even thermostatically controlled to prevent the oil from becoming too cool. This type of cooler also adds as much as 2 quarts to the volume of oil available to an engine.

### Oil Filters

Oil filters are remarkably unremarkable, usually. You change your filter when you change your oil, then forget about it until the next oil change. But not all filters are created equal.

Stock filters are usually sealed metal canisters with a mesh-type filter material inside, through which the oil must flow. As the oil flows through the mesh, dirt and metal particles are trapped in the mesh, so only clean oil flows out of the filter. Unfortunately, standard replacement oil filters do only a decent job of cleaning the oil. For one thing, the mesh can let smaller particles through that can still damage your engine. Another problem is that stock replacement filters can be quite restrictive to the flow of oil, especially as the filter traps more and more contaminants, blocking the mesh. Finally, because the stock filters are relatively small, they can quickly become plugged with dirt and debris, causing a bypass valve to open. This may allow your oil to bypass the filter entirely.

Aftermarket serviceable oil filters are available that you can periodically clean and reuse. This allows you to easily see the contaminants that are in your engine's oil; this is important diagnostic information. For instance, the presence of a lot of metal particles could indicate abnormal wear in your engine. (Stock replacement-type filters can be cut open and inspected, but the process is messy and time consuming, and the folded mesh makes inspection difficult.)

In addition, some aftermarket filters offer superior filtering properties, allowing the filter to trap much smaller particles.

### Oil

The most important part of your engine's oil system is its oil. It is the lifeblood of your engine, and without it, your engine will come to a grinding halt in a hurry.

You need to ensure your engine always has an ample supply of clean, cool oil to properly perform, so you need to change the oil every 3,000 miles for street use, or after every race for competition use.

What oil should you use? Any good-quality engine oil will generally do, though there are advantages to using synthetic oils, like Mobil 1. Synthetic oils are scientifically engineered to withstand heat extremes better, both hot and cold. They don't break down and thin out as much in extreme heat, so they protect your engine better. Plus, they flow more easily in extreme, cold weather, allowing oil to flow to your engine's vital parts more quickly. Tests have shown that the bulk of an engine's wear occurs during the first minute or so following startup, so anything you can do to speed up oil delivery will dramatically reduce wear.

Synthetic oils also result in increased power at high rpms; however, the increase is minimal and not a factor at normal engine speeds.

### Oil Additives

In recent years, oil additives have hit the shelves of auto parts stores claiming to do everything from eliminating engine wear to restoring engine performance. While there is generally some truth to the claims being made, the advertisements rarely provide the whole truth behind the claims.

The bottom line on engine oil additives is that a properly maintained engine that's in good condition shouldn't need them. As proof, just look to professional motorsports teams from NASCAR, NHRA, SCCA, and IRL or CART competition. If the additives provided true, valuable benefits, you can bet those teams would be using them to gain an edge on their competition. But they don't use them (and despite what one ad claims, it's not because the rules don't allow them to). You draw your own conclusions.

*Preoilers*—We discussed that most engine wear occurs at startup when the engine's oil is still down in the pan. Unfortunately, the way most oil systems work, you're faced with a Catch-22: they don't pump oil until they're spinning, but you don't want to spin them until they've been pumping oil. The solution is what is known as a preoiler. Just prior to the initial fireup following a rebuild (or healthy modification), it's common to preoil the engine using a drill-driven rod that engages the oil pump driveshaft and provides a needed bridge for an oil gallery. But this procedure requires removing the distributor, and therefore isn't practical for every time you're going to start the engine. Aftermarket preoilers use an electric motor to pump oil from a reserve tank throughout the engine. Prior to starting the car, you hit the switch for the preoiler and wait 30 seconds or so for oil to circulate everywhere. Then you twist the key and your engine can fire with little risk, because it's already protected by oil.

### Selection

A higher-volume oil pan will increase how much oil your engine has available. This can be especially important at higher engine speeds, when oil is drawn out of the pan more quickly than it returns to it. For many enthusiasts, a low-profile, high-volume pan and an appropriate pickup assembly is a good pick.

A stock oil pump will suffice in many instances. If bearing clearances are slightly larger in your engine for extended high-rpm use, a high-pressure or high-volume pump would make sense.

A windage tray—even just a basic one—is a sound investment, and so are oil coolers, high-performance filters, and a preoiler, though the last-mentioned is optional given that countless engines survive hundreds of thousands of miles without them. Oil-wise, any quality brand will do, but synthetics make the most sense (except, perhaps, from a cost perspective).

Last, it's critical that you use a high-quality oil pressure gauge to monitor oil pressure. It wouldn't hurt to install an oil temperature gauge to alert you to any unexpected hot times. Quality aftermarket electric gauges are usually more accurate than stock gauges; however, mechanical gauges react more quickly and accurately to changes in oil pressure and temperature so they are preferable to electric gauges.

### Modifications and Preparation

Believe it or not, there are several modifications you can make to your oiling system to improve its performance and reliability. Starting with the oil pump, you can deburr the pump's outlet and passages and blueprint its gear-to-cover clearance and gear-to-sidewall. Cover clearance can be corrected by milling or flat machining the pump's mating surface the required amount to achieve the low end of the tolerance. Adjusting sidewall clearance requires either different gears or a different case.

The oil pickup you use should be brazed or tack welded to the pump cover to ensure it remains properly installed and doesn't vibrate loose.

The oil pan should be suitably baffled and fitted with a magnetic drain plug to help collect any metal particles in the oil. A crank scraper should also be fitted to help remove excess oil from the crankshaft.

### Fasteners—Nuts and Bolts

Aftermarket bolts typically offer far better tensile and shear strength than stock bolts, allowing them to hold an engine together longer, under higher stress. Studs are even better because they distribute stresses throughout the length of the stud (unlike bolts, which concentrate the forces just below the head of the

Some applications, like small-block Chevy V8s, can greatly benefit from a cam button, like this roller unit from Crane Cams. The button keeps the cam from "walking" forward, which would affect cam timing.

# Long Block Assembly

A simple lock plate, like this one from Crane, is a cheap way to prevent your cam timing gear bolts from loosening.

bolt), and they don't damage the threads of the part into which they are installed. Instead, studs are installed once, and nuts are attached to the studs to secure the part. During subsequent rebuilds, so long as the stud isn't removed from the block, the only threads that can be damaged are the studs' exposed threads. And since the studs are easily replaced, damage to them is of little concern.

Studs are also available to allow the installation of a windage tray, which helps prevent oil (in the form of mist) from slowing the crankshaft rotation.

Aftermarket fasteners, such as those from Stage 8, are available with locking devices to prevent the fastener from loosening. Fasteners can also be modified to allow the use of safety wire to prevent them from loosening.

# Recommended Modifications

By now, if you've actually read this far and didn't just skip ahead, you're probably muttering something like, "Gee, this is all *really* fascinating, but what does it mean I should do with my engine?" A very good question, to which there are several very good answers; which one applies to you depends on how you will be using your engine.

## Block

While a two-bolt block will suffice for street use, a four-bolt block is preferable and also more than enough for the street. Four-bolt blocks are often a necessity for racing, and if you'll be competing for money, consider a splayed-bolt four-bolt main cap arrangement for added strength and rigidity. In every case, thoroughly deburr the block, lightly round every edge (except around the bores at the deck surface), remove excess casting flash, and smooth or paint the lifter valley to promote oil drainage. Only overbore the block if needed, because the process removes material, weakening the block. Make sure the block is dimensionally correct (main journal diameters and alignment; deck flatness, bores properly sized, and round top to bottom; and so on). It's also smart to replace stock fasteners—main bolts, rod bolts, and head bolts, specifically—with high-performance fasteners. Studs are better than bolts for mains and heads, but bolts will work fine in most cases.

## Crankshaft

Herb Couzins at Callaway Cars strongly advocates investing in a quality crankshaft, saying that some things just aren't worth skimping on. A high-performance crank, like those from Callies, Lunati, or other manufacturers, is like valuable insurance; you'll never have to worry about it failing. But if your budget can't handle $1,000 for a crankshaft, you can always modify the one you've got (or get a less expensive aftermarket unit). Enlarging the journals, deburring the crankshaft, balancing it, and hardening it will greatly increase its strength, and your peace of mind. Still, if you do splurge for an aftermarket crank, it makes sense to get a slightly longer stroke. There is little difference in price, but you can get substantial power gains.

A purpose-built, high-performance crankshaft should be considered a must for race-only applications. They're stronger, lighter, and usually have the bulk of the machining done for you, which at least saves you some time. Be sure to check any applicable racing rules, however, before considering a stroke change; this would affect displacement.

## Connecting Rods

Check with your chosen machine shop before you decide what to do about connecting rods. To properly prep them, your rods will need to be magnafluxed and resized; have new bolts installed; and have the area near the bolt head radiused, completely deburred, balanced, and then fitted to the pistons and pins. Find out what all that work will cost you, then compare that to the cost of buying new rods that have most of that work already done. If there's little difference in price, go for the aftermarket rods, which will usually be stronger and lighter. If you're buying new rods anyway, you may want to consider getting slightly longer rods, which reduce rod angularity for reduced friction and increase piston dwell for a more complete burn (longer rods require shorter pistons, though).

## Pistons, Wrist Pins, and Rings

New pistons are almost a given in a rebuild, as are new wrist pins and rings. While hypereutectic pistons are quite good—especially if you'll be using your engine in a daily driver—forged pistons are still stronger and comparably priced. A number of factors will dictate the pistons you select, including bore size, stroke length, and rod length. You will need to consider your desired compression ratio (and thus combustion chamber size too), but in general, flat-top pistons are best for making power, and you should keep compression under 10.0:1 for any vehicle that will run pump gas. If you're racing, class rules will usually dictate the maximum compression ratio allowed.

Wrist pins usually come with new pistons. If your engine is a race motor, you might want to consider lightweight wrist pins; however, bear in mind that lightweight pins are not as strong as a heavier pin of the same material. Naturally, the pins you use have to match your pistons and rods: full floating or floating in the rod only.

As for rings, plasma-coated rings don't require much run-in: They seal well, they're durable, and they're reasonably priced. Unless you're building a race-only motor, it's easier to stay away from file-to-fit rings, unless, of course, you need them to achieve a proper gap.

## Oil System

It's smart to run an oversized pan that adds a quart or two of capacity. This helps prevent oil starvation during performance driving. A high-volume oil pump with an appropriate pickup, a windage tray, and an oil cooler should round out the hardware. Make sure you deburr everything, and clean up oil passages on the block caps and inside the pump for better flow. Painting the nonmachined interior surfaces of the block can aid oil drain back, too, though it isn't absolutely necessary. When it comes to oil, it's largely your call: synthetic oil provides slightly better protection under hard use, but if you change your oil every 3,000 miles, conventional oil works perfectly well. Finally, always use a quality oil filter, and don't hesitate to change it more often than you change your oil.

## Main, Rod, and Cam Bearings

Choose quality bearings from a reputable manufacturer, and order them in the proper size. Your only real concern is to make sure the clearances between the bearings and their journals (main, rod, or cam) are within acceptable limits.

Wider clearances will reduce friction (to a point), but will eventually pound out the bearings due to increased movement of the part. Narrower clearances tighten up under use, which reduces the flow of oil between the bearing and part, increasing friction. As long as the clearance isn't too tight, however, wear is minimized because the part can't move around much. A constant, pressurized oil film keeps the part suspended off the bearing surfaces.

For street use, keep the clearances toward the tighter end of the accepted ranges to increase engine durability. Racing applications, however, will benefit from clearances toward the looser (larger) end of the recommendations.

**Top:** While it's possible to install a cam without degreeing to ensure it's accurately synced with piston positioning, degreeing isn't expensive, nor does it take much time. It's a crucial step in the "blueprinting" process. *Crane Cams photo*

**Above:** If degreeing shows that your cam is slightly out of adjustment, you can correct it using offset bushings, like these. *Crane Cams photo*

# Long Block Assembly

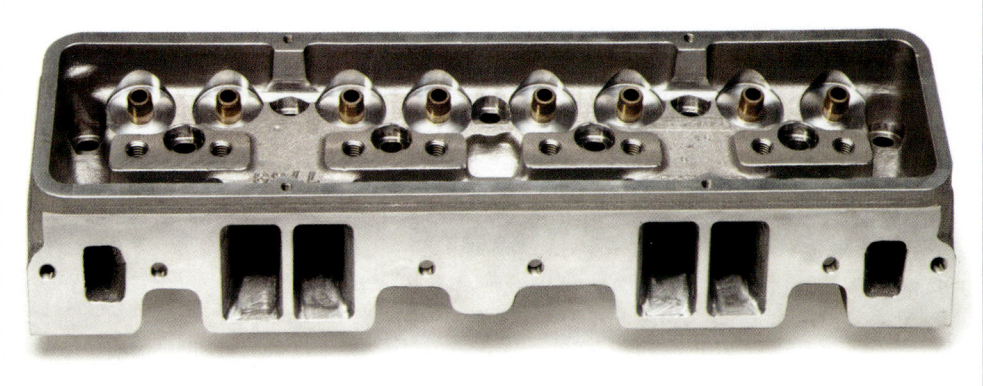

Cylinder heads largely determine how efficiently your engine can breathe. Stock heads are notorious for poor breathing characteristics. Aftermarket heads, like this aluminum Edelbrock Victor Jr, not only offer huge flow (and thus power) improvements, but reduce weight, too—which is just like adding more power to your engine. *Edelbrock photo*

## Cylinder Heads

Many engine components affect your engine's breathing abilities, but none are more critical than the cylinder heads. This is because they are the last possible restriction for air going into the engine, and the first possible restriction for exhaust going out. As such, no matter how free-breathing your induction and exhaust systems are, their effects can be nullified by poor heads.

Another way of thinking about cylinder heads is to consider that ideal cylinder heads (if such things existed) would allow an engine to produce its maximum power. Thus, good cylinder heads don't really *make* more power, but rather bad heads *restrict* power. The good heads are just a lot closer to being ideal heads, so they don't limit horsepower as much as the bad heads.

Of course, this is a gross oversimplification, since a good head for street use would be a horrible head for professional road racing competition. Like most other engine components, cylinder heads have to be selected for the specific application.

Four aspects of cylinder heads determine how well they will contribute to power production: ports, valves, combustion chambers, and the material from which the head is made.

## Intake and Exhaust Ports

Intake ports guide the air from the intake manifold runners toward the cylinder, while exhaust ports take the exhaust gases from the cylinder to the exhaust system. Each port's effectiveness depends on its shape and size. The goal is to minimize restrictions, which sounds an awful lot like "make them bigger," until you consider what goes on inside your engine and how port sizes affect airflow quality.

Quite simply, small ports flow a smaller volume of air but at higher velocities than large ports. Conversely, large-volume ports flow lots of air, but the air moves more slowly.

Here's a metaphor that might help this make sense: picture an old-fashioned bucket brigade where people are in a line passing buckets of water in order to fight a fire. If all the buckets are 1 gallon, everyone can pass the buckets quickly, but none dumps much water on the fire. Someone decides to switch to bigger 5-gallon buckets, figuring the fire will get put out faster that way. Unfortunately, the people on the brigade line can't handle the 5-gallon buckets so easily, so the line slows as people struggle to pass the bigger buckets. In the end, using the smaller buckets got more of the fire put out in a given period of time than using the bigger buckets.

That's a lot like the way cylinder head ports work at low- and midrange engine speeds: smaller ports may not be able to hold as much air as larger heads, but they're more efficient at getting that air to the cylinder.

However, assuming the brigade line could pass either size bucket at a high rate of speed, the brigade would be able to put out more of the fire (that is, make more power) with the larger buckets in the same amount of time than with the small buckets.

So at lower engine speeds smaller ports are more efficient, while at higher rpm the small ports can't move enough air through the engine, so power drops off.

Although it doesn't take port shape into account, one of the most common and effective ways to determine whether a cylinder head will work well for a given application is to examine the head's intake port volume.

Different engine designs have different port volumes, so you can't simply say "engines under 350 cubic inches need a port volume of X cubic centimeters." To give you an idea of how port volumes can be used to tailor engine performance, consider the following information on heads for the ubiquitous small-block Chevy.

In general, three flow ranges are typically used to group small-block Chevy heads. Ports of 179 cc or less are considered small-port heads and typically work well in street engines. Medium-port volumes range from 180 to 199 cc and are better for larger displacement street small blocks, or smaller engines that often need to turn high rpms. Finally, heads with port volumes of 200 cc or more are large-port heads and are usually race-only pieces.

Nearly all production Chevy heads fall into the small-port category, often far below the 179-cc cutoff. The aluminum L98 Corvette head used from the mid-1980s through 1991 is a prime example with its 163-cc intake ports. Many performance heads fall into the second grouping, including GM's own LT4 head with its sizable 195-cc intake ports for improved flow. Heads in the 200-plus category are often racing heads.

There is a fourth group—the *true* racing heads, which have massive intake port volumes. Good examples of these heads are GM's 18-degree and SB2 NASCAR heads; the former features 258-cc intake ports in computer numerically controlled (CNC) form, while the latter can stuff a full 280 cc of air and fuel in its intake ports (in CNC configuration). These heads have such cavernous ports that using them on the street would simply be foolish, unless you were to start with non-CNC versions (which measure 210 and 196 cc of intake port volume each, respectively) then do only minimal machine work.

Port shape can have just as much effect on airflow through the port as port volume, however. Ports should feature only gentle bends that guide the air to or from the cylinder. If the airflow encounters an abrupt, tight corner, it smashes into it, disrupting the flow. A smooth, gradual corner bends the air without disrupting flow.

Unfortunately, gradual corners require more room than tight ones, and the physical size of stock-style cylinder heads imposes unavoidable limitations. Again, using Chevrolet heads as the example, the company's first attempts at straightening out the small block's cylinder heads involved raising the port entry (intake) and exit (exhaust), resulting in the so-called raised port-style cylinder heads. The improvements were promising, so Chevy went a step further and developed the high-port race-only heads, which had ports elevated roughly 1/2 inch above their stock location. To make such a radical change, however, the heads are much taller than production heads, requiring special, matching intake manifolds. It also changes how exhaust systems connect and creates other problems, not to mention that they don't exactly look stock.

An area that presents a significant flow restriction through most cylinder head ports is the valve pocket, the area just beneath the valves in the ports. The valve pockets on many production heads are too small and restrictive. Unfortunately, this is one of the more difficult areas to modify, so most enthusiasts don't do any pocket porting, when small changes here can be more beneficial than large-port entry and gasket matching changes. A basic guideline is to try to enlarge the diameter of the pocket area beneath the valve to between 70 and 85 percent of the valve's diameter.

The valve guide support material in the valve pocket also tends to impede airflow, so streamlining the support will reduce the restriction, improving flow.

Polishing ports until they have a smooth finish is not as necessary as once believed. While it is still beneficial to remove casting irregularities (casting flash, casting marks, and so on), a glassy-smooth port finish may actually make it easier for fuel to fall out of suspension, thus decreasing efficiency.

## Valves

Nearly all American engines from the 1950s through the 1970s used two valves per cylinder—one intake and one exhaust—to control the flow of air and fuel into the cylinder and the flow of exhaust gases out of the cylinder. Stock valves are typically steel, and the valve face diameters vary depending on the particular engine.

Stock valves are reliable (at modest engine speeds), but their small sizes and inefficient valve seat and face cuts often

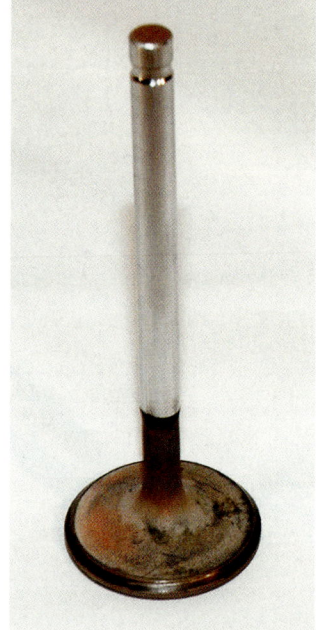

If you're opting to rebuild your existing heads, you'll want to fill them with high-performance valves that offer reduced weight and increased strength. Reducing valvetrain mass allows for higher engine rpm before you encounter valve float.

# Long Block Assembly

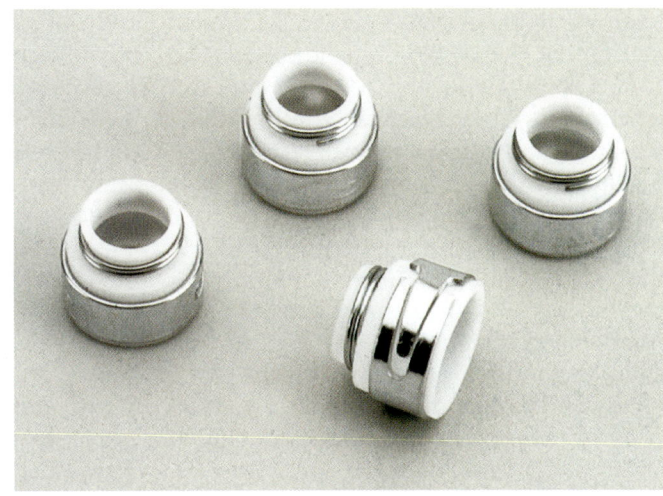

**Left:** High-performance valve springs, like this assortment from Crane Cams, are responsible for closing the valves when needed. High-strength (but lightweight) retainers and locks are also important. Note, however, that springs that are too stiff can result in accelerated valve and head wear, so choose carefully. *Crane Cams photo*

**Right:** PC-style valve seals with Teflon provide exceptional oil control—far better than stock-style umbrella seals. *Crane Cams photo*

limit performance. While a performance valve job will increase the efficiency of stock valves, the size of the valve may still restrict airflow. In addition, stock valves are not designed to withstand higher cylinder temperatures associated with high-performance engines.

Aftermarket valves are available in a variety of materials, most commonly stainless steel, and in a range of sizes. The size of valve you run depends on the design and airflow capabilities of your cylinder heads and your camshaft specifications. In addition, valves that are too large in diameter may contact the cylinder walls, causing immediate catastrophic engine damage.

Both stock and aftermarket valves are improved when treated to a multiangle valve job to smooth the flow of air. A triple-cut valve seat and double-cut valve face typically work best. Valve jobs are more science than mysterious art form, so it pays to have your heads worked on by someone with performance engine experience. For a cheap rebuild your local machinist is probably fine, but if you're hoping to make lots of power, a valve job is not a place to cut corners, if you'll pardon the expression. A bad valve job can kill a head's flow, plus lead to valve sealing problems and durability problems.

A number of exotic valve designs and materials are available. While some designs (such as hollow-stem valves that reduce weight) offer obvious advantages, they are not always well suited to street use. Necked-down valves have a smaller stem diameter for the portion of the stem that runs through the port. Necked-down valves do save a little weight, but their true benefit is reduced flow disruption. Since they are generally durable, they are good for nearly any application, with the possible exception of maximum effort competition engines.

One problem you definitely want to avoid is self-destructive wear from running unleaded fuel in older engines that were designed with leaded fuel in mind. The specific problem is erosion of the valve seats, particularly the exhaust valve seat. Tetraethyl lead in leaded gas lubricated and cooled the valves. It also cushioned the contact between the valve and the seat when the valve shut. But unleaded gas can't provide that protection, so the valve seats will eventually wear or recede into the head. To prevent this, you need to have hardened valve seats installed in your heads. The process is relatively inexpensive and well worth the money.

It's also not a bad idea to upgrade your valves for the same reason: older valves expected the presence of lead and can wear prematurely without it. Stainless-steel valves are an excellent replacement but won't cost you an arm and a leg.

## Valve Guides

Valve guides are replaceable sleeves through which the valves slide. Most production guides are iron, but bronze valve guides are popular replacements for performance engines. Instead of replacing guides, many machine shops ream out iron guides and fit them with bronze liners; the iron shell provides superior strength while the bronze lining reduces valve wear and friction.

Guide liners are an excellent solution, and one of the best designs is the interrupted spiral guide, which helps increase guide oiling for decreased friction and valve wear. A groove spirals down the inside of the guide liner, which allows oil to keep the valve stem well lubricated. The groove does not extend to the bottom of the guide (it's "interrupted"); this prevents excessive oil consumption.

Simple iron guides are actually a great solution for any application, except professional-level competition engines. Aside from being economical, they're durable.

Guides should be replaced (or relined) whenever cylinder heads are rebuilt. To save money, some machine shops knurl the valve guides, rather than replacing or relining them. But knurling digs up the inside of the guide and often results in accelerated guide wear.

## Combustion Chambers

A cylinder head's combustion chamber is where combustion takes place, and its size and shape have a lot to do with how efficiently the fuel/air mixture burns.

In the old days, combustion chambers were large, but as automakers learned the importance of an uninterrupted combustion process, they realized that domed pistons were inefficient. To switch to flat-topped or dished pistons (which don't obstruct the flame front as it travels through the cylinder), the size of the combustion chamber had to be reduced to maintain compression and good power. As a result, many modern heads have combustion chambers that are nearly one-third smaller than vintage heads.

This may pose a problem for someone trying to build a high-performance street engine because the small chambers of late-style performance heads may result in high compression, which would likely cause detonation when running pump gas. So if you plan on installing late-model heads, make sure they are compatible with the rest of your engine, specifically the piston domes.

### Cylinder Head Materials

Cylinder heads are typically available in either iron or aluminum. Iron was the material favored by the auto manufacturers because it is both inexpensive and extremely durable; however, many aftermarket companies—including the performance parts divisions of the Big Three—rely almost exclusively on aluminum for their performance heads.

A cylinder head's material doesn't affect airflow through the head, but it can affect power production. For example, aluminum heads run cooler and thus allow a more aggressive ignition curve before detonation sets in. Delaying the spark allows the air/fuel mixture to be more compressed, so it is easier to ignite, it burns hotter and quicker, and it produces more power. Aluminum heads also shave considerable weight from an engine in addition to being easier to repair when damaged, which is a factor in racing use.

Because of their softer metal, aluminum heads do require valve seat inserts, some form of valve spring seat cup, and also screw-in rocker studs. You'll also need head gaskets designed to survive the differences in expansion rates between the aluminum heads and an iron block.

Iron heads typically have combustion chambers and ports that are shaped during casting, so they have cylinder-to-cylinder variations in volume and shape of the combustion chambers and ports. On the other hand, most aftermarket heads' combustion chambers and ports are machined by CNC equipment. CNC machining ensures that each cylinder's combustion chamber and intake and exhaust ports are identical. This helps equalize power production from cylinder to cylinder, which results in a balanced, smoother-running engine.

### Cylinder Head Recommendations

Unless there is some overwhelming reason, such as competition class rules that require a cast-iron cylinder head, aluminum heads are generally preferable. Given the modest difference in price, they even make economic sense.

If your current cylinder heads have a lot of miles on them, or require extensive machining to configure them the way you want, you may find that replacement heads are a better buy. It's also quicker

Valve covers don't just look good—they serve several functions, too. They protect the engine from debris, allow your engine's crankcase to breathe, help dissipate heat, suppress noise, and even help direct oil back onto your valvetrain. These basic chrome covers are from Trans Dapt.

to order a replacement set of heads than it is to pull your current heads, get them machined, and then reinstall them. If you're in a rush, replacement heads may make even more sense.

If heads for your engine are available in a variety of port volumes, stick to the smaller sizes for any vehicles that will spend at least half their time on the street, because the smaller volumes will enhance throttle response and torque. If your engine will be powering a track-bound race car, then heads with larger port volumes may make sense. Just remember that heads with smaller port volumes can be enlarged for little expense, but purchasing heads with too-large ports would require costly replacement to reduce port size.

## Camshaft and Valvetrain

No other part determines as much of your engine's character as its camshaft. The camshaft determines when valves begin to open—both in relation to the crankshaft position and each other—how quickly they open, how far they open, how long they stay open, and how quickly they close. All of this dictates how much air can flow into and out of your engine.

Of course, a camshaft alone does nothing without the various components that it controls, especially the lifters (also called tappets), rocker arms and shafts, and valves. Together, these items and others make up your engine's valvetrain and fine-tune its airflow capabilities.

With rare exceptions, like Ford's legendary SOHC "Cammer" 427, most vintage V-8 engines use a single camshaft mounted in the engine block between the cylinder banks. The camshaft in a production engine is driven by a timing chain that runs around gears on the front of the crankshaft and camshaft. The camshaft spins at exactly one-half the speed of the crankshaft, thus creating the four strokes of modern internal-combustion engines: intake, compression, power, and exhaust.

Camshafts have egg-shaped lobes that raise lifters that ride on the lobes, which in turn raise the pushrods. Each pushrod raises one end of a rocker arm, causing the other end to push downward against the tip of the valve. As the lifter crests the peak of the cam lobe, a spring connected to the valve with a retainer and keepers closes the valve and keeps tension in the system to prevent parts from falling out.

Newer camshafts are often designed to work only with roller lifters, rather than the traditional flat-faced lifters. Roller camshafts offer a number of advantages that make them well worth considering, despite their added expense.

### Camshafts

Because your camshaft determines how and when your engine's valves open, it determines how much air moves in and out of the engine (intake, exhaust, and head flow capabilities notwithstanding). Changing your camshaft for a larger grind can radically alter the engine's performance.

Myron Cottrell, of Cottrell Racing Engines, recommends that customers swap camshafts first, rather than make a series of small changes with bolt-on parts that, combined, still won't yield the gains of the cam swap. Short of nitrous oxide or forced induction systems, swapping the camshaft is the quickest way to get the most noticeable power gains.

But choosing a camshaft isn't exactly child's play. For starters, there are two basic types of camshafts, each with two different types of lifters. Beyond that, you've got the characteristics of the cam lobes to consider, like valve lift and duration, plus the opening and closing timing events of each of the two valves. Then there are the lobe centerlines, the lobe separation angles (and overlap) and more, each of which will distinctly affect how your engine will perform.

Fortunately, unless you're trying to design your own custom-ground camshaft, you won't have to deal with all of this. Camshaft manufacturers have

High-performance cams come in all sizes, and a variety of types, based on the type of lifter they use. This Crane cam is designed for hydraulic roller lifters, which make it easy to maintain yet capable of helping your engine develop more power by letting it breathe better on both the intake and exhaust strokes. *Crane Cams photo*

already explored the possibilities and can help you select a camshaft that will work with the powertrain components you've installed.

Roller camshafts offer significant advantages in terms of valve opening and closing rates. Flat-lifter cams have to have gradual camshaft lobe opening and closing ramps so the lifter can follow the lobe profile without digging into it. Because of the large rolling wheel on their base, roller lifters can follow a much steeper ramp, allowing the valve to open and close more quickly. This means the valve can be open at maximum lift earlier and remain there longer than it could with a flat-lifter cam. To help you visualize it, a typical flat-lifter cam's lobe looks like an egg, but a roller lifter lobe looks more like a rectangle with a round bottom. While the two valves may be open the same amount of time (measured in crankshaft degrees), the roller cam will allow more air and fuel into the cylinder and more exhaust gases out, thus making more power. Aftermarket roller cams are available for many engines that were originally equipped with only flat-lifter cams, but they do require use of matching aftermarket roller lifters.

While it is possible to compare lift and lobe separation angles between flat-lifter and roller cams, you cannot directly compare duration figures—even duration at 0.050-inch figures. This is because roller cams will tolerate much more aggressive opening and closing ramps, which gives them longer duration figures.

## General Camshaft Recommendations

Making general camshaft recommendations for unspecified engines is like throwing darts at a moving target while blindfolded. While there are some general specs that will *usually* work well, ultimately the only way to determine whether a camshaft will work in your engine is to try it. Fortunately, aside from the several hours you'll spend performing the swap, the investment isn't outrageously expensive.

With that in mind, here are some recommendations that have to be taken with a very large grain of salt.

### High-Performance Street Driving

If you really want to have fun on the street, you want your engine to make gobs of power below 4,000 rpm, because that's about as fast as your engine will usually run. For that, you'll want a shorter duration cam because the valves will trap cylinder pressure at lower rpm, when there's plenty of time for the cylinders to fill. Wider lobe separation angles (less overlap) are desirable for the same reason: they don't bleed off cylinder pressure and they don't dilute the fresh air/fuel mixture with exhaust gases. Another figure that is often better when bigger is valve lift: the farther you lift the valve, the more air can flow past the valve to either enter or exit the cylinder.

If, by chance, you happen to be working on a big-inch stroker motor, you're in luck. Thanks to the torque advantages of larger displacement engines, these engines are less sensitive to changes that rob low-rpm power. For such engines, narrower lobe separations and longer duration often provide results worth smiling over.

### Drag Racing

Low-end response isn't of much concern on a drag strip, so you can select tighter lobe separations and longer duration to promote upper-rpm cylinder filling. Valve lifts, likewise, are generally much greater than on the street. Keep in mind that this requires careful attention to valve-to-piston clearance.

Cam installation is generally pretty straightforward once the cam bearings have been installed. Depending on your engine block, crank stroke, and rod design, you may need to consider a "small base-circle" cam to ensure things that shouldn't contact each other don't.

# Long Block Assembly

Most muscle car V8 engines featured a chain-drive system to turn the camshaft. The stock system should at least be replaced with a high-performance, double-roller chain and gear set, like this one from Edelbrock.

Recommendations are much more difficult to pin down on competition engines because there are endless combinations of equipment and modifications that may have been made to an engine, not to mention differences between vehicles the engines are in.

One general improvement for drag racing is to try retarding the camshaft a few degrees, which will usually boost top-end power.

## The Valvetrain

A camshaft is just a big lumpy stick of iron (or steel, in the case of roller cams). By itself, it doesn't do anything except take up space in the block. It needs an entire cast of supporting characters to even allow your engine to run.

Unfortunately, the parts it calls upon are among the weakest parts in your engine. Often it is not the reciprocating assembly of your engine that limits rpm, but the valvetrain assembly. Thus, as enthusiasts start making more power and looking for more speed (which ultimately results in increased engine speeds), they need more durable valvetrain components. The fact that aftermarket performance components also provide other benefits is icing on the cake.

### Understanding Your Valvetrain

The first thing to understand about the valvetrain is that its job is to convert the round-and-round motion of the camshaft into an up-and-down motion at the valves. Unfortunately, the antiquated design of many engines dictates complicated valvetrain geometry that impairs reliability and limits valvetrain upgrades.

The second thing to understand is that your instinct to replace everything with heavy-duty parts is wrong. Sure, heavy-duty pushrods, oversized springs, and other parts will make the valvetrain more reliable, but those parts will also increase valvetrain weight, which produces valve float at lower speeds. Essentially, the more mass your valvetrain has, the harder it is for the valve springs to close the valves. When the momentum (mass X velocity) of the valvetrain components is so great that the valve spring can't begin closing the valve when the lifter crests the peak of the cam lobe, the valve stays floating open in the cylinder longer than it should. If you're lucky, the worst that will happen when this occurs is that your valve springs will overheat, causing them to lose tension (which further reduces the speed where valve float will occur next time). If you're unlucky, the valve may contact the piston, bending the valve and maybe destroying the piston and combustion chamber. Or worse (yes, it can get worse), the valve spring retainer and keepers could lose their grip on the valve. If that happens, the valve drops into the cylinder, destroying the piston, cylinder walls, and combustion

Brass core (i.e., freeze) plugs will greatly outlast standard steel plugs. This set is from Milodon.

chamber. This can also cause damage throughout the engine as little bits of debris ricochet back into the intake and make their way to other cylinders.

**Planning Valvetrain Upgrades**

The goal of any valvetrain modification should be to increase reliability without increasing the mass. Even better, the modifications should decrease the mass, which extends the upper rpm limit.

Another problem that valvetrains encounter is flex, which typically occurs in pushrods and rocker arm studs, on engines that have them. Minimizing pushrod and rocker stud flex keeps valvetrain geometry precise, which minimizes the chance of problems and ensures that you get full and proper valve movement.

Speaking of valve movement, rocker arms are designed to amplify the cam lobe's lift. Stock rockers for many engines use 1.5:1 rocker ratios, which means that the valve end of the rocker travels 1.5 times farther than the pushrod end of the rocker. At least, that's what production rockers are supposed to do. Unfortunately, production stamped-steel rockers are not highly accurate, which causes different cylinders to have different valve lift and duration actions. This naturally affects cylinder-to-cylinder power balance. In addition to not being accurate, stamped-steel rockers aren't efficient either. In one fell swoop you can eliminate rocker ratio variations, and at the same time decrease friction and reduce valvetrain mass, simply by installing aftermarket aluminum roller (fulcrum) rockers. Going a step further, you can switch to rockers with a higher-than-stock ratio, which will cause the valve to lift farther from the valve seat.

Some engines, such as Mopar small-blocks, suffer from poor lubrication of the rocker assemblies. Obviously, improving lubrication can have dramatic benefits not only in terms of performance, but also durability, because increasing the volume of oil supplied to the valvetrain improves the cooling of those components, which extends their life.

The remaining possibilities involve upgrading the valves and their related hardware. Production valve springs are usually single-coil springs with a flat-wire

Harmonic dampers help minimize engine vibrations to keep your engine from literally shaking itself apart. They're also a vital part of balancing your rotating assembly. This Fluidampr unit uses a heavy, viscous fluid to dampen vibrations. *Fluidampr photo*

internal damper, except on some higher-performance engines. Although these are far from the hot race setup, they work well in high-performance street applications and even milder racing use. Aggressive cam profiles will exceed a stock spring's ability to control the valve, so whenever you change cams, make sure you throw in a set of compatible valve springs too.

If you end up changing valve springs, you may need to change valve spring retainers. Even if your new springs don't require them, you may want to install stronger, lighter replacements. Another aspect of spring retainers to consider upgrading is the angle of the valve keeper pocket in the retainer, though this is largely warranted only for race engines.

Two final concerns are the valve seals and the valve guides. The seals are designed to control the amount of oil that can travel down the valve guide into the valve pocket area of the cylinder head. For most high-performance applications, you will want to run Perfect Circle (PC)–style valve seals. The guide is simply a replaceable sleeve in which the valve travels up and down. Because the valve is mounted at an angle, some wear of the valve guide is inevitable. Guides make it easy to restore the valve's geometry so that it aligns properly with the seat.

## Valvetrain Components

The following section describes the basic functions of the various valvetrain components, the challenges those components face, and potential upgrades for different situations.

A gear drive timing set is another great option because it virtually never wears out and has no "chain slop" so cam timing doesn't fluctuate. *Lunati photo*

### Cam Drive (Timing) Sets

Every cam needs a drive system—something to turn it. A gear on the cam and another on the crank are connected by chains, gears, or ribbed belts. Each system has its advantages and disadvantages.

Chain-drive systems are inexpensive and relatively quiet; however, the chain can stretch over time, causing erratic timing. Double-row true roller chain-drive sets minimize this possibility, while reducing friction to free up power.

Gear drives are much stronger than chains, and they don't stretch. Yet because gear-drive systems so accurately transfer the crankshaft's rotation to the cam, they can cause unwanted harmonics to be transmitted too. Most gear drives are noisy, though more recent designs are quieter, and thus less objectionable for street use. Gear drives can use either a single gear between the cam and crank gears or twin gears, and the systems may or may not fit beneath stock timing chain covers.

Belt-drive systems are very quiet, very accurate, easily adjustable, and the belt is easily replaced. The catch is that the belts do stretch and need to be replaced rather frequently.

## CRANKSHAFT TERMINOLOGY

**Base Circle:** The portion of the camshaft lobe during which no lift is generated, after the intake valve has closed but before the exhaust valve begins to open.

**Duration:** How long, in crankshaft degrees, the valve remains open. Note that there are generally two figures quoted: "advertised" duration and duration "at 0.050-inch." The "at 0.050" figure is a standard for comparing two cams, whereas advertised figures are not consistently measured from one cam to the next or from one manufacturer to the next.

**Lash:** The clearance between the rocker arm and valve stem tip, in inches, required by mechanical tappet (flat or roller) camshafts to allow for heat expansion. Lash figures are usually different for intake valves than for exhaust valves and are provided on a camshaft specification card provided with new camshafts.

**Lift:** Expresses how high, in inches, a cam lobe rises above the cam's base circle (lobe lift) or how high the valve is raised from the valve seat (valve lift). Note that valve lift is the lobe lift multiplied by the rocker arm ratio. For example, a cam with 0.300-inch lobe lift and a 1.5:1 rocker produces 0.450-inch valve lift; but with a 1.6:1 rocker it produces 0.480-inch valve lift.

**Lobe Centerline:** The point, in crankshaft degrees, of the exact center (usually peak) of the cam lobe, either intake or exhaust.

**Lobe Separation:** The number of degrees of crankshaft rotation between the centerlines of the intake and exhaust valves of a given cylinder.

**Overlap:** The number of degrees of crankshaft rotation during which both the exhaust and intake valves of a given cylinder are both open (as the former is closing and the latter is opening). Can be calculated by adding the intake valve's opening point to the exhaust valve's closing point.

**Ramps:** The portion of the cam lobe during which the valve is either opening or closing.

**Single Pattern/Dual Pattern:** Single-pattern camshafts have the same lift and duration for both the intake and exhaust lobes. Dual-pattern cams have differing lift and/or duration specifications for the intake and exhaust lobes, usually to allow the exhaust valve to remain open longer to increase exhaust flow out of the cylinder to compensate for weaker cylinder head exhaust ports.

**Valve Timing:** The points, as measured in crankshaft rotational degrees, when the valves either open or close.

Because the driven gear mounts to the camshaft with bolts, you must ensure the bolts won't loosen over time, either by safety wiring them or by installing the bolts with a bolt lock plate, which features bendable ears that prevent the bolts from turning. Such lock plates are available for a number of engines, are inexpensive (less than $5), and provide excellent insurance against what could be a serious problem.

### Tappets/Lifters

Tappets—or lifters, as they're more often called—ride on the cam lobe. As the camshaft spins, the lobe's eccentric shape causes the tappet to move up and down in its bore. This, in turn, raises the pushrod, thus tipping the rocker arm, which pushes the valve open.

Four basic types of tappets are available: mechanical flat, hydraulic flat, mechanical roller, and hydraulic roller. Mechanical tappets (flat or roller) will sustain higher engine rpm before floating off the cam's lobe, making them popular choices for racing engines. Mechanical lifters require a slight clearance between the rocker arm nose and the tip of the valve (to allow for heat expansion), however, and this clearance causes a ticking noise during engine operation as the rocker strikes the valve tip. The vibrations and shock caused by the ticking also tend to loosen the rocker arm, requiring periodic adjustment.

Hydraulic tappets work similarly to shock absorbers: the oil within them cushions the movements of the valvetrain. This results in much quieter operation; however, because the tappet's pushrod seat takes time to reseat after the lifter crests the peak of the cam lobe, hydraulic lifters will lose contact with the cam lobe at engine speeds that are several hundred rpm slower than will mechanical lifters. Because of the cushioning effect hydraulic lifters provide, they do not induce harsh vibrations into the valvetrain and thus require far less frequent adjustment. This usually extends the life of other valvetrain components, such as pushrods and valve stems.

If you don't mind performing routine maintenance, solid or mechanical lifters allow higher rpms than hydraulic lifters, which tend to pump up much above 5,000 rpm. Note that the particular style of tappets, or lifters, that your engine requires is dictated by the camshaft you install. Each camshaft is designed to work only with a particular style of lifter.

In addition, old flat-tappet lifters should never be used with a new camshaft, because the lifters will have a wear pattern that may cause accelerated wear of the cam lobes. Likewise, if you ever remove old lifters and intend to reinstall them with the same camshaft, make sure that you reinstall each lifter in its original position, since lifters and lobe wear together to form compatible mating surfaces. There's no problem using new lifters with an old cam, and roller lifters aren't subject to these rules.

### Pushrods

Pushrods have two functions: First, they are responsible for transmitting the tappet's lift up to the rocker arm. Second, a hollow channel inside the pushrod acts as a passage to deliver oil to the rocker arm and valve assembly at the top of the cylinder head. One end of the pushrod rests in a cup in the tappet, and the other sits in a similar cup in the rocker arm. Holes in the lifter and rocker arm allow oil to enter and exit the pushrod.

**Left:** Modern performance cars usually rely on roller lifters (in either "solid" or hydraulic designs) to allow for faster, longer cam timing for more power and cleaner emissions. Most older engines can be upgraded with a cam designed for roller lifters. *Competition Cams photo*

**Below:** Any time you replace your cam, you've got to replace your lifters to ensure proper wear. Aftermarket hydraulic lifters are vastly improved over 1960s technology, so replace yours when you rebuild.

High-performance pushrods can further reduce valvetrain mass while increasing strength. *Crane Cams photo*

Unfortunately, pushrods suffer from a bad reputation that isn't entirely deserved. As pushrods attempt to transmit the lift from the lifter to the rocker arm, they are subjected to some complex, compound geometry. This is necessary because of the placement of intake ports and water passages in the head while the pushrod travels through an arc dictated by the rocker arm. This geometry causes the pushrod to experience some side loading, which can lead to bending. The forces become greater at higher rpm and with higher valve spring pressures. Still, pushrods—especially hardened performance units—are generally able to withstand these forces. Big monkey wrenches are thrown into the works, however, if the engine experiences valve float, because valve float introduces slack into the system. This allows the already complex valvetrain geometry to become even more complicated, increasing the side loading of the pushrods, causing them to bend.

Factory pushrods for many V-8 engines are usually about 5/16 inch in diameter and made of steel. They are reasonably strong but are not generally able to withstand sustained operation over 5,500 rpm without risk of bending. Aftermarket pushrods are available in both larger diameters (3/8 inch is a common upgrade) and stronger materials, such as chrome-moly steel. Despite the added weight, large-diameter, stronger pushrods are a worthy investment, especially for engines that will see sustained high rpm; they will increase engine reliability.

Depending on the type of rocker arms and rocker mount system being used, you may also need to run pushrod guide plates to minimize pushrod side-to-side movement. With the exception of one company's plastic parts, pushrod guide plates are made of steel, so hardened pushrods are required to prevent wear.

**Rocker Arms**

Rocker arms convert the pushrod's life into a downward push that lifts the valve off of its seat. They pivot on individual rocker arm studs or pedestals, or they all run together on a common shaft that runs the length of the head. Production rocker arms on many engines are made of stamped steel and do not feature roller tips or fulcrums.

The typical rocker arm ratio is 1.5:1, meaning that a camshaft lobe lift of 0.300 inch is amplified 1.5 times by the rocker arm, resulting in 0.450 inch of valve lift. Production tolerances, however, cause production rocker ratios to vary considerably. It's not uncommon for an engine to be equipped with one or more rockers that actually measure 1.48:1 and others that may be as high as 1.52:1 or more. While that may not sound like much, a 1.48:1 rocker ratio results in a 0.444-inch lift from a 0.300-inch lobe, while a 1.52:1 ratio will result in a 0.456-inch lift from the same lobe—a difference of 0.012 inch. An inconsistency like that can greatly affect overall engine efficiency and cause unbalanced cylinder-to-cylinder power output.

Aftermarket lifters are typically much more precise; however, a 1.5:1 ratio aftermarket rocker arm often opens the valve slightly more than 1.5 times the lobe lift, because as the top of the rocker swings through its arc, the leverage ratio changes slightly.

Nonroller stamped-steel rockers are available from aftermarket performance parts companies, but roller versions are preferable, especially rockers with roller fulcrums (pivots). These reduce friction and can result in a 10-degree or better reduction in oil temperatures, not to mention freeing up power. Fully rollerized aftermarket rockers are usually constructed of either cast or forged aluminum, while roller-tipped rockers are typically steel.

**Far left:** Rocker arms convert the upward motion of the pushrods to downward motion to open the valves. Most stock muscle car engines relied on stamped steel rockers that were durable but heavy and generated significant friction. Aftermarket arms are available cheap but are far more accurate than stock and often feature longer slots to function properly with high-lift cams. *Lunati photo*

**Left:** This Crane rocker arm features a roller tip and fulcrum to reduce friction, an aluminum body to reduce mass, plus an oversize 1.7:1 ratio (stock = 1.5:1), which effectively increases valve lift. *Crane Cams photo*

Because rocker arms multiply the lobe lift, using a rocker arm with a higher ratio (such as 1.6:1 or even 1.7:1) is essentially like swapping the camshaft for a bigger cam. For instance, a 0.300-inch lobe lift translates to 0.450 inch of valve lift with a 1.5:1 ratio; 0.480 inch of lift with a 1.6:1 ratio; and 0.510 inch with 1.7:1 rockers. Thus, an hour spent changing the rocker arms could boost valve lift by more than 0.060 inch! Some camshafts and cylinder heads respond well to a mixed rocker ratio setup, such as 1.5:1 rockers for the intake valves but 1.6:1 rockers for the exhaust valves. This allows the cylinders to empty out the exhaust more completely and reduce contamination of the fresh intake charge. Consult your camshaft and cylinder head manufacturers or machinists for their rocker ratio recommendations.

### Studs, Shafts, and Pedestals

Rocker arms need to pivot on something, and typically that something is a rocker stud, a rocker shaft, or a pedestal of some sort. Chevy and other vintage engines often relied on stud-mounted rocker arms, while Mopar engineers favored shaft systems, and Ford engineers often called for pedestal-based systems. Each has its strengths and weaknesses, and for the most part, there's not much you can do to change from one system to another. You're pretty much stuck with whatever rocker system the engine's engineers gave it, but you can improve on the factory's efforts.

Rocker studs have the seemingly simple job of locating the rocker arm in a fixed position. Stock rocker studs are usually about 3/8 inch in diameter and are either pressed into the cylinder heads or screwed in. Aluminum cylinder heads often use screw-in rocker studs, which are always preferable, since pressed-in studs can loosen and actually pull out of the head. Heads that have pressed-in studs can be machined to receive screw-in studs. Screw-in studs require pushrod guide plates, which typically require hardened pushrods. If you use guide plates on a cylinder head not originally equipped with them, you may also have to enlarge the holes in the cylinder head through which the pushrods travel for added clearance.

Studs are available in larger 7/16-inch diameter, which will resist bending and flexing better than the thinner 3/8-inch units, and thus result in more accurate valvetrain action. And since the portion of the studs that thread into the head are usually the same size for both the 3/8-inch and 7/16-inch rocker studs, swapping to the beefier studs is a simple task. Note, however, that larger diameter rocker studs do require rockers designed for them.

For racing applications that will see extremely high rpm, you may want to use a rocker stud girdle, which is two long pieces of metal (usually aluminum) that are bolted together, one on each side of the studs. The girdle ties each stud to all the others on that head for additional strength and rigidity.

Rocker pedestals are similar in concept to rocker studs, except the pedestals are typically cast as part of the head, and the rocker assemblies bolt to them. Because the pedestals are an integral part of the head, they're very stable. Unfortunately, they don't allow much adjustment and tuning flexibility without aftermarket shims or adapters.

Rocker shafts offer superior strength because a bank of rocker arms (all intakes, all exhausts, or both) mount to a single tubular steel cylinder that is secured to several pedestals along the length of the head. The design offers several advantages: they're strong, and they prevent the rockers from cocking sideways as they move, which would alter valvetrain geometry and induce side loads on the valve tip. Those side loads ultimately lead to accelerated valve guide wear.

### Valve Seals

Valve seals are used to limit the amount of oil that is used to lubricate the valve stem and valve guide. Two basic types are used: the production-style O-rings and the performance-oriented PC or umbrella seals that clamp around the head of the valve guide.

PC-style guides are preferable to the stock O-rings. PC seals may require modifying the valve guides for proper installation and clearance between the seal and the spring or spring retainer.

O-rings deserve a quick installation note too. Novice engine builders often unwittingly install them incorrectly; they must be installed *after* the spring retainer, while the spring is compressed. Then the keepers can be installed and the spring can be decompressed.

### Valve Springs

While the camshaft is responsible for opening the valve, the valve spring closes the valve, once the lifter crests the peak of the cam lobe. Valve springs must be matched to the camshaft; too strong a spring can cause the lifter to wear the cam lobe.

Valve springs weaken with age and mileage, and new springs should always be used when installing a new camshaft. Get the springs that the cam manufacturer recommends.

When installing valve springs, make sure they are all at the specified installed height. That is, each spring should be the same height, top to bottom, as the others. Use shims between the spring and the head to reduce the spring height, or have the head's spring seats machined if the installed height is shorter than specified.

If the spring heights aren't equal, the actual spring tension from valve to valve will be different, which will alter power production, cylinder to cylinder. The shims essentially just compensate for differences in the height of valve seats and spring pockets.

It's also important to inspect for coil binding, especially with high-lift cams or thick-wire springs. With large-diameter springs and roller rockers, it's especially important to check for interference with the rocker arm.

### Valve Spring Retainers and Keepers

Valve spring retainers are metal discs that do exactly as their name implies: they keep the valve springs in place. The valve runs through a hole in the center of the retainer. Production valve spring retainers are made of steel and are typically adequate for general high-performance and mild-racing use. Aftermarket retainers are often made of higher-strength or lighter weight materials, and are available for oversized springs.

Valve spring retainers are held in place by angled valve keepers, and the angle of the bore in which the keepers rest must match that of the keepers. Production keepers typically have a 7-degree angle, while racing keepers often have a 10-degree angle. The sharper angle helps prevent the keepers from pulling through the retainers at high rpm or with exceptionally strong spring pressures.

It's important to verify that there is sufficient clearance between the bottom of the spring retainer and the top of the valve guide and valve seal when the cam is at peak lift.

# Chapter 5
# Gas and Spark

**S**upplying adequate fuel and fire to your engine is essential in achieving optimum performance. Matching these systems to the rest of your combination requires careful consideration.

## Induction System

The induction system is one of the most visible systems of your engine. It has a considerable effect on the engine's appearance, as well as its performance. The engine breathes through its induction system, which also mixes fuel with the incoming air. There are two basic types of induction systems: carbureted and fuel-injected, with some variations within each type. The induction system generally is credited with (or blamed for) fuel efficiency, reliability, and drivability.

Your induction system delivers two vital elements to your engine: air and fuel. The amount of fuel delivered is proportional to the amount of air the engine can ingest. If your induction system restricts how much air the engine can inhale, it reduces how much fuel can be mixed with the air, and thus power is decreased. Alternatively, if your induction system can't supply a sufficient volume of fuel to mix with the air, the engine will run lean, limiting power.

A stock induction system's limitations often appear following other modifications to the engine. Cam changes, better cylinder heads, higher compression, and a free-flowing exhaust system all change the engine's air requirements and can quickly exceed the abilities of a production carb and intake.

When it comes to high-performance upgrades, you have a number of options, including improving what you already have for an intake and carb, swapping it for a hotter factory system, installing an aftermarket carb and intake, or going to a modern fuel-injection system.

Each path has its good and bad points, and we'll explore a few of those in the following sections. But before you worry about the equipment that you'll use to mix the air and fuel, you need to ensure you have enough of each.

### Air Induction System

The air induction system's job on vintage engines was merely to supply air to the carburetor. In most cases, the system consisted of just an air cleaner housing, which may or may not have had an air snorkel (or two). Some engines also incorporated a butterfly valve in the air cleaner snorkels. The butterfly controlled whether air was drawn through the snorkel (and possibly from ducting that lead to the vehicle's exterior) or through a hose that drew hot air from around the exhaust manifolds for better cold weather drivability.

### Cold-Air Induction Systems

Many performance models used cold-air and ram-air induction systems to improve performance. Cold-air induction systems drew cold, dense air from outside the engine compartment. Denser air can support more fuel, which leads to more potential heat energy and more power. Although hood scoops were the most common methods of drawing cold air into the engine, there were others. Ford's Thunderbolts used the inboard headlight buckets as scoops to funnel air to two massive hoses (they actually resembled clothes dryer ducts) that funneled air to the air cleaner. One system that was briefly optional on Oldsmobile 4-4-2s employed a scoop mounted beneath the front bumper and a duct that funneled the air from the scoop to the air cleaner assembly. Chevrolet pioneered

Your high-performance engine needs a free-flowing induction system that won't "choke" the engine, leaving it starving for air or fuel. Fortunately, choices are numerous, from a simple four-barrel carb on an aluminum intake, as shown here, to modern fuel injection systems.

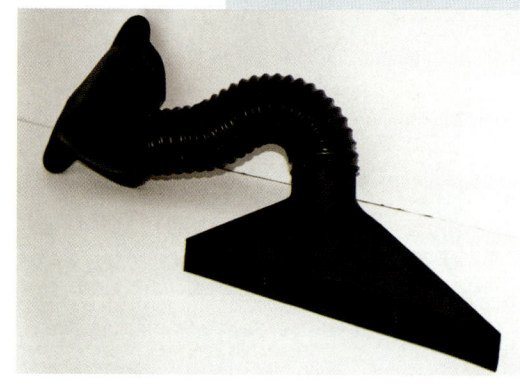

Aftermarket cold-air induction kits are available, like this one that positions a scoop under the front bumper, similar to those available on Oldsmobile 4-4-2 and Hurst-Olds models.

# Gas and Spark

This crate engine from Edelbrock features a dual-quad setup to feed the engine enough air and fuel to develop 315 horsepower. *Edelbrock photo*

**Left:** Many 1960s muscle cars came with air cleaner assemblies that helped funnel cooler outside air into the carburetor, that could hold more fuel in suspension than hot, underhood air. More air and fuel leads to more power, when properly tuned. This is a "Ram Air" air cleaner and hood seal on a Pontiac GTO.

**Right:** 1967 and 1968 Camaro Z/28s came with an ingenious "cowl induction" system that drew cold air from the cowl area below the windshield, through a special duct to the air cleaner.

cowl-induction systems that tapped into a natural low-pressure zone at the base of the windshield. The original 1967 Z/28 system used an oversized snorkel that connected to a hole in the firewall on the passenger side. It drew air from beneath the car's cowl panel. Later cowl-induction systems used hood scoops that ingested air from above the cowl panel.

If your vehicle isn't equipped with a cold-air induction system, you can easily fabricate one. Aftermarket hoods may be available with integrated scoops or ducts that will make the job easier. Or you may have to graft a scoop or duct to a non-scooped hood (of course, using a factory-style scoop is preferable, in order to maintain a stock appearance). Or you might forgo body modifications by running ducts to the grille or headlight areas, or take a cue from many late-model sports cars and draw cool air from beneath the car.

Fans of NASCAR should know that cowl-induction systems are still used, which validates their effectiveness (NASCAR doesn't allow scooped or ducted hoods, or you can bet the racers would use them!), and they can be easily fabricated for almost any vehicle.

### Ram-Air Induction Systems

While cold air alone boosts performance, the benefits of forced-air induction systems were not lost on auto manufacturers. They struggled to provide the benefits of forced-air induction without adding cost-prohibitive superchargers or turbochargers. Thus ram-air systems were developed.

The principle was simple: forward-facing scoops could funnel air directly to air cleaner assembly. The faster the vehicle traveled, the higher the pressure within the system, and the more air was rammed into the engine. Naturally, more air entering the engine meant more fuel was packed into it, so potential heat energy increased, along with power. The early Thunderbolt system, with its forward-facing headlight-bucket scoops and incredible hoses, shoved a massive volume of air into the engine. Chrysler and Oldsmobile, however, made the most radical contributions to ram-air technology, with their cutting-edge hood scoop designs. Chrysler's 440+6 fiberglass hood resulted from wind-tunnel tests. These tests showed that air velocity was low at the hood surface, but the air velocity picked up considerably about 2 inches above the surface. That's where Chrysler stuck the 440+6's hood scoop, and they made the scoop big so it gulped plenty of air.

Oldsmobile, and later Pontiac, realized that positioning hood scoops at the leading edge of the hood, rather than above the carburetor, as was traditionally done, increased the volume of air collected. In addition, the forward position improved the ram-air effect because it provided a less disruptive path to the carburetor, since the air didn't have to abruptly turn

downward once it entered the scoop. Both companies also raised their scoops above the hood to get them up in the air stream.

As with cold-air induction systems, ram-air systems can be created for nearly any vehicle. You can follow the Thunderbolt plan and install large hoses to pick up air from the grille or headlamp area (perhaps you remove a headlamp or two at the track to reveal ducts behind the headlamp buckets). Or you can use the Oldsmobile approach by installing a scoop beneath the front bumper. Naturally, hoods with ram-air scoops would make the job easier.

## Air Cleaner Housings

Ram-air scoops and flow-directing hoses all dumped air into the air cleaner housing. In the old days, air cleaner housings mostly did one job: hold the air filter. Engineers eventually realized that air-cleaner housing design influenced power production. This led to dual snorkel housings and large-diameter, open-element housings.

Beyond just the size of the openings in the housing, though, the shapes of the housing base and lid also affect power production. They help direct the flow of air between the filter and the air horn of the carburetor or fuel-injection throttle body. The shape of the air cleaner components is especially important for low-profile assemblies for vehicles with limited hood clearance. In such circumstances, the base of the air cleaner assembly may be considerably lower than the entry point into the air horn, so the base must direct the airflow upward, then the lid must redirect it downward into the air horn.

Many vehicles left the factory with undersized air cleaners, and one of the easiest upgrades for an air cleaner is to increase the diameter. For example, an air cleaner with a 9-inch diameter has a circumference of about 28 inches, but a 14-inch air cleaner is roughly 44 inches around—a significantly larger surface area to draw air through. This is especially important because most air filters are restrictive; larger air cleaners compensate for the restriction with increased surface area.

Fully enclosed air cleaner assemblies help minimize induction system noise. They also present a significant power restriction because your engine must breathe through the small snorkel (or if you're lucky, dual

Cross-ram intakes, like this Edelbrock unit, feature longer, straighter intake runners that tend to help an engine make more power because the air and fuel flow doesn't have to turn sharp corners, minimizing turbulence and improving airflow velocity.

If two carbs are good, three must be better, right? Chevy's "Tri-Power" system used on 1960s Corvettes uses three Holley two-barrels, though it normally runs only on the center carb until you sink your foot into the throttle. Two Tri-Power 427s were available: a 400-horsepower oval-port and a rectangular port making 35 more horses.

**Left:** Ford's "shaker" hood scoop on the Boss 302 mounted the scoop to the engine, then poked it up through the hood to ingest fresh, cool air.

**Right:** If you're really into tuning carbs, you can pull out all the stops and run a six-pack of Webers, like this set for a Ford.

snorkels), which is like a marathon runner having to breathe through a straw. The air demands of even a stock engine are typically greater than the snorkel's flow capabilities. (Just picture how much smaller that snorkel is compared to just a single cylinder of your engine, let alone all of its cylinders together.)

While a number of aftermarket assemblies are just image enhancements, a few actually provide performance benefits, including a few designs that make it easy to fashion your own cold-air induction system.

### Filtration Systems

Air filters are an absolute necessity. To even consider running without one is tempting fate. The smallest airborne particles can cause catastrophic engine damage, and your sole protection against them is your air filter.

As you might expect, not all air filters are created equal. While the traditional, tried-and-true, paper-element filter is satisfactory for a low-performance vehicle, it neither filters nor flows well enough for use on a high-performance vehicle.

One performance filter uses an oiled gauze-like cloth to extract dirt and other particles from the air. The cloth material is much less restrictive than paper filter elements, plus the oil on the cloth traps contaminants.

Another style of performance filter uses an oiled foam material for even better flow and filtration. The foam has large passages that flow a lot of air; however, the filter is considerably thicker—nearly an inch for most applications—than a thin gauze filter

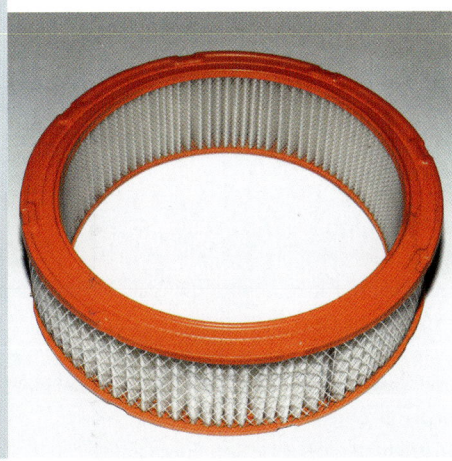

**Left:** Dirty air filters choke your engine. A new filter lets it breathe freely, while a reusable oiled-cotton high-performance filter improves filtration, yet minimizes restrictions. *K&N photo*

**Right:** An air cleaner assembly is needed to prevent dirt and other contaminants from entering your engine and causing damage. This is a simple, round 14-inch air cleaner assembly like those used on a number of 1960s vehicles. It comes from Trans-Dapt with a 3-inch folder paper filter.

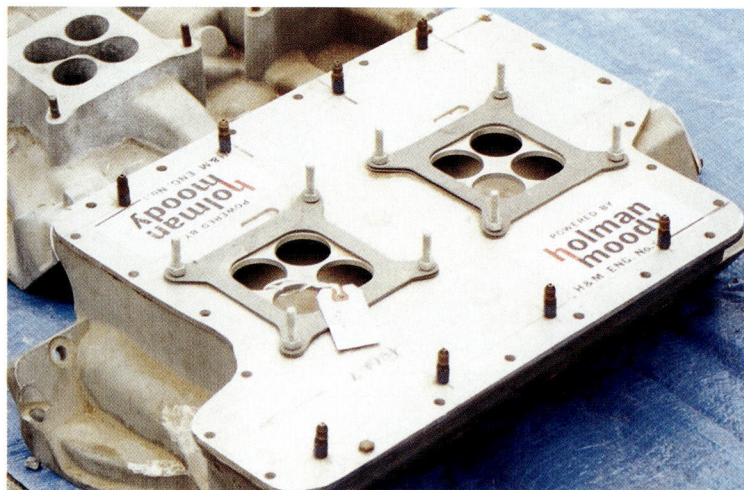

element that's roughly 1/16 inch thick. As with the gauze filters, oil applied to the foam element improves in dirt-trapping abilities.

In addition to the filtration and performance benefits of gauze and foam air filter elements, both are cleanable and reusable. While they will typically cost three to four times the price of a paper element filter, you theoretically would never have to replace your performance filter again. When it gets dirty, simply clean it, re-oil it, and reinstall it.

## Fuel System

Air alone won't create any power within your engine. It needs to be mixed with fuel to create a combustible mixture. As you improve your engine, you change the amount of air it can and will pump through its cylinders, and that means you change how much fuel will be required to achieve the optimal 14.7:1 stoichiometric ratio of air to fuel. If you change the air and fuel requirements of your engine enough, the stock fuel delivery system might not be up to the task.

Most production fuel systems on 1950s, 1960s, and 1970s cars are pretty similar and pretty basic, even those with complicated-looking emissions components tacked on. In their simplest form, the fuel systems consist of a fuel tank, a pickup assembly in the tank, fuel lines, a fuel pump (typically mechanical), fuel filters, and the carburetor or fuel-injection system. Your vehicle might also have a fuel pressure regulator. The parts that deserve the most attention are the fuel pump, the fuel lines, and the fuel pressure regulator.

Production, mechanical fuel pumps use a rubber diaphragm to draw fuel from the fuel tank, then force it to the carburetor. The pump itself is generally mounted to the side of the engine and is driven by a fuel pump pushrod that rides against a lobe on the camshaft. Most production pumps will develop around 8 psi of pressure under normal driving conditions. At higher rpm, the fuel pump isn't efficient enough to sustain that pressure, so the engine begins to lean out and loses power.

Aftermarket mechanical pumps deliver higher pressures at streetable engine speeds, but they also deliver higher pressure at higher rpm, which makes them suitable for racing. In many cases, aftermarket fuel pumps will require a fuel-pressure regulator so excess pressure doesn't force the carburetor's needle valve from its seat, which would flood the engine with fuel.

A better solution —or perhaps an auxiliary one—is to install an electric fuel pump in the fuel line, much like the automakers use on today's cars. The trick is to make the pump's power supply dependent on

**Left:** Swap meets can be a great place to pick up used intakes, like this Edelbrock 2x4 cross-ram for a Ford small-block. Just be careful to inspect intakes for cracks, stripped threads or machining that may make it more difficult to use on your vehicle.

**Right:** Another swap meet treasure: an original Holman & Moody large-plenum 2x4 box intake from a vintage race engine. While overkill for the street, it would look killer on the right vehicle.

Dual-plane intakes, like this Holley unit, are excellent for the street because they feature smaller passages to keep the air velocity up (which helps maintain good fuel atomization), plus a divided plenum, which helps keep the vacuum signal high and helps minimize turbulence to further improve flow characteristics.

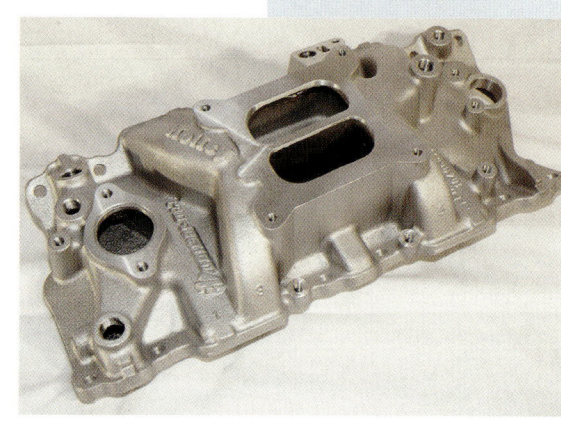

# Gas and Spark

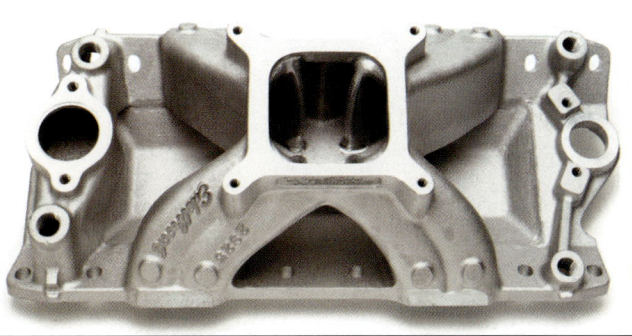

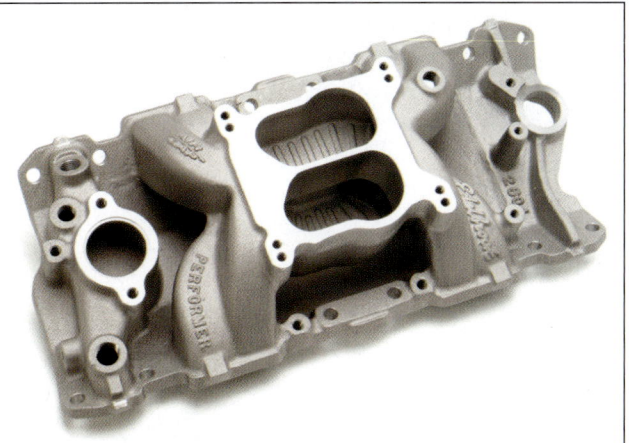

**Top:** Single-plane intakes, like this Edelbrock Victor Jr. model, use large passages that are less restrictive at high rpm, but are usually overkill for the street. Another benefit of most single-plane intakes is the air gap beneath and between the runners, which helps keep the intake and air/fuel mixture cool. *Edelbrock photo*

**Above:** Edelbrock combines some of the features of the dual-plane and single-plane intakes in its Performer AirGap intake. Like a single-plane, air can flow around the runners to keep things cool and maximize power. *Edelbrock photo*

Here's a good view of Edelbrock's 2x4 intake for Pontiac V-8s. It's essentially a dual-plane intake with shared plenums. Two carbs can help lessen the lean-out condition that can happen with end cylinders, but they can cause the opposite condition—over-rich—for middle cylinders, so carbs have to be jetted properly to compensate. *Edelbrock photo*

sufficient oil pressure. That way if you are ever in an accident but the key is left on, your pump won't continue to run, which could present a fire hazard. An electric fuel pump eliminates vapor lock, which results from an air pocket entering a mechanical pump and preventing it from moving fuel. Electric pumps also ensure a constant, steady stream of fuel to the engine, because their speed doesn't depend on engine speed.

Electric fuel pumps are available in a range of pressure capabilities. Carbureted and throttle-body-injected fuel systems require relatively little fuel pressure—typically around 15 psi or less, depending on the system. Multipoint fuel-injection systems require fuel pressures as high as 45 psi.

Aftermarket fuel pressure regulators are typically adjustable, which allows them to be tuned to deliver the proper pressure for nearly any vehicle's fuel system. Stock regulators, on the other hand, deliver a fixed pressure and are unadjustable.

Whether you're running a fuel pressure regulator or not, it's often beneficial to plumb a fuel-pressure gauge into your fuel delivery system. The gauge should be installed after any fuel pumps and pressure regulators but before the carburetor or fuel-injection assembly, to accurately reflect the pressure being delivered.

Fuel filters are your engine's only defense against contaminants in your fuel. Dirt and other debris can clog the minuscule passageways inside a carburetor or damage a delicate fuel injector, so your fuel needs to be as clean as possible. Stock fuel filters on many carbureted vehicles consisted of either a paper or sintered-bronze filter element that was installed in the carburetor's inlet. Although better than nothing, the filters were often too small and too restrictive. Plus, most designs provided a bypass system, which would allow the vehicle to continue to operate even if the filter became completely clogged. In such cases, raw, unfiltered gas entered your engine, which is never good.

Aftermarket fuel filters, even inexpensive inline canister-style units, provide a significant improvement in filtration and flow over the small stock filters. Filters with a glass case let you see both the condition of the filter and the flow rate and condition (cleanliness) of your fuel.

Performance filters are available from a number of companies, many of whom advertise in racing publications. The advantages are improved filtration (trapping smaller particles) and reduced flow restriction. Some are also cleanable and reusable, or offer a quick-replace filter cartridge to minimize downtime and expense.

As with air, cooler fuel is better for making power, and racers have discovered that running a "cool can" can help reduce the temperature of the fuel. This makes it denser, plus it cools the combustion chamber slightly, delaying detonation. A cool can is just a section of spiraled fuel line inside a coffee can–sized can. When ice is poured into

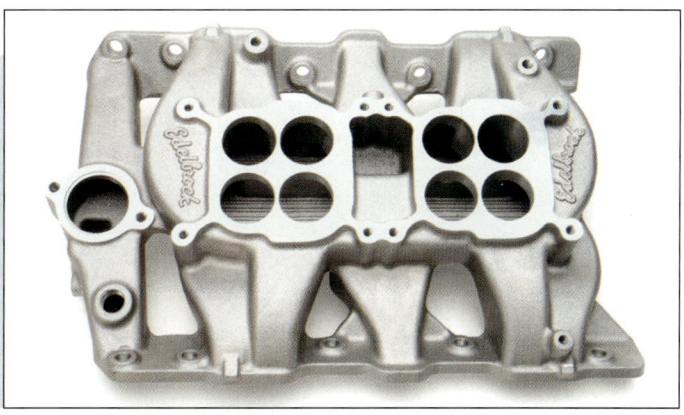

the can, it chills the fuel as it passes through the coils.

You can also increase the inside diameter of your fuel supply lines from the fuel tank to the carburetor or fuel-injection system. While most vintage vehicles used 5/16-inch lines and hoses, many big-block performance engines required more fuel than those small lines could carry. So the factories used larger lines and hoses. Depending on the demands of your engine, you might consider 3/8- or 1/2-inch lines and hoses to prevent fuel starvation.

Finally, it may be beneficial to equip your high-performance vehicle with a fuel return line, which helps keep the fuel cooler (and denser) by removing it from the fuel line near the hot engine. Instead, fuel flows from the tank to the carb or injectors, then excess fuel quickly returns to the fuel tank to start the process over again. Fuel return lines are standard features of modern fuel-injected vehicles, but can be difficult to retrofit on vintage vehicles.

## Carburetion Systems

Although somewhat crude by today's standards, carburetors were the dominant fuel metering devices used during the 1950s, 1960s, and 1970s. They're also elegantly simple and efficient, within certain limitations. In fact, carburetors are so good at what they do that when testing racing engines with both fuel injection and carburetors, the folks at Cottrell Racing Engines routinely develop more peak power with the carbureted systems. The catch is that carbs are really only efficient at the specific air velocity (through the venturis) and pressure for which they're tuned. Fuel-injection systems are much more flexible, and thus deliver better fuel economy, torque, and emissions virtually everywhere else on the power curve but the peak.

There are a number of ways to improve your vintage vehicle's carburetion system. If your engine's fuel needs have not greatly changed, you may want to simply use your stock carburetor and intake manifold. If you converted your low-performance engine into a factory-style, high-performance engine, you will likely need to install an induction system designed for the high-performance factory engine you copied. On the other hand, if your engine is a custom-built fire-breather, it will probably work best with

When it comes to carburetors, the classic Holley four-barrel is still an excellent choice for street driving or racing. *Holley photo*

**Left:** In the old days, carbs came in one color: dichromate gold. Not so today, though. This Holley 4150 was anodized by Holley's Custom Shop (where they work on more than just Holley carbs) to match the car's paint.

**Right:** Edelbrock's AVS four-barrel carburetor (which was based on the original Carter AFB, as used on so many 1960s Mopars) is as state of the art as carburetors come—right down to its chrome-like "Endurashine" finish. *Edelbrock photo*

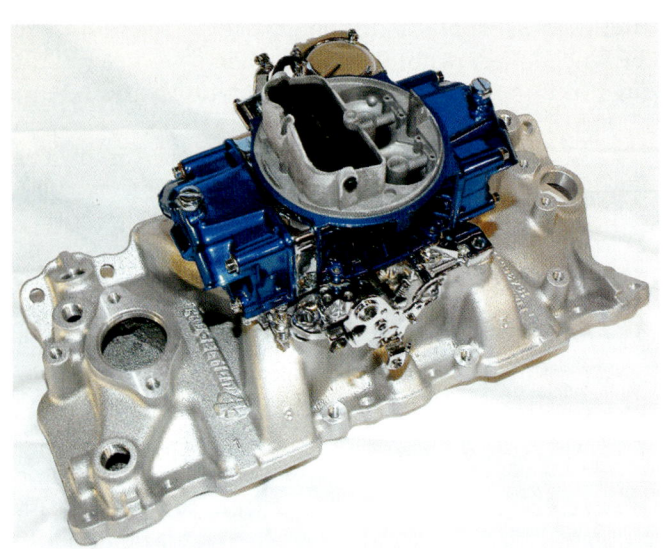

## THIRSTY OR THRIFTY?
## HOW LARGE SHOULD YOUR ENGINE'S CARBURETOR BE?

Picking the proper size carburetor for your application isn't a guessing game. There's actually a scientific method to get you not just in the ballpark, but right down by the dugout. The formula looks like this:

Carb. cfm = ( (Engine cid x Max. rpm) / 3,456 ) * Volumetric Efficiency

As an example, let's take a typical high-performance engine like a 427-cubic-inch big block, since most manufacturers offered engines at least close to that size.

We'll assume a maximum rpm (at the track, on weekends) of 6,000 and a typical volumetric efficiency of about 80 percent (0.80), which is common for street engines.

Carb. cfm = ( ( 427 x 6,000) / 3,456 ) * 0.80

Carb. cfm = 593.1

Based on this formula, a street-driven 427-inch V-8 needs a 593.1-cfm carb, and the closest out-of-the-box carb to that is a 600-cfm unit, which is a far cry from the 735, 780-cfm, or larger carbs that were routinely fitted to these engines from the factory.

A typical 350, operating with the same rpm limit and volumetric efficiency, would need a 486.1-cfm carb. Carter and Edelbrock each offer 500-cfm four-barrel carburetors, while Holley has a handful of carbs sized at 450 and 585 cfm.

Carburetors with vacuum-operated secondary venturis can continually vary their airflow based on the needs of your engine, so a 750-cfm carb may actually only flow 600 cfm, if that's all your engine demands.

an aftermarket system designed to maximize power.

### Upgrades and Modifications

There are two great reasons to upgrade your vehicle's stock carburetion system rather than simply replace it: First, you won't have to concern yourself about whether the carburetion will look stock or not—it will, because it is. Second, it's generally less expensive to tune your carb properly or spend a little time grinding the intake ports than it is to buy a bunch of parts that might need additional work.

You can take a number of different steps to improve your stock carburetion system. A good first step is to ensure that your carburetor is in proper working order. If you're knowledgeable enough, you can tear it down, inspect the parts for wear (particularly the throttle shafts, which tend to become sloppy as the bushings in the throttle plate wear), make any necessary repairs, then put the carb back together using a quality rebuild kit. Make the proper adjustments and you're done. Sounds easy, right? Well, it's not. But it's not exactly rocket science either.

Rebushing the throttle shaft isn't a simple project, so you're better off farming it out to some place such as the Carb Shop or Holley's Custom Shop, both of which offer professional rebuilding and restoration services.

Rebuilding a carb also gives you the chance to remove all the gunk that has built up inside it for years and replace deteriorated gaskets. You can replace and adjust the float assembly and power valves (on Holleys), change jets, and change metering rods and other parts to fine-tune the carb's performance.

Depending on how and when you drive your vehicle, and what type of carburetor(s) it has, you may want to make other modifications. A simple change that's popular for many Holley

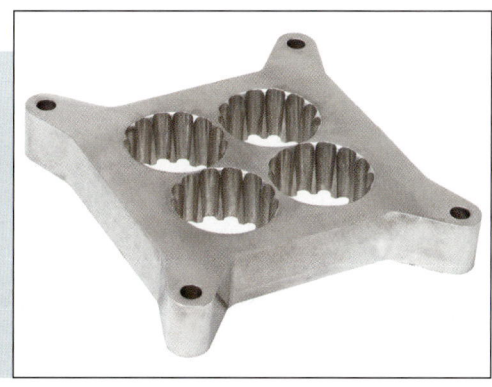

If you're still running a carburetor, a spacer plate, like this one from Crane Cams, can provide an inexpensive, modest power boost and improve throttle response by adding volume to the plenum and straightening the airflow to the ports to improve velocity. But they can create hood-clearance problems. *Crane Cams photo*

carbs is to angle-cut the top of the fuel bowl vent tube, because low-profile air cleaner assemblies can contact the vent tube, plugging it if it's cut straight.

Another Holley change is to remove the air horn by cutting and grinding it. Doing this will eliminate your choke assembly, which will worsen drivability until the engine is warmed up, especially in colder weather. It will also clean up the airflow path to the venturis, however. The same trick works for other carbs with tall air horns, such as Rochester QuadraJets and various Carter carbs.

Holley carbs have a wealth of performance parts to maximize their performance in different situations and operating conditions. One of the best upgrades is adding a quick change–style fuel bowl and metering block assembly, which allows you to change the jets without removing the fuel bowls.

**Top:** Throttle body fuel injection—like Holley's Pro-Jection system—is like an ultra-high-tech carburetor. Fuel injectors are perched atop the throttle body assembly and respond to commands from the Electronic Control Module (the black box) based on various sensor inputs. They're generally more precise and efficient than carbs, but can still result in fuel falling out of suspension before it reaches the cylinders.

**Bottom:** As with carburetors, throttle body injection (TBI) systems use a free-flowing intake manifold that is largely the same as a carbureted intake.

When it comes to adjusting your carburetor, the idea is to hone in on a 14.7:1 air/fuel ratio. One of the easiest and most accurate methods of achieving this is by installing an aftermarket air/fuel meter, which is just an oxygen sensor tied to a display unit. While the air/fuel sensors require some fabrication work to install, they make it easy for you to see whether your engine is running rich or lean in real time, rather than waiting until after the engine is shut off to read spark plugs.

In some cases, it helps to install a heat deflector between the carburetor and the intake manifold. This prevents engine heat from warming the carburetor and the fuel in it, which reduces the density of the fuel. The deflectors are generally a thin sheet of aluminum or other metal with the necessary holes for the throttle blades and carb mounting studs.

Another change that reduces heat in the induction system is blocking off any heat crossover passages in the intake. These passages, which are common on many intakes (especially factory small- and big-block Chevrolet units) route hot exhaust gases through the intake manifold to heat it, to improve cold-weather drivability. Raising the temperature of the air/fuel mixture reduces its density, however, and the engine produces less power.

If you have enough hood clearance, installing an aluminum or plastic carburetor spacer will effectively add plenum volume to your intake manifold, which aids upper-rpm performance. This can be especially useful on street engines, which tend to have smallish plenums in their two-plane intakes; however, carb spacers provide that higher-rpm gain at the expense of low-end torque, so they may not be right for everyone. Fortunately, they're very inexpensive, so if it doesn't work, at least it hasn't cost much.

An intake change that won't cost you a cent (unless you mess it up so bad, you trash your intake) is to remove part of the plenum divider in some intake designs. This makes two smaller plenums (one for each plane of a

# Gas and Spark

dual-plane, street-type intake) act like one larger plenum.

Still working in the plenum area, you can smooth the transition to the runners by knife-edging any runner dividers that you can access. This is easier on single-plane intakes, though it is possible on some dual-planes, as well. By grinding blunt divider walls into knife-like leading edges, you reduce turbulence and improve airflow.

You can also add a flow director to the plenum floor, to help the air/fuel mixture make the transition from its vertical dive to a horizontal flow. Aftermarket flow directors are available, though you could fabricate one. For dual-plane intakes, you would actually need two directors, one for each bank of runners. They should be short, triangular-shaped humps that go across the runners, with the peak centered between the carburetor throttle blades. Single-plane intakes, on the other hand, would use a cone-shaped director with its point centered between the carburetor throttle blades.

It also helps to port-match the intake's ports to the heads' ports, by matching both sets of ports to a specific gasket set. Port-matching minimizes turbulence as the air/fuel mixture flows from the intake to the head. When port-matching, taper any changes to a depth of about 1 inch into the runners to blend the runner shapes for minimal airflow disruption.

One intake modification you *don't* want to make is to polish the inside surfaces of the intake runners. Wet intakes—those through which both air and fuel flow—require some turbulence in the runners to help keep fuel in suspension.

If the air stalls anywhere in the intake, the fuel will fall out of suspension and collect on the intake floor. It then streams toward the cylinder head and into the combustion chamber, causing mixture problems and hurting drivability.

## Stock Replacements

If your engine started life as a low-performance economy powerplant, its induction system is probably poorly suited for a high-performance engine. Yet the induction systems of many factory high-performance engines were quite good. In fact, some—such as Chevrolet's famous Z/28 intake from 1969 and 1970—remain the standard against which all other induction systems are compared.

Aside from the potential power increases that a high-performance, factory induction system may offer, it also has the advantage of retaining stock appearance for your engine.

Some factory systems actually have the added attraction of looking quite exotic, such as the triple-two-barrel systems offered by nearly every muscle car manufacturer during the 1960s and early 1970s. Chevy, Chrysler, Ford, Oldsmobile, and Pontiac all offered three deuces on their performance engines at one time or another, and those systems perform well (despite often being grossly oversized for stock engines) and add visual appeal to an engine. Several manufacturers also offered dual quad induction systems in either inline or trick-looking cross-ram styles.

The downside to using a stock induction system is that many of the more

**Left:** Carburetors typically rely on a mechanical fuel pump, usually driven by a rod that rides along the camshaft. High-volume fuel pumps can prevent fuel starvation under heavy-load (or racing) conditions. Adding an electric pump can prevent vapor lock—a condition that happens when air pockets appear within the fuel line or pump, preventing fuel to flow to the carb.

**Right:** Whether you add a high-volume mechanical pump or an electric one (or both) to your fuel system, you'll need a fuel-pressure regulator to ensure you don't push too much fuel through your carb or injection system, which could cause puddling ... or worse.

desirable, high-performance systems are rare and expensive. From a performance-per-dollar standpoint, factory high-performance systems are rarely the hot setup. However, in recent years, a number of reproduction castings have been released, including the legendary Z/28 2x4 cross-ram intake and some of the Hemi intakes, among others. These reproductions aren't necessarily cheap, but they are cheaper than the original.

**Aftermarket Systems**

If you're determined to stick with carburetors, yet want to maximize performance, an aftermarket induction system is the way to go. Aftermarket systems aren't designed under the same limitations that factory-designed intakes were subjected to. So a factory intake designed 30 or more years ago won't be as capable as a new one based on countless research, design, and manufacturing advances made in those three decades.

Of course, the more we've learned about induction systems, the more we've realized that there really is no such thing as an "ideal" one, because ideal is a relative term. What's ideal for one type of driving (say, drag racing) isn't going to be ideal for another (such as street driving).

Basically, there are two categories of carbureted induction systems: single-plane and dual-plane.

In single-plane intake manifolds, all runners feed from a common plenum, and both cylinder banks have the same runner design. Single-plane intakes are often high-rise intakes, with straight runners leading to the intake valve—the straighter the runner, the more efficient the air/fuel flow through it. This efficiency produces more power, especially at high rpm.

Dual-plane intakes use two separate plenums, one for each bank of the engine, and because the runners have to crisscross the intake (a result of the firing sequence of the engine), the intake halves must be split into upper and lower planes. This change makes the shapes of the runners different from cylinder to cylinder, which affects power output. Dual-plane intakes improve torque. The split design helps keep velocities up in the intake, because at any given moment, fewer cylinders are attempting to ingest the air and fuel in the intake. The run-

An appropriate fuel pressure gauge is a must. Note that mechanical pumps typically deliver under 15 psi of pressure, whereas fuel injection systems often require as much as 50 psi or more.

ners on dual-plane intakes also tend to be longer, which further aids torque production for the same reason: each cylinder gets a stronger intake signal.

Intake manufacturers have learned a lot about runner sizes and contours, and manufacturing processes have improved so that runner lengths are more equal (promoting good cylinder-to-cylinder balance). There are even trick improvements like air cavities beneath the runners (as on most single-plane intakes) that help cool the intake charge.

There are some grossly generalized statements about aftermarket intake designs. In truth, many subtle differences exist from one intake to the next; these differences make one intake more suited to a given use than another. In fact, when you shop for an intake, you are likely to find dozens for your engine, each intended to perform well at a given engine rpm, which is partially dictated by minute differences in runner volumes, shapes, lengths, finishes, and other factors.

Depending on the year of your vehicle and whether it was sold in California, you may need to contend with the Environmental Protection Agency's edict that you keep your engine's emissions control devices, including the exhaust gas recirculation valve, vacuum ports to run other emissions devices, and more. Fortunately, most aftermarket performance intakes (at least those designed for street use) have provisions for this equipment.

The intake manifold is only half the equation; you also need a carburetor. Several carburetor manufacturers supplied a number of different models for vehicles built during the 1950s, 1960s, and 1970s. The most popular models came from Holley, Rochester (a GM division), Motorcraft (a division of Ford), and Carter.

As with most parts, though, decades of advances and developments have improved modern-day carbs. There are also many performance parts to fine-tune carbs for your engine's needs.

One feature to look for is a one-piece main body, because it practically guarantees the carb will never spring a leak. For years this was a problem on Holley carbs with their end-mounted fuel bowls. For the street, a spread-bore design (primary venturis are smaller diameter than secondary ones) also tends to work better than a square bore (all venturis are the same size). The small primaries provide crisp throttle response and better fuel economy, yet when you jump on it, the massive secondary throttle blades open to provide ample air and fuel for high-performance runs.

Aftermarket intakes are also available for multiple carburetors; however, unless you're running a gargantuan motor or your vehicle will be strictly used for show or racing purposes, this will likely be overkill and will actually hurt performance. When it comes to picking a carburetor, it's better to err on the small side than the large, because your engine will still be fine with the smaller carb during most driving conditions (basically anything except wide-open throttle, or near to it). If you really want them, aftermarket systems are available to mount twin four-barrel carbs or a trio of two-barrels. (See the "Thirsty or Thrifty?" sidebar for the formula to calculate what size carburetor your engine needs.)

**Fuel-Injection Systems**

When it comes to automotive technology, advances are more evident—or more important—in the development of highly efficient electronic fuel-injection (EFI) systems.

EFI systems mix air and fuel in a precise ratio based on a number of conditions, including intake air volume, air temperature, air density, air pressure within the intake manifold, engine rpm, throttle position, throttle travel rate, exhaust gas contents, and other factors. The fuel-injection system's computer checks these vital signs of the engine thousands of times per second, and continually adjusts the fuel injector on time, which controls how much fuel is sprayed into the intake air. A longer on time injects more fuel, which richens the air/fuel mixture, while a shorter on time leans the mixture. Using an oxygen sensor creates what is known as a closed-loop system. While checking the properties of the intake air plus the throttle and speed characteristics tells the computer how much fuel the engine *should* need, readings from the oxygen sensor tell how much air and fuel the engine really needed. If the oxygen content of the exhaust gas is high, then the mixture was too lean; there wasn't enough fuel to mix with all the air. If the oxygen content is too low, then the mixture was too rich; there wasn't enough air for all the fuel. The computer can then compensate injector on times to achieve the theoretical ideal air: fuel ratio for 14.7:1.

By comparison, carburetors introduce fuel in response to the volume of air flowing through the carb's venturis and the density of that fuel. Manifold pressure and throttle position (but not rate) determine the volume of air flowing through the venturis. Hotter, less dense air simply won't hold as much fuel as

This Edelbrock crate motor sports the company's Pro-Flo Multi-Point EFI system and develops 440 horsepower! *Edelbrock photo*

cooler air. Perhaps worst of all, however, is the fact that jets and metering rods are fixed-size devices in carburetors, so fuel output is fairly constant. In contrast, fuel injector on time is continually variable over a fairly broad range, allowing EFI systems to flow more or less fuel as engine needs dictate.

Despite operating on the same basic principles, some fuel-injection systems are more efficient than others. This stems from the differences between the two basic types of fuel-injection systems: throttle-body injection versus multipoint fuel injection.

## Throttle-Body Injection (TBI) Systems

The earliest EFI systems, throttle-body injection, were actually little more than electronically controlled carburetors. TBI systems, which are still common, use a carburetor-like assembly to control airflow into the engine (as limited by the position of the throttle blades). Instead of using intricate fuel passages within the unit, however, a fuel injector sits atop each venturi and sprays fuel into the venturi when the EFI system's computer tells it to do so. Because the system uses a variable-duration injector, rather than a fixed-size jet or metering rod, the mixture can be adjusted to compensate for different operating conditions.

Although early TBI-style systems were less than ideal, modern systems—including aftermarket ones for vintage vehicles—are highly reliable, efficient systems that deliver good performance at an affordable price.

But TBI systems have their drawbacks. Their most notable weakness is that they are wet-style systems, which means they flow air and fuel through the intake, just like a carbureted system. Naturally, air laden with fuel is heavier than air alone, so a wet-flow induction system is less efficient than a dry system. The air/fuel charge flows more slowly, which slows cylinder filling, and the fuel can fall out of suspension in the intake, causing puddles on the intake floor. Those puddles will eventually stream to the cylinders, causing erratic, unpredictable changes to the fuel mixture. Even without puddling, though, mixtures in wet-flow systems aren't evenly distributed, because the intake runners are not identical. In addition, the engine's firing order causes two side-by-side cylinders to fire in sequence, so the two cylinders compete for the same air/fuel supply in the intake (the later-firing cylinder always loses out in such competitions).

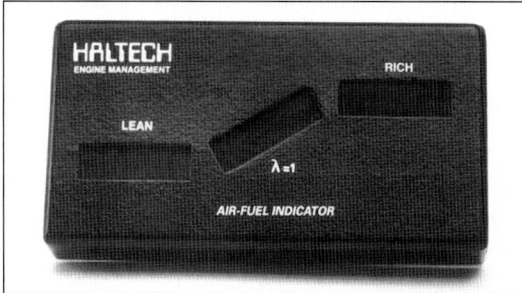

One reason that EFI engines typically outperform carbureted engines is that they continuously monitor their own efficiency by monitoring the oxygen content in the exhaust, then adjusting the air/fuel mixture ratio accordingly. While you can't make a carb variably adjust the mixture, an aftermarket air-fuel monitor, like this one from Haltech, can help you tune your setup for the best overall efficiency. *Haltech photo*

Still, TBI systems—because they're so similar to a carburetor—are easy to retrofit onto vintage vehicles and with a little artful concealment of wires and hoses, look quite stock (at least until you remove the air cleaner assembly). Kits are available from a number of companies, including Holley Performance Parts, ACCEL, and Howell Engine Developments, that include everything needed to replace your low-tech carb with a high-tech EFI system. Most systems allow you to retain your stock manifold, or you can bolt on a modern intake designed specifically to complement a TBI unit.

## Multipoint Fuel Injection (MPFI)

The alternative to TBI-style fuel-injection systems are multipoint fuel-injection (MPFI) systems (which are sometimes referred to as multi*port* fuel-injection systems). MPFI systems flow only air through the intake manifold, so they're dry systems. Fuel is injected at the end of each intake runner, often aimed at the intake valve. With one injector per cylinder, and only air flowing through the intake, air/fuel mixtures are extremely equal cylinder to cylinder, which helps balance the power output across all cylinders.

MPFI systems also eliminate fuel falling out of suspension, or puddling along the runner floors, because no fuel flows through the intake.

Because there is one injector per cylinder, each injector can be triggered to fire only when its intake valve is about

MSD popularized "multi-spark" boxes, which literally fire the spark plug several times per ignition event to improve combustion efficiency. They're also an easy weekend upgrade.

of short, around-town trips that may not burn the spark plugs clean of soot and carbon. But in racing applications, stock plugs may not cool quickly enough and may begin to melt. You may want to switch to a cooler-than-stock plug. There would rarely be a reason to switch to a hotter-than-stock plug, especially if you upgrade other parts of the ignition system.

### Auxiliary Ignition System Accessories

High-performance use and racing often place special demands on an ignition system. Your engine may benefit from using certain aftermarket ignition products designed to increase spark output. The most common of these are multiple-discharge spark systems and rev limiters, but there are others depending on your application.

### Multiple-Discharge Spark Systems

Multiple-discharge spark boxes deliver a rapid series of spark pulses to more completely burn the air and fuel in a cylinder. While the initial pulse ignites the air and fuel and is responsible for burning most of the mixture, follow-up sparks can ignite pockets of air and fuel that may have escaped the initial burn cycle, resulting in greater overall efficiency. Many of these multiple-discharge spark boxes deliver a single, extended-duration spark at higher rpm, rather than multiple discharges. High engine speeds do not leave sufficient time to fire a plug multiple times, but a longer-duration single spark can provide the same benefit.

Installing a multiple-discharge spark box is a recommended upgrade for all high-performance applications except restored show vehicles.

**Left:** A rev-limiter is a good way to keep you from mistakenly over-revving your engine, which could cause expensive (or even irreparable) internal damage.

**Right:** A timing computer can both eliminate the need for a mechanical advance mechanism, plus allow for on-demand timing changes at high rpm or when running nitrous to ensure sufficient time for the energy to fire the spark plug.

# Gas and Spark

**Right:** ACCEL's unique "U-groove" spark plugs feature a specially shaped ground electrode that features a channel in which the flame front can grow before spreading, instead of being "quenched" like standard plugs. ACCEL claims improved throttle response, better fuel efficiency and reduced emissions. *ACCEL photo*

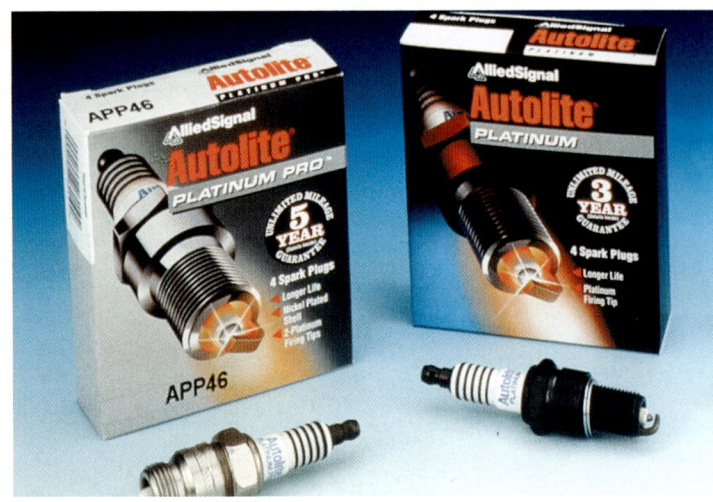

**Far right:** The easiest upgrade to your ignition system is to replace your spark plugs with performance plugs, like these Autolite Platinum or Platinum Pro plugs. They'll produce a more intense, more focused spark, plus will last longer than traditional plugs. *Autolite photo*

High-performance plug wires are a second great, easy ignition system upgrade. Replacement wires should feature minimal resistance (under 50 ohms/foot) and good suppression of electronic emissions, so your stereo and other electronics gadgets operate clearly. Other niceties are stain-resistant sleeves and boots, plus improved terminals. *MSD Ignition photo*

headers, which are notorious for melting ignition wires. Ignition wires are available in a number of different sizes, and 8 mm wires should be considered a minimum diameter. Because of all of the interference-sensitive electronics in late-model cars, you should always use RF-suppression wires. They suppress radio frequencies that could disrupt some systems, especially radio/stereo equipment.

## Spark Plugs

Spark plugs are spark plugs, right? Well, not exactly. Years ago there were few choices in spark plugs; you replaced old spark plugs with new versions of the same thing. Today, however, we have many spark plug choices. There are choices in heat ranges (which we've had for many years) and choices in construction materials, electrode designs, tip designs, and more. There are so many choices and so many claims made about why one is better than the others that picking the best plugs for your engine can be frustrating and tiresome.

For years, automakers relied on standard resistor plugs. Today, platinum-tipped spark plugs are used to extend general service intervals to 100,000 miles. (Remember when it used to be amazing to have an engine live to 100,000 miles? Now that's the first recommended tune-up interval.) Platinum plugs just use platinum electrode tips, which resist wear better than standard plug materials. The result is a plug that preserves its gap and spark quality, so it maintains optimal performance longer.

Several companies produce spark plugs with unique design features, such as a forked tip, grooved electrodes, or other innovative elements. While it is possible that these qualities will increase your engine's power output, it's also likely that a fresh set of standard plugs will provide the same benefits. In other words, the high-tech features really don't provide much more performance than a set of new, standard plugs, particularly on the street.

How you use your engine, and what performance equipment you've added, can affect the spark plug specifications necessary to maintain optimal efficiency and power. One typical adjustment involves the plug heat range: how quickly or slowly the plug can cool itself. Most manufacturers typically specify a hot plug for production use, since most vehicles are driven on lots

stock system's existing parts, often by replacing them with aftermarket performance parts that offer specific improvements. The second possibility is to extend the abilities of your ignition system with the addition of performance ignition accessories, such as multispark boxes. The goal, however, is always the same: to deliver a hotter spark that will thoroughly burn the intake charge, thereby maximizing heat production and power.

## Ignition System Components and Upgrades

### Ignition Coil

An ignition coil is a remarkable little device. It takes a lowly 12-volt battery signal and steps it up to as much as 60,000 volts or more. All that voltage is needed to create a spark strong enough to touch off a roaring, instantaneous inferno that it is hoped will burn all of the air and fuel in a cylinder.

Stock coils work well, but when loads are highest and engine rpms are soaring, the coil can't recharge quickly enough or with enough electricity to produce an intense spark across the spark plug gap. Aftermarket coils typically have increased windings to induce a higher discharge voltage into the secondary windings. Many aftermarket coils also offer quicker refresh times to improve performance at high rpm.

### Distributors, Caps, and Rotors

Vintage engines used traditional distributors to control where a spark signal was sent and when. Such engines can use a number of performance distributors that provide more accurate timing, thanks to roller bearings for the distributor shaft and a more accurately machined housing.

Some vehicles have tight engine compartments and may need to use a small-diameter distributor cap, unless you can create enough room for a full-size cap like those used on GM's HEI systems or Ford's large-diameter distributor cap. Of course, Ford and Chrysler engines that use front-mounted distributors rarely have such space problems.

Distributor caps and rotors should always be replaced as units, and parts from different manufacturers should not be mixed and matched because of differing design and manufacturing methods that can make parts incompatible.

### Ignition Wires

An ignition wire carries the spark to a spark plug. Stock wires aren't designed for performance use. They typically feature high resistance, as much as 5,000 ohms per foot, which reduces the current available at the spark plug.

For performance applications, replacement wires offer lower resistance, some as low as 150 ohms per foot, allowing more spark energy to reach the spark plug. Many use superior insulating materials that protect against spark induction from one wire to another (known as cross-firing). The insulators also reduce radio frequency interference, so onboard computers, radios, and communications equipment function properly.

Some wires also protect against high heat. This is especially useful on engines equipped with exhaust

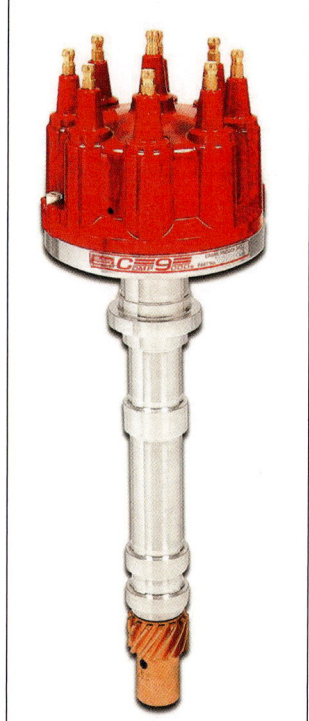

Replacing your stock distributor with an aftermarket performance model can benefit your engine in several ways. First, distributors get "sloppy" with age as bushings wear, leading to erratic timing. Second, many aftermarket distributors feature large-diameter caps to minimize the chance of spark scatter or jump, and a breaker-less triggering system for improved performance at any rpm. *Mallory photo*

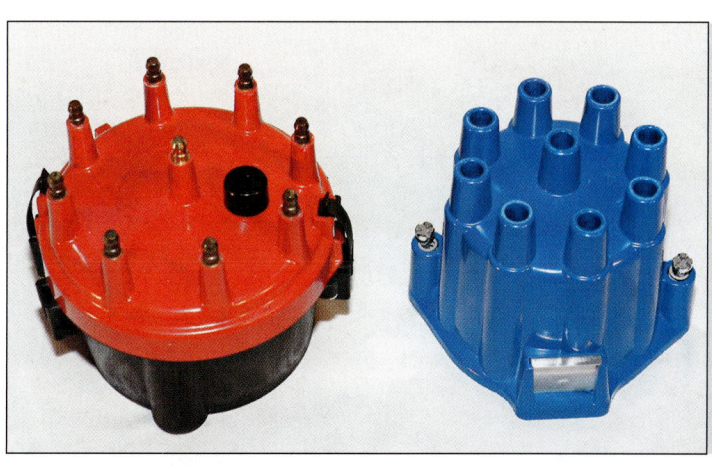

**Far left:** High-performance coils are another easy upgrade. Some, like this MSD Blaster 2 Coil, resemble a stock-type canister coil—especially if treated to a stealthy, stock-like paint finish.

**Left:** Here you can see the difference between two distributor caps available for a small-block Chevy. The large cap positions the electrodes farther apart, which greatly lessens the chance that the spark will jump from the rotor to the wrong plug, which could have disastrous results under heavy load.

to open, minimizing wasted fuel. Such systems are termed sequential port fuel injection. Simpler batch-fire systems trigger all injectors on one side of the engine at the same time.

An additional advantage of dry induction systems is that the runner designs can be radically different from those of wet-style induction systems, since there is no fear of fuel falling out of suspension. The shining example of this is Chevrolet's Tuned Port Injection system that was introduced in 1985 in the Corvette. With its large box-like upper plenum, long curved tubular runners, and cross-ram style manifold base, the system was designed to promote torque below 5,000 rpm. Prior to MPFI systems, an induction system design like this would have been impossible.

Depending on your engine, you may be able to retrofit a late-model factory MPFI system, or you may need to go with an aftermarket system, which are designed for a wide variety of engines.

Although a factory-style system may be available for your engine, you may want to opt for an aftermarket system because it offers advanced tuning and adjustment possibilities that aren't built into factory systems. Some systems feature a control box that allows you to easily adjust various operating parameters while you're driving. Other systems allow you to hook up a laptop (or standard PC) computer to the EFI system's computer to fine-tune fuel maps and other settings. You can also view the sensor inputs being fed to the computer, which can help diagnose problems or plan improvements.

Whether you go with a factory system or an aftermarket one, MPFI systems won't look stock, even if you go to extraordinary lengths to camouflage them. Although some aftermarket systems are based on somewhat traditional-looking intake manifolds, the fuel rails and injectors plugged into the ends of the runners are virtually impossible to conceal. And depending on your view of the high-performance restoration Golden Rule (keep it looking stock), the visual deviation may be worth the many performance advantages MPFI systems provide.

**Forced Induction and Other Fun Stuff**

Chapter 7 focuses on the benefits of adding forced induction to your engine buildup plans, typically a supercharger, turbocharger, or nitrous oxide system.

These systems place extraordinary demands on your induction system. With nitrous oxide kits, installation of additional fuel injectors (usually in the form of an injector plate that gets sandwiched between the throttle body or carburetor and the intake manifold) is necessary because the stock injectors simply can't deliver the required amount of fuel.

# Ignition Systems

Whatever air and fuel you get into your engine needs to be burned, which is the job of the ignition system. In most cars it consists of a distributor, coil, plug wires, plugs, and a few other components, but for a high-performance restoration, you will likely want to improve its performance with additional equipment.

The goal of the ignition system isn't just to ignite the air and fuel mixture, but rather to burn it as completely as possible. The more complete the burn, the more power will be produced, because you're not wasting fuel.

There are two ways to upgrade your ignition system, and it's likely you will use parts of each. The first steps usually involve improving the

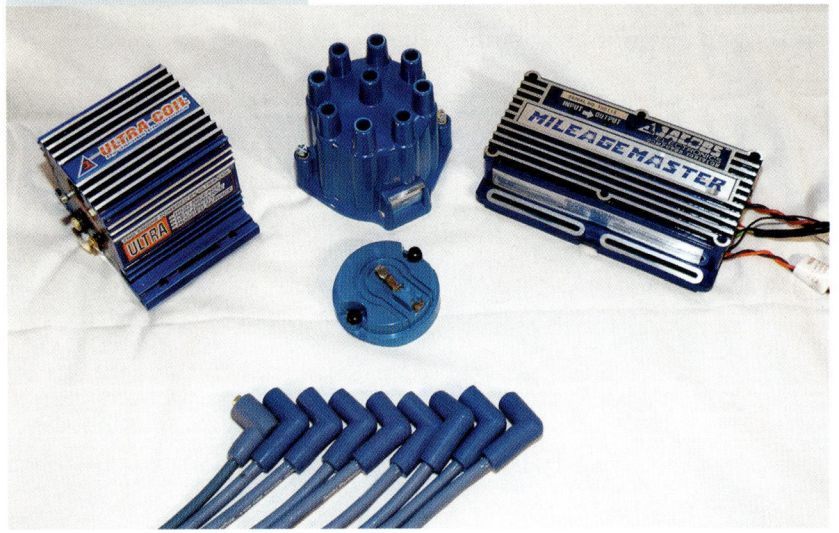

Jacob's Electronics offers upgrade kits that feature a high-performance cap and rotor, plug wires, a high-output coil, and a multispark box to really pump up your ignition system's output.

Speaking of timing, another easy upgrade is an adjustable timing tab, which will let you accurately set your timing, compensating for production errors that can result in timing marks being several degrees off from correct. They also tend to be easier to read. *Mr. Gasket photo*

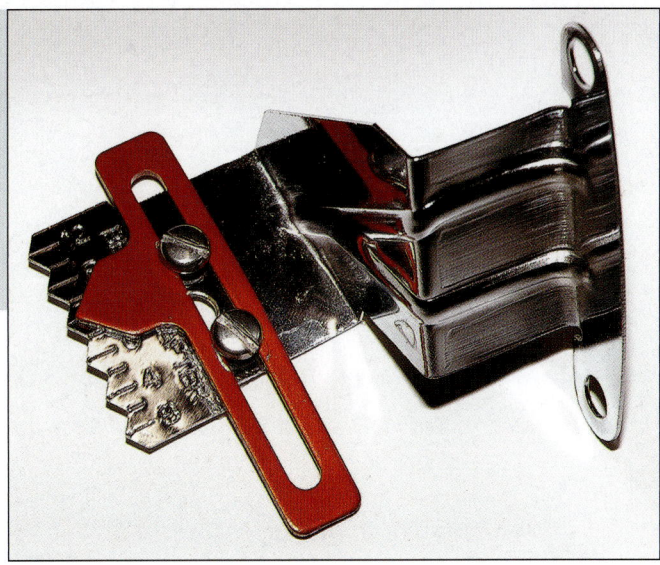

### Rev Limiters

Whether racing or just playing around on the streets, it's easy to forget about watching the tachometer to avoid exceeding the engine's redline (maximum recommended rpm). Over-revving the engine can damage internal engine components, most notably pushrods and valve springs, though damage deeper in the motor is possible too. A rev limiter can eliminate excessive engine rpm by preventing the engine from exceeding a specific rpm, which is typically user-programmable. When the engine reaches the specified maximum rpm, the rev limiter begins dropping spark pulses to keep the engine from speeding up (or even sustaining the speed it has).

Sophisticated rev limiters offer different rpm settings for different situations. In drag racing, for example, it's often useful to perform a burn-out to heat and clean the tires. Then, when staged and awaiting the green light, a different maximum rpm is needed. Finally, during the run, a still different rpm is needed to maximize power without sacrificing engine components or reliability. While some systems only provide a single maximum rpm, others allow multiple settings.

Remember, however, that rev limiters won't prevent accidental over-revving caused by downshifting at high speed. For example, if you attempt a full-throttle shift from second to third but accidentally hit first gear, engine rpm will quickly race beyond redline. This can cause extensive (and expensive) internal damage, because neither an ignition nor fuel cut-off-based system has any effect.

### Timing Retard Systems

Timing retard systems are used to retard the timing under certain conditions, such as when running nitrous oxide, or during extended runs that cause the engine to run extremely hot. Some systems use a computer to delay timing events, and most of these units allow you to specify the degree of retard to dial-in. Other systems use a fixed secondary triggering mechanism in the distributor. When running off the primary triggering system, the timing is as you set it, but by switching over to a secondary ignition system, you can alter the timing by a few degrees advanced or retarded, depending on how you set up the system.

### Backup Ignition Systems

NASCAR fans are probably familiar with drivers suddenly slowing on the racetrack, only to pick up speed again as though nothing had happened. When asked about it, the driver or crew chief often mutters something about having to switch ignition systems. What he or she is referring to is equipping a car with a backup ignition system that duplicates the failure-prone components, namely the coil, multiple-discharge spark box, rev limiter, and other components. A toggle switch selects which ignition system is used. Some systems are available with a triggering mechanism for the secondary ignition system advanced or retarded a few degrees. This allows the system to work as a backup system and an on-track performance tuning device.

# Chapter 6
# Cooling and Breathing

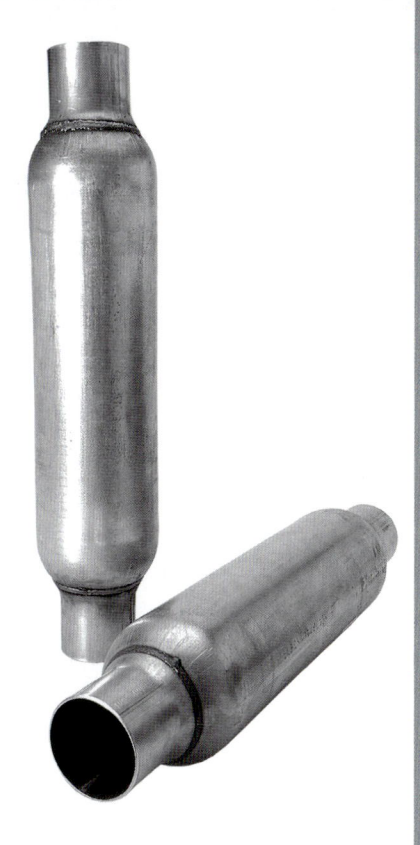
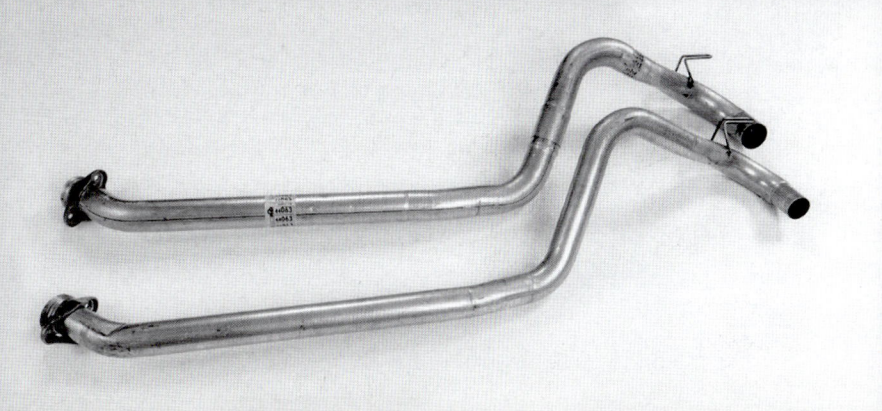

A performance car simply doesn't live up to its name without the right exhaust system. And a muscle car that overheats is even worse. Avoid these two pitfalls with thoughtful parts selection and meticulous installation.

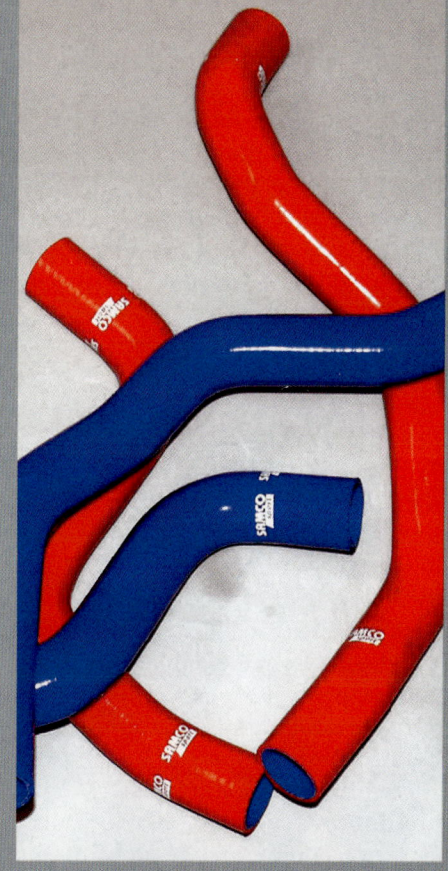
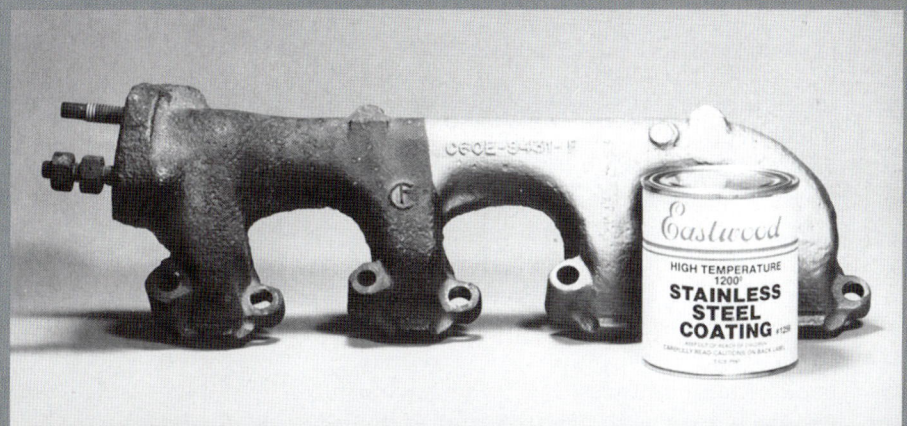

# Cooling System

## Primary Cooling System Basics

Of course, burning anything creates heat. And while your engine needs to create and retain a certain amount of heat, the *cooling system* has the daunting task of maintaining an optimum operating temperature and preventing the engine from overheating.

Your vehicle's cooling system has two basic functions: to cool the engine and prevent it from overheating and to provide a source of heat for the passenger compartment on cold days.

Most vintage cooling systems achieved these goals the same way, with the same equipment. A crank-driven water pump circulated coolant through passages in the engine block and cylinder heads, where it absorbed heat. The hot coolant flowed out of the engine through a thermostat, then through a flexible rubber hose to the radiator where the air rushing through the radiator removed heat before the coolant returned to the engine to repeat the process. A fan was typically attached to the front of the water pump to help draw air through the radiator and increase cooling, especially at low vehicle speeds. Some of the coolant was redirected through heater hoses to the heater core located in the passenger compartment just through the firewall.

Such systems are simple and effective, as attested to by decades of trusty service that continues to this very day, but they have flaws. The most significant is that the coolant heats up considerably in the block, so by the time it reaches the heads, it can't absorb much more heat. This means the combustion chambers stay pretty hot, which promotes detonation. And since today's fuels have a lower octane rating than fuels that were available in the 1960s and 1970s, compression ratios need to be kept down to avoid costly engine damage.

The biggest improvements to these sorts of cooling systems are made with better water pumps and better radiators. It's worth mentioning that switching to aluminum cylinder heads will also improve cooling, since aluminum gives up heat much more quickly than cast iron, making them less prone to detonation with higher compression or less total ignition advance.

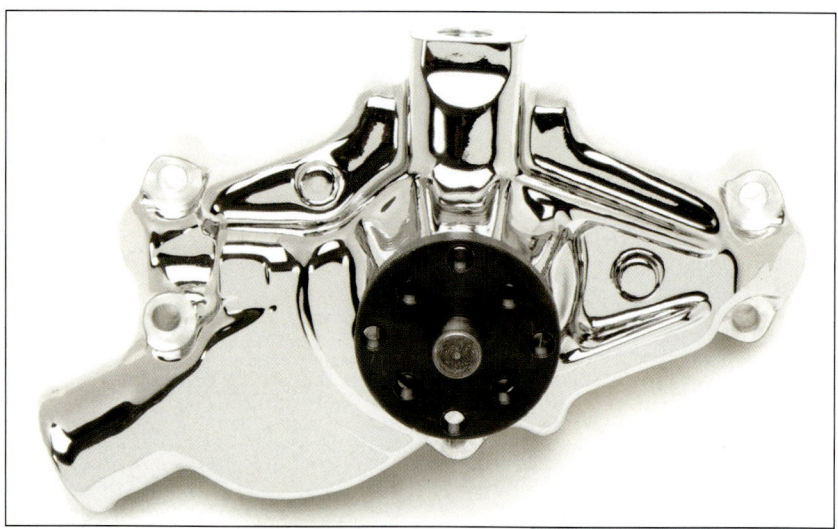

High-volume water pumps, like this one from Edelbrock, typically feature aluminum housings for light weight and better heat dissipation, plus heavy-duty bearings and seals for longer life. *Edelbrock photo*

## Water Pumps

Water pump upgrades depend on the make and model of engine you're working on. In general, the biggest improvements result from redesigned impellers to increase flow through the engine, the size of the impeller shaft bearings, and possibly the housing material.

Some water pumps use straight water pump impeller vanes, which are less effective than curved vanes. In addition, impellers on most performance water pumps have a solid backing plate, which helps the impeller better direct the flow of the coolant. Finally, the impeller material might be improved. Many factory-style pumps used cast-iron impellers, which are heavy and take up most of the space in the pump housing. Cast-aluminum impellers weigh less, so they are easier on bearings. Impellers fashioned from thin sheet metal, however, are lightweight and take up very little space, leaving more room for coolant that can be pumped to the engine more quickly.

Water pump housings are made of either cast iron or aluminum. Cast iron can be more durable, but aluminum's lighter weight is usually welcome. Aluminum also dissipates heat more readily, so an aluminum pump helps reduce coolant temperatures. So if you have a choice between an iron or aluminum

# Cooling and Breathing

water pump housing, go with the aluminum if you can afford it.

Finally, most aftermarket performance water pumps are designed with heavy-duty bearings to increase durability. This can add years to the pump's life, especially under severe service conditions, such as racing.

## Radiator

When people think of the cooling system, one of the first two things that comes to mind is the radiator. Although technically not a part of your engine, your engine wouldn't live very long without the radiator because the radiator is what takes the hot coolant from the engine and cools it off by sending it through thin tubes (arranged in rows) over which air flows. Additionally, thousands of tiny fins zigzag back and forth between the rows, absorbing additional heat from the tubes and shedding that heat into the air flowing past them.

Generally speaking, the more rows and columns of tubes a radiator has, the better it can dissipate heat. But there is a practical limit to how thick a radiator can be before it reaches a point of diminishing returns. For instance, a four-row radiator is probably the widest radiator useful in a street car. Any wider and the radiator becomes so thick that it acts as a wall, preventing air from flowing through it. Even if air could flow through it, the air would be so hot from the heat given off by the first four rows of tubes that the fifth row couldn't dissipate any heat.

Most vintage radiators used metal tanks on the ends (or top and bottom) of a copper radiator core and were generally reliable. The size of the radiator—the number of rows of coolant tubes—depended on the options ordered. High-performance models got heavy-duty four-row radiators, as did most air conditioned V-8-powered vehicles.

Most aftermarket performance or racing radiators are made of aluminum, which weighs less and dissipates heat more quickly, increasing efficiency. Along with the aluminum core, most aftermarket radiators have aluminum end tanks. The aftermarket units are generally available in various thicknesses (rows of cooling tubes), with many cooling tube sizes and even different fins-per-inch counts, allowing you to customize your radiator to suit your exact requirements.

## Thermostat

The thermostat controls the minimum coolant temperature once the engine is thoroughly warmed up.

The thermostat presents a minimal restriction to coolant flow, and if left unchecked, coolant could flow through the engine so quickly that it wouldn't have time to cool the engine, causing the engine to easily overheat. Conversely, the coolant may flow through the radiator so quickly that the heat in the coolant can't be dissipated, so the coolant returns to the engine still hot, causing the engine to overheat. Either way, the end result is a problem, so don't replace a thermostat with simple flow-restrictor disks.

Most vintage V-8 engines work well with a 160- to 180-degree (Fahrenheit) thermostat.

## Hoses

The cooling system hoses—both the upper and lower radiator hoses, as well as heater hoses—are the weakest spots in your engine's cooling system. Over time the hoses become brittle and crack, releasing coolant, or they could become so weak that rather than cracking they simply burst, spewing as much coolant as your engine can pump out.

From the factory, most engines had rubber cooling system hoses. These should be inspected regularly for cracks and replaced approximately every three years or so—much more often for competition engines. Bear in mind, though,

**Below:** High-performance engines require a high-performance cooling system to shed the extra heat they generate. An aluminum radiator, like this AFCO unit, is an excellent foundation for your cooling system upgrades. It will weigh less and shed heat more effectively. *AFCO photo*

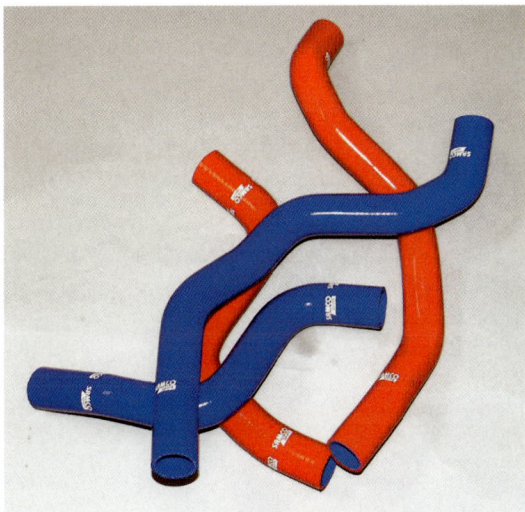

**Bottom:** High-performance radiator and heater hoses can not only improve durability under extreme conditions, but they can add some visual appeal underhood, too. *Samco photo*

**Left:** Fans create airflow through the radiator when you're cruising slowly. Performance replacement fans often feature more and better-designed fan blades to improve airflow while drawing less power. *AFCO photo*

**Middle:** An electric fan can be used either as your primary fan, or as an auxiliary fan. If you've swapped in a big block, it's possible that engine-to-radiator clearance may not allow you to run an engine-turned fan. Or, if your high-performance engine still runs hot, consider adding an electric fan to increase airflow through the radiator. *AFCO photo*

**Right:** Conventional fans can be improved with a thermostatic clutch, which acts as a sort of inverse torque converter. At slower engine speeds, the water pump's rotation causes the fan to turn, but as the pump's speed increases, the input shaft spins through the fluid, allowing the fan to freewheel, thus drawing little power from the engine.

that hoses deteriorate from the inside out, so external appearance isn't always a good indicator.

A good upgrade would be silicone hoses. They are stronger and last longer than rubber hoses and can prove quite reliable, even in competition use; however, the applications they are available for are quite limited (mostly just late-model vehicles).

Even better than silicone hoses are braided steel hoses, which are exceptionally strong and can withstand higher pressures. Just don't confuse braided steel hose covers for actual braided steel hoses.

Finally, it is possible to replace the bulk of the hoses under your vehicle's hood with rigid tubing, using only short sections of hose to connect the rigid tubes to the radiator, water pump, thermostat gooseneck, and so on. Rigid tubes can also make quite a fashion statement if anodized or powder coated. Another option is the Cool-Flex corrugated flexible metal hoses. They bend and flex but don't crack, and they dissipate heat.

In any event, flexible, one-hose-fits-all discount hoses should be avoided, because they disrupt coolant flow and fail quicker where the hoses bend. Quality molded hoses are much more reliable.

## Coolant

Coolant is probably what comes to most people's minds when they first think of cooling systems. The coolant is the blood of the system, traveling through the engine, picking up heat, then going to the radiator to dissipate that heat, before returning to the engine.

The factories filled cooling systems for most engines with a near 50/50 mixture of antifreeze and water. Unlike most mixtures, a mix of antifreeze and water actually lowers the mixture's freezing point, while raising its boiling point at the same time. The usually ideal 50/50 mix will typically freeze at around –30 degrees Fahrenheit and will boil at roughly 250 degrees Fahrenheit. By comparison, straight water freezes at 32 degrees Fahrenheit and boils at 212 degrees Fahrenheit.

If you happen to live in a warm climate, you may be able to mix water with a product called Water Wetter, which improves the water's ability to absorb and dissipate heat, plus raises the boiling point of the water. In colder climates, however, using this product could allow the coolant to freeze in the engine, which could crack the block or cylinder heads, destroying them.

Note that until the mid-1990s, most auto manufacturers used ethylene-glycol antifreeze. The mixture was a fluorescent lime-green color and needed to be changed every two years or so to maintain optimal efficiency. Beginning in the mid-1990s, however, new orange-colored antifreeze became available and is generally called DexCool. It is designed to last for up to 100,000 miles before needing to be changed. The two types of coolant cannot be mixed, or internal engine damage may result.

In terms of cooling ability, regular ethylene-glycol coolant, DexCool, and even Water Wetter are roughly equal. DexCool should last longer, and Water

# Cooling and Breathing

Wetter doesn't offer any antifreeze protection, so again, it's not suited to colder climates. Some say you should only use distilled water, not tap water. There are no distinct advantages to running distilled water except perhaps for slightly fewer deposits forming in the water over time. But if you change your coolant and flush the system regularly, deposit build-up shouldn't be a problem.

## Fan(s)

Radiators need to have air flowing through them to cool the coolant; however, a number of factors can limit the amount of air that reaches a radiator, minimizing its cooling abilities. Most older vehicles have generous grille openings, so airflow through the radiator is rarely a problem when the vehicle is moving. When the vehicle sits still, there would be very little air flowing through the radiator, if it weren't for a fan.

Most older vehicles relied upon engine-turned fans. Some fans had a thermostatically controlled clutch in the hub. The clutch locked up when hot so the fan would spin. When cool, the clutch disengaged so the fan could freewheel. This reduced the fan's parasitic power drain on the engine.

Aftermarket fans are available with more fan blades (usually up to seven or eight) to help increase the fan's draw through the radiator. In addition, flex-style fans have flexible fan blades that straighten out at higher rotational speeds to further reduce any parasitic power losses. Most aftermarket fans are made of lightweight aluminum, which reduces weight and can extend the life of water pump bearings. Another option is electric thermostat–controlled fans, which are nearly invisible if mounted ahead of the radiator.

## Secondary Cooling Systems

Anything that indirectly helps cool the engine or its auxiliary equipment is a secondary cooling system. While improvements to these secondary systems may not have as dramatic an effect on engine coolant temperature, they can have a considerable effect on performance or other engine characteristics. At the very least, paying careful attention to each will pay off in extended engine life.

### Oiling System

Next to lubricating your engine's moving parts, cooling parts is your oil's most important function. Many parts in your engine never have coolant anywhere near them. Bearings, the crankshaft, connecting rods, pistons, piston rings, cam drive systems, the camshaft, rocker arms—none of these parts are cooled (not directly, anyway) by engine coolant. Each relies on engine oil to absorb heat and carry it away.

Of course, your oil can't absorb much heat if it's already overheating. Oil overheats when there's not enough oil in the engine; because of insufficient flow through the engine, perhaps due to a restriction somewhere; because of excessive engine temperatures (due to a malfunctioning cooling system or extreme operating conditions); or, of course, due to insufficient cooling of the oil.

Each of these problems usually has a fairly simple solution: Insufficient quantity could be because the engine is simply low on oil; it may have leaked some out, or perhaps it is burning oil. Your engine may also run out of oil if it is operated at high rpm for extended periods of time, especially if you are running a high-volume oil pump. Since oil is under pressure when flowing out of the oil pan, but returns by gravity, it's easy to understand how, at high rpm, the oil pump may empty the oil pan faster than the oil returns to it. A higher-capacity oil pan could be one solution: by simply increasing the quantity of oil available, you decrease the chance all of it will be pumped out of the pan. You could switch to a standard-volume oil pump, which actually provides ample pressure and volume (with close-to-stock bearing clearances) as proven by the countless small blocks that endure hundreds of thousands of miles with no oil-pressure problems.

Professional racers, such as those on the NASCAR or SCCA Trans-Am circuits, rely on dry sump oiling systems that actually draw oil from the engine after it is circulated to ensure oil doesn't linger in the engine any longer than it needs to.

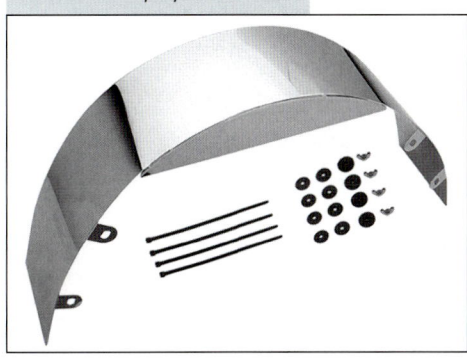

A fan shroud improves cooling by focusing your fan's efforts at drawing air through the radiator, much like a wind tunnel. If your car didn't originally come with a shroud, you can usually add an aftermarket one like this Trans Dapt piece. If you're concerned about the non-stock appearance, scuff it with sandpaper and spray it an appropriate shade of black and it will blend right in. *Trans Dapt photo*

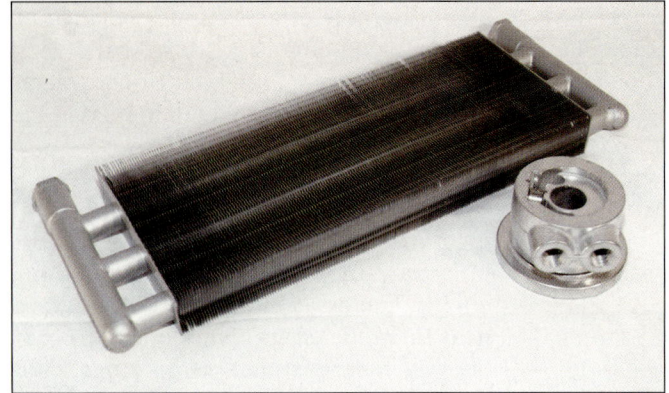 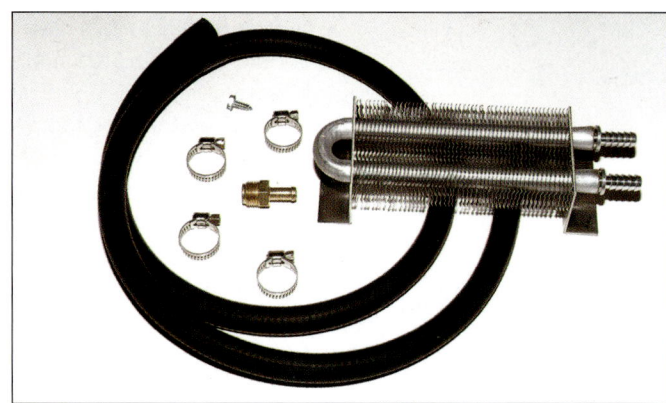

**Left:** Your engine's oiling system does double duty as a cooling system, too, so a high-performance oil cooler should be used. Coupling one with remote-mount filters adds extra oil capacity, extra filtering capability, plus convenience.

**Right:** Don't forget to keep your power steering system cool. GM, Ford, and Chrysler have all supplied them on various "performance" cars, including police cars and high-performance models. Aftermarket kits generally offer greater cooling performance plus more flexible installation options. *Perma-Cool photo*

(Dry sump systems typically have storage tanks that hold 10 or more quarts of oil, too, as compared to the 4 quarts held by standard V-8 oil pans.)

Of course, no matter how much oil you have, you can still get it too hot. In those cases, you need to cool the oil. First and foremost are dedicated oil coolers. Two basic types are available: oil-to-coolant and oil-to-air.

GM installed oil-to-coolant oil coolers on many late-model V-8 models, including Corvettes, Camaros, Firebirds, Caprices, Impalas, and others. These coolers help oil reach its proper operating temperature quickly (because the coolant heats up quickly), and they help maintain that temperature by shedding excess heat to the coolant. If the coolant is overheating, however, it can cause your oil to run hot, which can worsen overheating conditions by thinning the oil. Conversely, if the oil is running hot, it can cause the coolant flowing through the adapter to pick up additional heat.

Oil-to-air coolers, on the other hand, work similarly to your cooling system's radiator. An adapter between the block and filter routes oil to the mini radiator. Heat transfers from the oil to the cooler's tubes, then to its fins, then to the air flowing through the cooler. These coolers are the type typically used in competition engines, where the complexity of an oil-to-coolant system would pose an unnecessary risk of a coolant leak or where high coolant temperatures may cause the oil to heat up. Oil-to-air cooling systems are more easily adapted to various vehicles as well.

You can also improve cooling by simply using smarter replacement parts for some of your oil system's existing parts. Aluminum oil pans, for instance, dissipate heat more readily than stamped-steel pans. Likewise, rocker (valve) covers with built-in oil drippers—or better yet, oil sprayers—can increase oiling of the valve springs, which reduces their temperature.

Of course, the oil has a lot to do with your oil system's ability to cool—and protect—your engine. While any high-quality conventional oil will work well when changed regularly (every 3,000 miles or six months, whichever comes first), synthetic oils provide added insurance. Synthetic oils are engineered to withstand higher temperatures than conventional oils, so they don't thin out as quickly when they get hot, and they can get hotter before burning off. An old Mobil 1 television ad features two frying pans, one with conventional oil and the other with Mobil 1 synthetic, subjected to high heat. The ad showed the conventional oil burning and turning to a thick, tar-like substance, while the Mobil 1 was still golden brown and flowed smoothly. Advertising theatrics? Probably. But the premise is sound, and if you require proof, look what oils professional motorsports teams use.

**Induction System**

Stretching the concept of cooling systems a bit further, we can include providing cool, dense air for the combustion process. Cooler air will hold more fuel than hotter air, so it burns hotter in the chamber, which produces more power. The problem is, a lot of things are working against you when it comes to delivering cool air to the engine. Underhood temperatures on high-performance vehicles can be staggeringly hot, and the

# Cooling and Breathing

designs of some systems and components you add can accentuate any problems.

Because underhood air is typically so hot, the best way to minimize the heat being drawn into your engine is to draw it from outside the vehicle with a cold-air induction or ram-air-type kit, as discussed in the chapter on induction.

Once you have nice, cool air flowing toward your engine, you need to ensure that it stays nice and cool. That involves minimizing the temperature of parts the air contacts, specifically the intake manifold.

Your intake manifold heats intake air, because the manifold is heated by coolant flowing through it, and in some engines, the manifold is heated by the oil flung off the camshaft against the bottom of the intake. Many intakes also face an additional heat source: the heat crossover passage that directs some exhaust gases from the center exhaust ports through the intake to aid in engine warmup and prevent manifold icing. The crossover is only useful for wet-style intakes—those that flow both air and atomized fuel—because a too-cold intake could cause the atomized fuel to form ice along the inside walls of the intake runners.

To solve the problem of oil splashing on the bottom of the intake, you can install an oil splash shield. Sheetmetal shields can be bought or fabricated to block oil from contacting the intake.

As for the heat crossover, you can either minimize its effect or eliminate it. Most intake manifold gasket sets contain heat crossover passage restrictors, which reduce the size of the passage but still allow some exhaust to flow through the intake for cold-weather driving. To block the crossover entirely, you can install gaskets that do just that, or, if you're swapping intake manifolds or cylinder heads, you can select pieces without crossover passages.

A last note about induction system cooling: drag racers ice down the intake manifold between runs to cool it. As crude as this trick is, it does work, briefly. The key is to keep the engine off until the last possible second, because as soon as you start the engine, the heating process begins.

## Fuel System

In the old days, it was common for an engine to suffer vapor lock: when the fuel boiled in the line, it created an air pocket that blocked fuel from reaching the carburetor. Vapor lock is virtually unheard of on engines equipped with an electric fuel pump.

EFI systems minimize the chance of vapor lock by using a fuel return line that sends unused fuel back to the fuel tank. Because the fuel never sits still near a heat source, it stays cooler.

It is still possible to improve the system using another old racer's trick—fuel-line cool cans, which are described in Chapter 5. You can buy one or make a cool can using nearly any canister (a large coffee can works well, or even a large plastic jug) and a coil of fuel line. Just remember that EFI systems are under high pressure and should only be used with solid steel or stainless-steel lines.

## Accessory Systems

A few other engine components need some help shedding, or fighting off, heat if they are to work reliably and properly.

Chevrolet V-8s are notorious for starting difficulties when it's hot. The problem (generally) stems from exhaust manifold or header heat that causes the starter-mounted solenoid to temporarily fail. The easiest cure is to purchase or fabricate a simple sheetmetal heat shield that's positioned around the solenoid, but with an air gap to allow the solenoid to dissipate heat.

Late-model and aftermarket high-torque gear-reduction starters are designed to withstand the heat of cramped engine

Air conditioning will help keep you cool while you're cruising. If your muscle car came with air, you can rebuild its system. If it didn't come with air, you can add it using a high-quality aftermarket kit, like this one from Vintage Auto Air. *Vintage Auto Air photo*

compartments, so they generally do not experience the hard starting conditions. Gear-reduction starters also deliver higher cranking rpm for faster starts, as well as higher-torque cranking for high-compression engines. As if that weren't enough, they are significantly smaller and lighter than standard starter motors.

A third option is to modify the starter to use a remote-mounted solenoid, similar to those used on Ford vehicles. If your vehicle uses an integral solenoid/starter assembly, the gear-reduction replacement starter motor is generally an easier solution and provides additional benefits the solenoid swap won't.

Another accessory that experiences a fair amount of heat is the power steering pump. When run for extended periods of time, or worked very hard (such as during autocross runs), power steering fluid heats up considerably. The solution is to install a power steering fluid cooler. A few options exist here. First, General Motors equips some late-model vehicles with power steering coolers that were just lengths of tubing mounted where they received moderate airflow. The fluid flows through the tube, and air blowing across the tube whisks away heat.

A similar system was employed for many years on police cars built by GM, Ford, and Chrysler. This system mounted a miniature radiator about the size of a thick candy bar off the power steering pump assembly. A tube running through the fins of the radiator carried power steering fluid, and air flowing through the fins dissipated the heat. Simple and effective. Such units are often available in salvage yards or can sometimes be ordered new through dealerships or parts stores.

# Exhaust System

After the air and fuel charge is burned, it's up to the *exhaust system* to shuttle the waste products out of the engine, to make room for a fresh air and fuel charge. The more exhaust that gets out, the more pure—and thus more *potent*—the fresh air/fuel charge will be.

A performance engine needs an efficient exhaust system, because an engine can't draw in new air and fuel unless the old, burned exhaust gases are removed from the cylinders first.

What kind of system you assemble depends on the vehicle. For instance, a Corvette's exhaust system is different from a Mustang's, which in turn is different from a truck's set of pipes.

## Stock Systems—Understanding the "Standard"

To save on production costs, nearly every vintage vehicle features cast-iron, log-style exhaust manifolds. Although hardly ideal, cast-iron manifolds do have some redeeming qualities: they're durable and they absorb noise, but their weight and poor airflow characteristics make them ill-suited to high-performance use, except for highly detailed, original show cars.

As they exit the manifolds, exhaust gases travel through steel head (or header) pipes to the intermediate pipes, which connect to the mufflers. From the muffler, exhaust gases exit into a tailpipe, then dump into the atmosphere. Beginning in 1974 and 1975, auto manufacturers installed catalytic converters into production exhaust systems to reduce some harmful exhaust emissions. The converters were installed between the

If you do a lot of racing, exhaust cutouts like this one from Hedman make it super-convenient to uncork your exhaust when at the track. *Hedman photo*

**Left:** For many, the first exhaust system upgrade that comes to mind is replacing stock exhaust manifolds with free-flowing tubular headers. Long equal-length tubes make it easier for each cylinder to empty itself on the exhaust stroke, which allows more fresh air/fuel mixture into the cylinder for the next burn cycle. This Dynomax Cyclone header features a metallic thermal-barrier coating that really resists rust and corrosion. *Dynomax photo*

**Right:** If you're committed to sticking with your stock cast-iron exhaust manifolds, you may want to consider coating them with a stainless-steel coating to keep them looking like new for years. *The Eastwood Company photo*

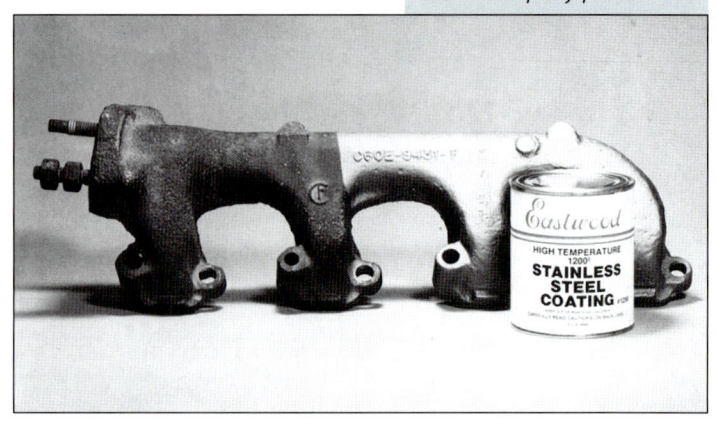

# Cooling and Breathing 115

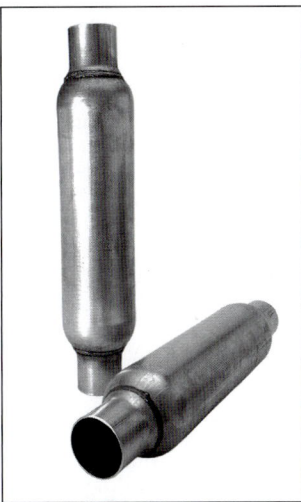

**Top:** Edelbrock's Sound Deflection Technology—SDT, for short—mufflers use specially designed internal flow directors to "manipulate sound waves" without choking your engine. And thanks to its Ti-Tech coating or optional 304 stainless-steel finish, the SDT muffler will retain its good looks long after you install it. *Edelbrock photo*

**Above:** Or you can dig a little deeper into history and run a pair of 'glass-pack mufflers. *Hedman photo*

head pipe and the intermediate pipe, beneath the passenger's footwell.

Some production vehicles had unique exhaust systems or optional features. Chevrolet offered chambered exhaust systems on a number of models, including Camaros and Chevelles. These systems didn't use traditional mufflers, but perforated exhaust pipes that featured an outer shell that was crimped in various places to form different-sized chambers. These chambers tuned out different frequencies of exhaust sound without packing material. Other vehicles, such as Pontiac's 1970 GTO, featured exhaust cutouts that bypassed the mufflers when activated, for a racier sound. Unfortunately, both these systems were short-lived because they exceeded maximum sound levels in many states and municipalities.

Although never factory installed, some vehicles, including the 1969 Camaro Z/28, were available with equal-length tubular steel exhaust headers. The headers were supplied in the trunk of the vehicle, from the factory, and it was up to the delivering dealer or the owner to install them.

As with most things on production cars, stock exhaust systems work reasonably well, but aren't designed for peak performance. Unfortunately, depending on the year of your vehicle and where you live, there may not be much that you can legally change to improve your vehicle's exhaust system, given the Environmental Protection Agency's hard-line stance against any modifications that may alter or defeat emissions control devices. In this case, the only viable option is to replace components with Environmental Protection Agency–approved replacement parts.

**Exhaust System Improvements**

Assuming it's legal to improve your vehicle's exhaust system, the changes you make may be dictated by the floor pan design of your vehicle. While custom-built street rods may feature plenty of wide-open space for installing headers and a free-flowing dual-exhaust system, other cars may not be so accommodating.

While custom exhaust systems may be a possibility for your application, the reality is that most enthusiasts will be limited by the availability of ready-to-bolt-on systems. Fortunately, there are a lot of options, thanks to aftermarket companies.

The goal is to increase exhaust flow out of the engine. In the information that follows, we'll examine each (typical) exhaust system component, run through the problems that the components present, and discuss how to solve those problems.

## Cylinder Head

Lots of people believe that their exhaust system starts with their exhaust manifolds or headers. It doesn't. It starts inside your engine, in each cylinder.

For the sake of simplicity, we'll say the first part of your exhaust system is the cylinder head; yet a case could easily be made that your pistons and block are also parts of the exhaust system. As each piston travels back up the cylinder (following the power stroke), the piston actually pushes some of the burned gases out of the cylinder and into the cylinder head.

The two-cylinder head parts that affect exhaust flow are the exhaust valve and the exhaust port, which were both covered in Chapter 4. It's important to remember that your heads are part of the exhaust system, because they represent the first possible obstruction to exhaust flow. If your exhaust system starts out choked off, any changes you make downstream of the heads can't possibly produce maximum flow.

## Exhaust Manifolds/Headers

Once the exhaust leaves the head, it enters the exhaust manifold or header.

Most production cars use cast-iron, log-type exhaust manifolds. Cast-iron manifolds are super quiet and last virtually forever, but they're also restrictive and heavy, neither of which suits them to performance use. Weight-wise, the problem is obvious: they're made of cast iron—lots of cast iron. In terms of flow restriction, the problem is that all four

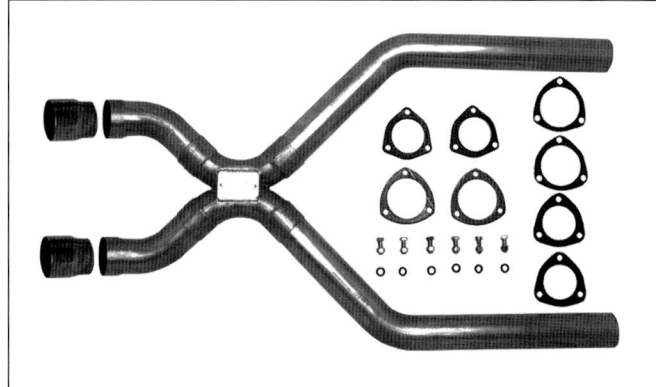
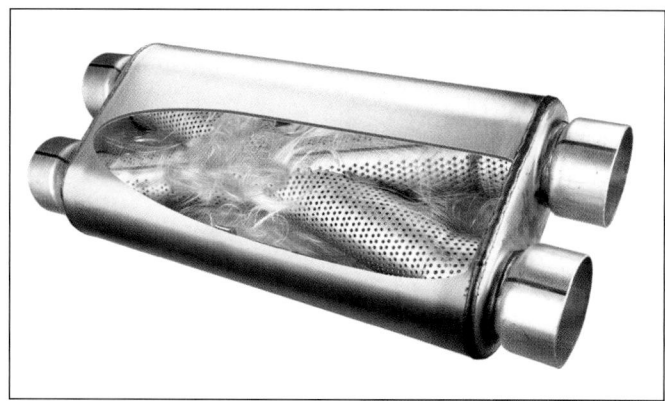

**Left:** Dual exhaust was state of the art 40 years ago. Since then, we've learned that the exhaust pulse traveling down one pipe can help draw the pulse down the opposite pipe if the systems utilize a properly designed crossover connection. *Hedman photo*

**Right:** An alternative to cross-connecting your exhaust pipes is Dynomax's new Ultra Flo X Performance muffler, which incorporates a crossover internally. Just run both exhaust pipes in and two pipes out and you've got a cross-connected system—and less weight than one with a second hefty muffler. *Dynomax photo*

cylinders on one side of the engine feed into one common plenum. But if that plenum is already full of exhaust from, say, cylinder number one, then the gases from cylinder number three have nowhere to go. Most of cylinder three's exhaust gas will eventually get out but not all. Some will be trapped in the cylinder when the exhaust valve closes, and that means less fresh air and fuel can be drawn into the cylinder.

The factories knew about the shortcomings of stock, cast-iron manifolds, so for certain performance engines, the factories took the time to design freer-flowing iron manifolds. Chevrolet modified its legendary Ram's Horn manifolds with larger ports and outlets for use on high-performance small-blocks in the Corvette. Ford fitted exotic manifolds to engines like the Boss 429. Chrysler's 426 Hemi had massive, header-like exhaust manifolds with relatively long individual runners for each cylinder. And Pontiac even went so far as to equip some of its lightweight Super Duty models with free-flowing manifolds of cast aluminum to save weight, too.

Aftermarket tubular exhaust headers, on the other hand, typically flow much better, since each cylinder has its own primary header tube, and pulses of exhaust gases from individual cylinders don't have to fight for space in the single runner of the stock manifold. Long equal-length primary tubes work better than shorter tubes of unequal length. The longer equal-length tubes deliver each exhaust pulse to the collector tube in the same order as the engine's firing order, so pulses of exhaust gases don't even have to fight for space in the collector. In fact, by preserving the firing order, each exhaust pulse that reaches the collector helps to scavenge the next pulse from the next cylinder (in the firing order on that side of the engine) by creating a low-pressure zone behind it, which the next pulse rushes to fill.

Since tubular headers are made of relatively thin-wall steel tubing, they weigh less than manifolds. This reduces the amount of power needed to move the vehicle and helps vehicle handling. Unfortunately, the two areas headers don't excel in are durability and noise; however, the noise emitted from headers generally isn't considered objectionable (not by performance enthusiasts, anyway) nor is it overly loud. Furthermore, advances in ceramic header coatings now allow headers to last almost indefinitely without rusting, corroding, or discoloring.

Metallic-ceramic coatings do more than just make headers (or other exhaust system components) look good and last longer. The coatings help the header retain heat, which keeps the exhaust pulses hotter for longer. And since hot air moves more quickly than cool air, coated headers actually do a better job of expelling exhaust gases than do noncoated headers. This also keeps underhood and interior temperatures down. Note, though, that some budget headers are coated only on the outside. Headers coated both inside and out are preferable.

Header wraps and blankets do the same thing as header coatings, in terms of retaining heat, only the wraps and blankets do it better—too well, in fact. Wraps and blankets retain so much heat that the header tubes get hot enough to

# Cooling and Breathing

change the structure of the metal. The metal then gets brittle enough to actually crumble like a cookie after a relatively short time. For racing applications this isn't necessarily a problem, especially if you can justify replacing headers every season or so. In that case, the benefits of the wraps and blankets far outweigh the detriments. On the street, however, the benefits header wraps and blankets provide aren't needed and their side effects are a nuisance.

## Oxygen Sensor(s)

Vintage vehicles didn't come with oxygen sensors, but you might want to install one because they are the key to determining whether your air/fuel mixture is truly what your vehicle needs.

Oxygen sensors, which mount in the exhaust manifold or header, measure the amount of oxygen in the exhaust gases to determine how efficiently the engine is burning its air/fuel mixture. All modern EFI systems use an oxygen sensor so they can run in the far more efficient closed-loop mode.

But you don't need an EFI system to use an oxygen sensor. Aftermarket air/fuel ratio monitors show you whether your engine is running rich or lean while it's running, which is invaluable information for performance tuning.

## Primary Exhaust (Header) Pipes

Not to be confused with the pipes that make up a set of exhaust headers, the primary exhaust pipes—often called header pipes—connect the exhaust manifolds or headers to the catalytic converter(s) in vehicles that have them, or to the exhaust pipe in older vehicles. In most cases there is little that can be changed about your header pipes, since their size and shape are dictated by the vehicle.

One upgrade to consider is using header pipes made from stainless steel or aluminized pipe. Although the different material won't make the pipe flow any better, it will have a dramatic effect on appearance. Stock, mild-steel pipes rust quickly, and eventually the rust will ruin the pipe. Stainless and aluminized pipes resist corrosion, so they'll look great (or need only minimal effort to restore the look) and will last virtually forever.

## Catalytic Converters

Catalytic converters clean the exhaust emissions by converting the harmful gases into less toxic gases, thanks to a chemical reaction and the injection of oxygen into the exhaust system. The oxygen mixes with the deadly carbon monoxide and converts it to carbon dioxide, which plants and trees need to breathe.

Since catalytic converters were first introduced in the mid-1970s, they have had the reputation of being power-robbing emissions junk. In fairness to the anti–clean air crowd, the early pellet-type catalytic converters were highly restrictive and did kill engine power. But by the 1980s, the pellet-type converters had been replaced by the monolith brick-type converters, which we still have today. Brick-type converters restrict airflow to a small degree and have a minimal impact on an engine's power. So-called high flow catalytic converters are available from aftermarket sources, but most use merely the same type of brick, just in a larger size and with larger openings and exits.

**Left:** In the 1960s, Chevy offered chambered exhaust as an option on a number of muscle cars, including Chevelles and Camaros. Rather than using sound-absorbing material inside, the system used different-sized outer "chambers" around a perforated inner tube to trap and deaden certain sound waves.

**Right:** Exhaust systems that use aluminized pipes will last virtually forever and look great the entire time. These pipes are from Dynomax.

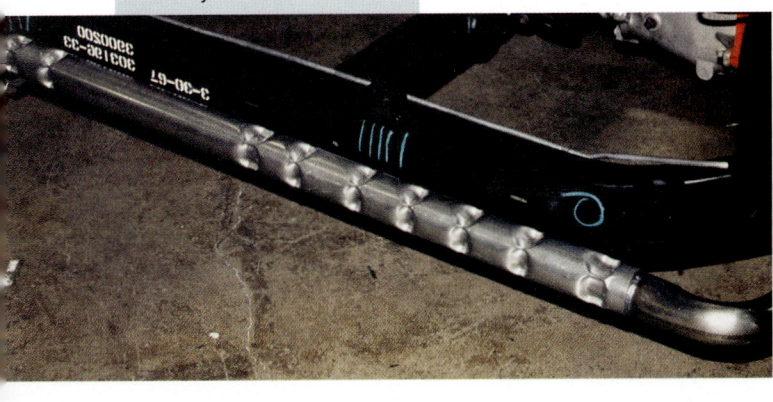

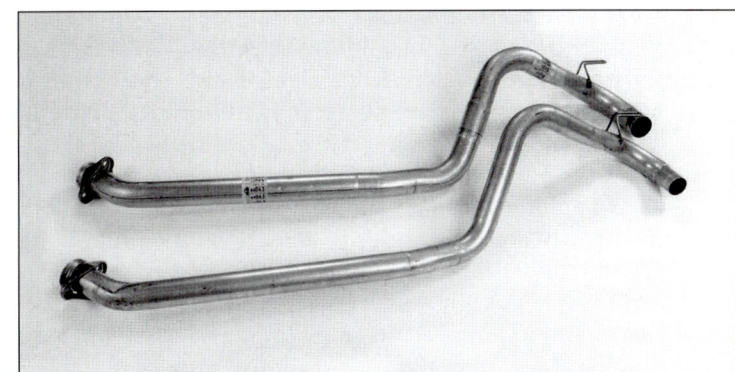

**Far left:** Some cars, such as 1967–1968 Mustangs, look awesome with a quad-tip appearance. *Hedman photo*

**Left:** Though not necessarily stock-looking, resonators mounted as tailpipes can add some visual flare to the underside of your car's rear end. This Hedman resonator also features a 'glass-pack muffler built in to help keep your ride quiet. *Hedman photo*

Modifying catalytic converters is not necessary or permitted, nor are they replaceable until the chemicals inside the converter have been used up, allowing engine emissions to become dirty again.

## Mufflers

Once upon a time, picking a muffler (or mufflers) for your vehicle was a simple matter: either you went with a replacement for the factory muffler, or you ran 'glass packs ... or you dumped the mufflers altogether and went with straight pipe. Today, we have a multitude of choices, including the stock replacement-type mufflers, 'glass packs are still around, turbo-style mufflers are still popular, chambered-exhaust never quite caught on, and we've even got high-tech electronic mufflers that cancel out sound with inverse sound waves. Then there are the different materials with which mufflers are constructed, particularly stainless steel and aluminized steel.

In general, most vintage cars are well served by turbo-style mufflers, because they not only flow quite well, but they look pretty similar to stock mufflers. And if constructed of aluminized or stainless steel, they'll last almost forever. Most turbos also just so happen to have a nice, mellow tone that nicely complements a high-performance engine.

'Glass packs (so-named for the fiberglass packing material encased in them to absorb sound), though legendary, are hardly the ultimate muffler, in terms of flow. In fact, they're quite restrictive compared to more modern muffler developments.

Chambered exhaust pipes, like those available on late-1960s Camaros and Chevelles, are very tricky, and don't use any kind of sound-absorbing material. Instead, they rely on chambers of different sizes to tune out specific frequencies. Chambered pipes are available in reproduction form, but, like 'glass packs, are hardly efficient flow-wise.

One of the big things to look for in a muffler is actually the size of its inlets and outlets. Obviously, they should match the sizes of the exhaust pipes you'll be connecting to the muffler, but the inlets and outlets shouldn't neck down when they enter the muffler; the muffler should retain the same size passages throughout, to ensure unrestricted flow.

### Cat-Back Exhaust Pipe/Muffler Systems

Since the Environmental Protection Agency (EPA) made it illegal to alter any emissions devices on a vehicle exhaust system, manufacturers have focused on cat-back exhaust systems, systems that replace all the exhaust system parts rearward of the catalytic converter. This keeps the EPA happy and provides a noticeable power boost and improved sound.

Most cat-back exhaust systems employ larger-diameter exhaust pipes, typically with smooth mandrel bends, plus a low-restriction muffler with a larger inlet and one or more large outlets. Most are available in either aluminized or stainless steel for long life.

# Cooling and Breathing

## Exhaust Recommendations

Ideally, every car would run long-tube, equal-length coated headers, a high-flow catalytic converter (if required), and a free-flowing exhaust system for maximum efficiency. But that's not always possible, nor is it always necessary.

Depending on how you use your car and whether you feel it's important enough to shoehorn in a set of full-length headers, you will likely find a comfortable system somewhere in between bone-stock and the ideal just mentioned in the previous paragraph.

### Street High-Performance Driving

Street driving doesn't require an all-out exhaust system, but that doesn't mean there's no point in upgrading things a little. Headers are worth the money and time to install, but don't get a set without a protective thermal barrier coating inside and out (unless you particularly like the thought of replacing them in a couple of years). If you happen to have a catalytic converter and it needs to be replaced, get a high-flow unit. A high-performance, cat-back exhaust system won't usually break the bank and will generally provide a modest power increase (just don't expect too much of it if it's installed behind restrictive manifolds).

If your car is a daily driver and you value reliability, you might want to stick with the production exhaust manifolds. They rarely ever leak, they're nice and quiet, and they never wear out. Of course, they will cost you some power and the weight won't help your handling any.

Most vintage vehicles have the room to run true dual-exhaust pipes, and they're almost a requirement for a performance vehicle (if only for the image they convey). But don't get too crazy on the diameters of the exhaust pipes for your dual-exhaust system. Most 350- to 400-cubic-inch street engines will work fine with 2 1/4-inch or 2 1/2-inch exhaust pipes and turbo-style mufflers. Tailpipes don't need to be as large, so 2-inch pipes are usually sufficient. These modest pipe sizes will help keep the flow velocity up throughout the system.

### Drag Racing

If you're serious about racing, your only real choice is a set of equal-length, long-tube headers. At the track—depending on class rules—you can probably uncork the headers by disconnecting the exhaust at the end of the header collector for a few extra horses.

If you are going to all the trouble to run equal-length, long-tube headers, you also want to consider the tube sizes you'll be running. While street-driven small blocks respond better to 1 5/8-inch primary pipes, race engines (which typically spend more time at higher rpm) can benefit from 1 3/4-inch or even 1 7/8-inch primary tubes. The larger-diameter tubes flow enough air to prevent the engine from choking on its own exhaust. Keeping the primary tubes relatively long—around 30 inches or so—will aid low-end torque too.

Collectors also affect power. Good headers will have collectors that measure at least 3 inches in diameter and are about 1 foot long. Extending them will usually increase low-end torque even further, but you'll have to experiment with the length because it varies based on camshaft profile, head flow, and the remainder of your exhaust system (or lack of one, if you're running at the track).

If the class you compete in requires you to run through the mufflers, then focus on low-restriction exhaust pipes and mufflers, and, of course, a high-flow catalytic converter if your vehicle requires one.

**Below:** Many muscle cars came with—or could benefit from—tasteful exhaust tips. These oval-shaped tips from Hedman resemble tips used on Chevelles for several years. *Hedman photo*

**Bottom:** A number of muscle cars featured megaphone-like tips. *Hedman photo*

# Chapter 7
# Underhood Extras

Power adders are more popular than ever, and for good reason. How else can you bolt on several hundred additional horsepower in just a few hours? Whether your power addition of choice is nitrous oxide, a turbo or a supercharger, there are many decisions to be made.

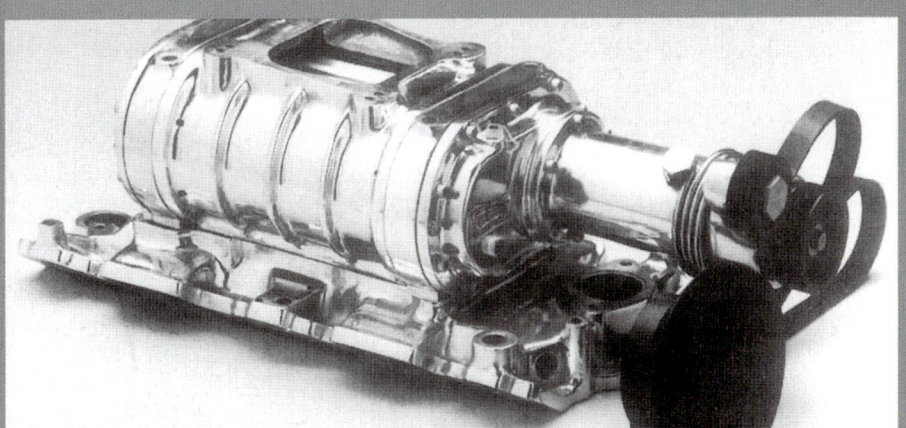

# Nitrous, Superchargers, and Turbos

Internal-combustion engines are merely air pumps; they draw it in (mixing it with fuel in the process), burn it, then blow it out. The better your engine is at doing this, the more power it can make. That's why engine builders spend so much time working on free-flowing intake manifolds, cylinder head ports, and exhaust systems.

But if you're not so handy with a grinder, or if you've already done all that and still want more power, consider artificial means of increasing your engine's breathing efficiency.

Nitrous oxide systems, superchargers, and turbochargers all make even a stock engine act like a purpose-built race engine. And they transform race engines into better, more powerful race engines.

## What Do They Do?

Don't blame us, but no matter how good you are at tuning your naturally aspirated engine, it's still pathetically inefficient. The problem is this: your engine's cylinders are relatively large, but the time that the intake valves are open is brief, so there is little time for the fresh air/fuel mixture to fill the cylinder.

Fortunately, there are a few ways to increase an engine's efficiency, and they're nothing new to the automotive world. Nitrous oxide kits, turbochargers, and superchargers all increase an engine's power output by increasing the volume of air and fuel an engine can inhale. Each does this in a different manner and with differing advantages and disadvantages.

Despite the common goal, each of these systems operates on the same basic premise. They get more air and fuel into your engine. Essentially, each system overfills each cylinder with more air and fuel than it would normally ingest.

The bottom line is that each of these systems can transform a ho-hum engine into a blazingly fast rocket. In many cases, they can boost a stock engine's output by 100 or more horsepower, resulting in better performance than an expensive, purpose-built engine.

## Nitrous Oxide

Nitrous oxide is a popular and effective power booster for stock and race engines alike. Nitrous oxide (also known as laughing gas because of the effect it has on people if inhaled, which you should never do without medical supervision) increases engine power in two ways: First, it super-oxygenates the air-fuel mixture, allowing it to burn more fuel, so the combustion process produces more heat. Second, nitrous oxide cools the air/fuel mixture, which allows the air/fuel mixture to hold even more fuel, and it reduces hot spots in the cylinder that could lead to detonation. Since the intake air can absorb so much more fuel, nitrous kits inject more fuel to prevent the engine from running lean, which could cause it to burn a piston or detonate so severely that it could damage the engine.

Easy-to-install, bolt-on nitrous kits are available for nearly any engine from a number of manufacturers and can generally boost power anywhere from

Nitrous oxide is another quick way to quicker ETs. The basic gist is that the nitrous both cools the intake air (which allows it to hold more fuel) plus super-oxygenates it (which allows it to hold even *more* fuel). Kits like this one from Nitrous Oxide Systems can boost power anywhere from 50 to more than 500 horsepower! *Nitrous Oxide Systems photo*

75 to 150 horsepower for a stock engine. Modified engines can handle additional power boosts, up to around 250 horsepower, while full-race motors with heavy-duty reciprocating assemblies may be able to withstand as much as 400 nitrous-generated horsepower or more!

Carbureted and TBI-equipped engines can use a normal injector plate that gets sandwiched between the intake manifold and the throttle body assembly. MPFI systems may require a slightly different solution that may result in fuel flowing through the intake manifold. That can lead to uneven fuel mixtures cylinder-to-cylinder, or even puddling. More exotic systems solve this problem by using additional fuel injectors that feed directly into the intake manifold runners, aimed toward the intake valves.

Nitrous kits are easy, cost effective, and safe methods of increasing engine output for short periods of time, such as a drag race; however, you have to be cautious about how much extra power you attempt to make with a nitrous kit because it is possible to overstress parts and cause them to fail, or to at least increase wear. When in doubt, be conservative with nitrous system jetting and careful in its use, limiting nitrous use to 15 seconds or less, and only at full throttle.

Additionally, it helps to use timing retard devices with nitrous oxide systems. Nitrous-assisted engines create higher cylinder pressures, so ignition timing should be retarded. But since you only use nitrous sporadically (and never on the street!) you don't want to hamper engine performance when the nitrous is not in use. An ignition-retard device can be wired to activate when the nitrous is activated, so timing is only retarded when needed.

### Nitrous Benefits

Based on all that, you should be able to spot the good points of running nitrous: it's inexpensive (initially, at least); it's easy to install; it doesn't affect around-town driving; and some systems can be tuned to deliver more power as your needs or cravings increase.

Serious drag racers may like the fact that it's possible to hook up nitrous kits in stages. You can have a relatively modest kit for launch, when cylinder pressures are greatest as the engine strains to get the car moving. Then, when the car is moving, a higher-power kit can kick in to boost power even more for continued acceleration.

### Nitrous Drawbacks

There's no such thing as a free lunch, so it should come as little surprise that nitrous systems do have drawbacks. First, it costs money to refill those nitrous bottles. Sure the system is cheap to install, but if you use it regularly, you'll find that refilling the bottle will empty your wallet. The fact that your nitrous supply dwindles with each use also means that you could run out at the least opportune time—either between rounds at the track or, worse, in the middle of a run. At the very least, you're likely to lose races that way. But there's also the possibility of engine or drivetrain damage if the nitrous starts sputtering in midrun.

Beyond that, nitrous isn't well-suited to street use because it creates a sudden explosion of power that can make a car difficult to control on the street, around other cars, or around people. Rarely will you encounter conditions on the street where nitrous helps.

There is always the issue of whether nitrous oxide will increase wear in your engine or cause something to break. That is possible, but it shouldn't be a problem if you properly match the nitrous system to your engine's abilities. In other words, stock engines—especially ones with lots of miles on them—won't be able to withstand the increased cylinder pressures and forces created by high-horsepower nitrous kits, but a low-power kit should work just fine.

## Forced-Induction Systems

With the exception of a handful of Oldsmobiles with turbocharged Jetfire V-8s, some Paxton supercharged Shelby Mustangs, and a few other rarities, stock engines of the 1950s, 1960s, and 1970s were normally aspirated. The only fuel and air they could get into their cylinders was what they could suck in. But by pressurizing the induction system, it is possible to force-feed an engine more air and fuel than it would normally use. With more air and fuel in the cylinders, you create more power.

There are two basic kinds of forced induction systems: turbochargers and superchargers. Each has its own strengths and weaknesses. Use of them should be considered carefully, because they place added stress on engines and could cause parts to fail. In addition, you may need to rebuild your engine with a different cam and pistons to get the most from a forced induction system.

## Turbochargers

Turbochargers use exhaust flow to turn an impeller. As the impeller spins, the impeller's shaft spins. On the opposite end of the shaft is another impeller, which spins too. This second impeller blows additional air into the engine. As more air enters the engine, more fuel is mixed with it, and the cylinders become fully filled with fresh air and fuel (the pressurization also helps to evacuate exhaust gases), so the combustion process produces higher-than-usual levels of power.

Because turbochargers are driven by the flow of exhaust gases, the engine must reach a certain rpm before the turbo builds enough boost to be of value. This spin-up or spool-up time is known as turbo lag. Using exhaust gases to run the turbo creates an excess heat problem. The exhaust heats the turbo, which heats the air flowing through it to the intake manifold. This makes the air less dense and reduces the amount of fuel the air can hold. This problem is compounded by the fact that as you pressurize the air, it naturally heats up. The problem escalates as the turbo continues to run, since exhaust gases are hotter from the pressurized combustion cycles.

Using an intercooler helps combat the heat problems, because it lowers the intake air temperature substantially. It does this in much the same manner as a radiator, only, instead of coolant flowing through the intercooler, (hot) air flows through it. Air-to-air intercoolers are most common, because they're simple: hot air from the supercharger or turbocharger enters the intercooler, cooling fins absorb the heat from the internal air, then wind blowing through the cooling fins whisks the heat away from the fins. Air-to-water intercoolers are also available.

Because turbos get so hot, they are extremely hard on engine oil that is supplied to the turbo for lubrication. In fact, the number one cause of turbo failure is improper lubrication, usually due to oil that has thinned out due to the extreme heat. Synthetic oils are highly recommended for turbocharged applications. Heat also damages internal seals in turbos, causing the lubricating oil to get into the intake stream resulting in the too-common blue smoke and fouled plugs.

Also, as with nitrous oxide kits, turbochargers require retarded ignition timing because of the increased cylinder pressures. They also require reduced compression to avoid detonation on pump fuels.

**Left:** Today's superchargers operate on the same time-tested and track-proven principle as those early systems: the supercharger screw is turned by a belt driven off the crank. But today's superchargers can benefit from modern intercooler technology that cools the intake charge so it holds more fuel and thus makes more power. *ProCharger photo*

**Right:** Paxton chargers turned up in the 1960s as an option for Shelby Mustangs, too.

# Underhood Extras

**Left:** Turbos are another forced induction option. This Gale Banks twin-turbo setup is about as exotic as they come—and equally powerful, producing up to 1,100 horsepower! They do take a bit of effort to fit between the fenders, but the effort is worth it. *Gale Banks Engineering photo*

**Right:** Engine output is a function of how much air can flow through it. Supercharging forces more air through the engine to raise power output significantly. Even a supercharger running modest boost can double power output—they're a great way to wake up a mild engine. *ProCharger photo*

Turbocharger kits aren't as popular today as they once were, but there are still a number of companies that produce turbo kits, and it is always possible to homebrew one, using parts from different suppliers and fabricated brackets and miscellaneous pieces.

## Turbocharger Benefits

The good news is that turbochargers are the closest thing to free power as you can get: they take a waste product (exhaust gas) and use it to force more air into the engine, and the process feeds itself. The more air the turbo forces in, the more exhaust blows out and at greater speeds, so it can blow even more air into the engine. These are important differences from superchargers, which use some of the engine's power to turn their impellers.

Turbos are no-brainers as far as their use goes: if exhaust flow is high enough (engine speeds and cylinder pressures demand it), then the turbo kicks in. Otherwise it passively sits there. And while it's idle, it's not creating unnecessary strain on the engine.

## Turbocharger Drawbacks

Nothing's perfect, and turbochargers are no exception. One of the biggest problems is trying to find a ready-to-install kit for your vehicle. When you do find one, it probably won't come cheap.

If those two problems don't scare you away from a turbo setup, you'll need to prepare yourself for setting up your car to work with a turbo. Beyond simply installing the turbo system, which typically requires a low-compression ratio in order to run a reasonable boost, you will also need to work on a chassis setup that will let you get your engine's power to the ground. This can be especially challenging, because you will have to contend with turbo lag. The problem, in a nutshell, is that you essentially have two engines. When the turbo isn't making boost, it's naturally aspirated and making relatively little power. When it is making boost, you'll have an insane level of power. Finding a good chassis setup that balances these two extremes isn't easy. Time spent working with waste gates and careful selection of the turbo size you run will make life easier, but it still won't be easy.

Once you do get the turbo set up and your chassis dialed in, there is the issue of heat buildup, both in your intake air and in your engine's oil.

An intercooler—either air-to-air or air-to-water—cools the intake air charge, so it remains dense and holds more fuel. But intercoolers and their plumbing can be difficult to package in a tight engine compartment.

As for the oil, the solution is twofold: One, run synthetic oils, which are designed to withstand higher temperatures better. Two, use an oil cooler.

## Superchargers

While turbochargers are part-time power builders, superchargers run full time and always keep the intake tract pressurized because they run off of the crankshaft via a drive belt. This extra drag on the engine results in a minor parasitic power loss, but the benefits of a supercharger far outweigh that minor drawback. Otherwise, turbochargers and superchargers are essentially similar in function.

Because superchargers do not suffer from lag, it's easier to tune a supercharged engine. Superchargers don't have the heat problems caused by running off the exhaust gases, but they still raise the intake air temperature as a result of pressurization.

Using an intercooler will lower the intake air temperature, which allows the air to hold more fuel and thus makes a supercharger even more efficient. Use of synthetic engine oils also helps superchargers.

Because of the increased cylinder pressures generated under boost, superchargers also require retarded ignition timing and reduced compression. Off-the-shelf units are generally designed to deliver relatively little boost because of the compression ratio of stock engines; however, if you purpose-build an engine to use a supercharger, you can tailor the compression ratio and the boost for maximum power.

**Supercharger Benefits**

The allure of superchargers is that they create full-time power increases at any engine speed, any throttle position, and in every driving situation. Since the supercharger is always providing boost, power application is smooth, though amplified compared to a normally aspirated engine. This makes setting up a chassis easier, and it also aids drivability and control, since the engine's reactions to throttle are predictable.

Installing a supercharger is more straightforward as well, since the units bolt on and don't require replacement of or modifications to exhaust manifolds and systems. Placement of the system and the lack of a modified exhaust system mean superchargers are generally easier to fit into a factory engine compartment, though they will hardly look stock.

If you rebuild your engine so that it can withstand more power (stronger pistons and connecting rods, better pistons and rings, and so on) then you can increase supercharger boost by simply changing the pulley ratio. Turn the supercharger faster and you get more boost and more power; slower supercharger speeds yield less boost but increased engine life.

It's also possible to combine supercharging with nitrous oxide for even more racing power.

**Supercharger Drawbacks**

The number one drawback of superchargers is the price. Although a number of companies offer kits for almost any engine, they don't exactly give them away. Supercharger kits tend to be all-inclusive, right down to the hardware, the drive belt, mounting brackets, and necessary ductwork.

As with turbos and nitrous, superchargers increase cylinder pressures and power, and they increase the stresses and forces on your engine. Any weaknesses will quickly appear, usually in the form of failures.

The science of superchargers hasn't been lost on the auto industry. In 1957, Ford produced a limited number of Thunderbirds with Paxton superchargers. The engines developed 300 horsepower.

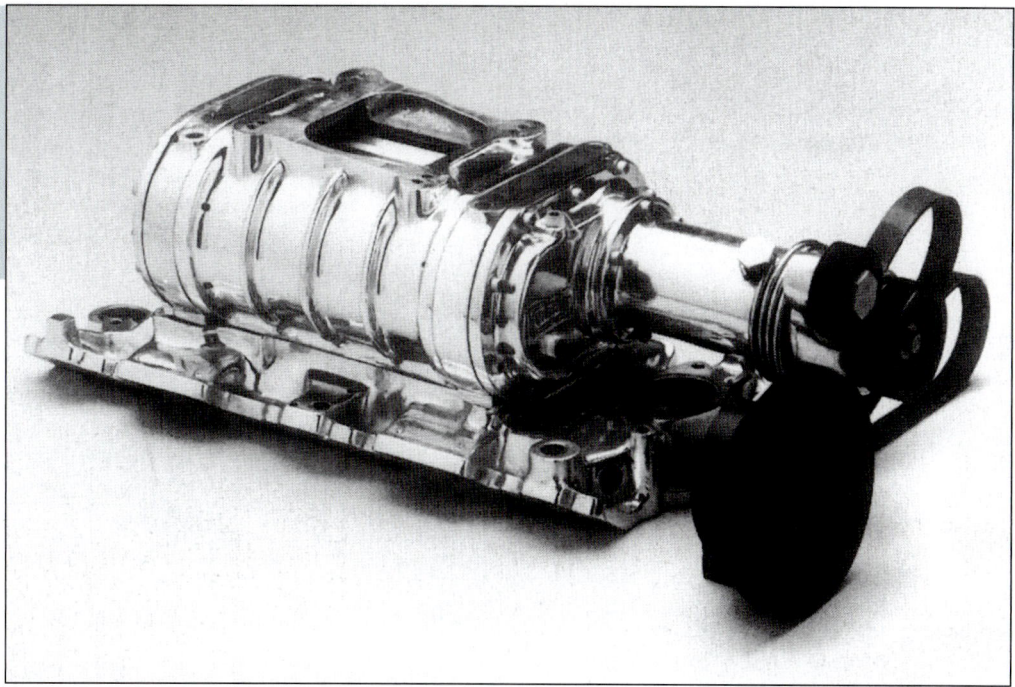

Pro Street–style superchargers are a tad easier to set up, but they're harder to conceal, due to their size. But you can't beat them for reliability—just check out any NHRA or IHRA event and you'll spot more x-71-style superchargers than you can count. *Weiand photo*

Although this is a somewhat subjective drawback, superchargers—and turbos to an extent—are noisy. All that air rushing through them creates a whining whistle that some people find objectionable. To be entirely fair, the noise isn't overwhelming and most enthusiasts would more than gladly sacrifice a little quiet for the impressive power gains.

Superchargers heat intake air because of the pressurization, but an intercooler reduces the air charge temperature. Oil also gets heated up, but synthetic oil and an oil cooler dispense with that worry.

## Which One Is Right for You?

If you've been reading this book—or if you've been involved in performance cars for any length of time—you should already know that there is never a simple answer to that sort of question.

Depending on how your engine will be used and the parts and preparation that you are putting into it, any one of these solutions could work. Or any one of them could be disastrous.

The following information should be viewed as a set of very generalized guidelines, since it's impossible to account for every possible engine and chassis combination, driving conditions, driver skill, and more.

### High-Performance Street Driving

Supercharging is usually your best bet for street use because of the smooth, consistent, predictable delivery of power. Superchargers work well with either manual or automatic transmissions, and you could even run one pulley to produce modest boost on the street, then swap on a different pulley for more boost at the track.

### Drag Racing

Drag racers have long employed both nitrous oxide and superchargers, individually and together, to get down the quarter-mile in a hurry. The short runs, steady throttle action, and controlled environment make drag racing perfect for nitrous oxide.

Turbochargers would be more popular in drag racing if it weren't for turbo lag. Since superchargers provide the same benefit without lag, they're a favorite way of boosting a drag engine's output.

# Chapter 8
# DRIVETRAIN

Harnessing the power of your freshly built engine can be a challenge, particularly if you're using substandard or worn-out factory parts. Selecting the right transmission and rear end components is the next step in maximizing the performance of your modified muscle car.

A high-performance vehicle's drivetrain—its transmission, rear axle, and related parts—is what turns your engine's power into motion. If the drivetrain isn't sturdy enough to survive behind your high-performance engine, you're going to find yourself watching your competition race off into the sunset.

Fortunately, drivetrains are perhaps the easiest vehicle systems to understand. Despite certain mysterious parts (just try to figure out how an automatic transmission works sometime—it's mind-boggling), the basics of how the crankshaft turns the transmission's gears, which turns the driveshaft, which turns the pinion gear that rotates the ring gear, which spins the axles, is pretty straightforward. You've got a simple flow of power through the system.

Of course, things are a bit more complicated than that. You've got to think about clutches for manual transmissions and torque converters for automatics, about torque-multiplying gear ratios in both the tranny and the rear-axle assembly, about pinion angles, limited slip differentials, and even wheel studs. But if you step through the system one piece at a time, it will make sense, and you'll figure out what your high-performance vehicle needs to perform reliably.

## The Good, the Bad, and the Ugly

Unfortunately, few vintage vehicles are known for having bullet-proof drivetrains. In stock form, the transmissions, driveshafts, and rear-axle assemblies are, at best, adequate for the job. But if you start piling on power parts, like hotter camshafts, headers, wider and stickier tires, and especially superchargers or nitrous oxide, you'll start breaking drivetrain parts like you change your underwear (which might be more frequent, too, given the scary driving that can follow certain drivetrain failures).

More engine power stresses the transmission, especially in drag racing, where shifts are typically fast and furious and at high rpm. Sustained high rpms can cause a stock driveshaft to spin itself to pieces. Stickier tires will wrench every ounce of life from a rear-axle assembly, since the tires may still be gripping when internal rear-end damage occurs.

## Blood, Sweat, and Gears

One of the hardest concepts of automotive mechanics to grasp is that of gearing on overall performance. The principle is straightforward: gearing should allow the engine to operate at or near its peak efficiency under given conditions.

If we oversimplify things, the concept becomes clearer. If your engine develops peak torque at 3,000 rpm, your vehicle would be most efficient cruising with the engine at that speed. Divide the engine speed by the transmission gear ratio, then divide that by the rear-axle gear ratio, and multiply that by circumference of the wheel and tire combination to find the speed at which the vehicle is most efficient.

(Engine RPM ÷ Transmission gear ratio) x Tire circumference = Speed Axle gear ratio

For example, 3,000 rpm divided by a one-to-one (1:1) transmission gear (typical high gear) results in a 3,000-rpm driveshaft speed; divide driveshaft speed by a 3.00:1 rear-axle gear ratio to determine an axle speed of 1,000 rpm, which must then be multiplied by tire circumference to determine a vehicle speed. A typical 28-inch-tall tire would then yield a speed of 83.3 miles per hour, when all the calculations are done.

Of course, a vehicle that was only efficient at 83 miles per hour would be pretty impractical on the street, so we have transmissions that allow us to change gear ratios, which effectively changes what speed the vehicle is efficient at. For example, changing to a 2:1 transmission gear (roughly second-gear range) cuts driveshaft speed in half (1,500 rpm), then dividing that by the rear-axle ratio (3.0:1) yields an axle speed of 500 rpm and a resulting speed of about 42 miles per hour, which is much more streetable.

Naturally, the more gear choices you have, the more speeds at which your vehicle will operate efficiently. Racers work with this information to determine the gearing they need to go through certain portions of a race course at a given rpm or vehicle speed.

Unfortunately, you can only alter gear ratios in manual

**Below:** Many racing classes require a scatter-proof bell housing, like this Lakewood unit. Even if you're not racing, a steel bell housing is good insurance against a very ugly (and painful) clutch explosion. *Lakewood photo*

**Bottom:** Muncies, TopLoaders, and "Hemi" four-speeds are great transmissions, but there are better ones available, like Richmond's 4+1. Based on race technology, the 4+1 will not only survive behind a high-output engine, it'll make it more tolerant of street use, thanks to an overdrive fifth gear. *Richmond photo*

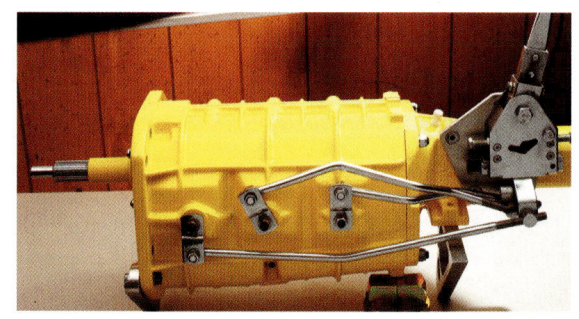

## WHO'S GOT THE TOUGHEST DRIVETRAIN?

On average, high-performance Mopars get high marks for heavy-duty components, like the TorqueFlite 727 automatic transmission, the legendary Hemi four-speed, and not one but *two* super-strong rear-axle assemblies: Chrysler's own 8¾-inch rear end, plus the Dana 60 units the company stuffed under some vehicles.

On the other hand, Chevrolet gets fairly low marks. Muncie four-speeds are ill-suited to life behind engines like the 450-horsepower LS6 454. And Chevy's sole performance rear-axle assembly—the 12-bolt—was a far cry from the Mopar units or Ford's 9-inch. The shining point in GM's drivetrain lineup was its Turbo Hydramatic 400 automatic. Dubbed the "bang-screech" tranny for its ability to consistently chirp the tires during full-throttle upshifts, it was a superb transmission behind a variety of engines.

Ford fell squarely in the middle between GM and Chrysler: its 9-inch is so tough it's still the predominant axle assembly in professional and amateur racing. And while its TopLoader four-speed manual gearbox and C6 automatic are considered durable, they just don't compare to the Mopar equivalents.

So what should you go with if building up your high-performance muscle car or truck? Transmission choice is probably best left to what the factory offered you (unless you go with an aftermarket unit, like a Richmond or Jerico). Rear axle–wise, the Ford 9-inch will give you the most flexibility in terms of gear ratios, heavy-duty axles, and other performance-oriented parts.

## Transmissions

Most vintage vehicles were available with a choice of manual or automatic transmissions, sometimes depending on what engine was ordered.

Manual transmissions have the edge in performance mystique, but when put to the test on a drag strip it was often the automatics that ran quicker, or at least more consistently.

When it comes to upgrading your vehicle's transmission, you have a few methods of attacking whatever problem you have, real or perceived. First, you can improve the transmission that you have. Second, you can swap it for a transmission that was optional. Or third, you can retrofit a modern transmission (either factory or performance aftermarket) to your vehicle.

### Manual Transmissions

Factory manual transmissions were fairly simple, generally with either three or four forward gears, plus reverse. First-gear ratios were around 2.20:1 for close-ratio boxes, while wide-ratio first gears were closer to 2.50:1 for more torque off the line. Top gear (third for three-speeds, fourth for four-speeds) was always 1:1.

The cases for most manual transmissions were cast iron, because it was cheap and durable. It was also heavy, which doesn't make it fun to change even a small cast-iron gearbox, like a GM Saginaw three-speed. GM's Muncie four-speeds—known by their RPO codes M20 (wide ratio), M21 (close ratio), and M22 (heavy-duty close ratio)—used aluminum cases, for a considerable weight savings, though they still tip the scales at roughly 100 pounds each. Chrysler's Hemi four-speed was even more of a cast-iron monster, and the Ford TopLoader wasn't much more svelte.

#### Upgrading What You've Got

As far as upgrading vintage transmissions, you should always start off by

transmissions and rear-axle assemblies. Since automatics don't have gears that you can feasibly change on your own, you're left to deal with whatever the manufacturer of your transmission has blessed you with.

The formula also points out that if your engine has a nice, broad torque curve, your vehicle will be efficient at a broad range of speeds in each transmission gear. If your engine has a spiked torque curve, your vehicle will be efficient at only narrow ranges of speeds.

Manual transmissions, like this GM "Muncie" four-speed with its aluminum case, are highly sought after. Of course, for performance use, there are a number of worthwhile upgrades that make your drivetrain more reliable.

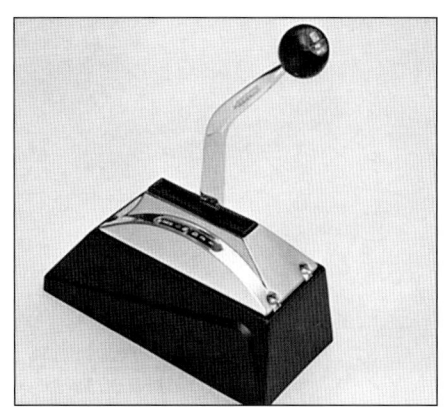
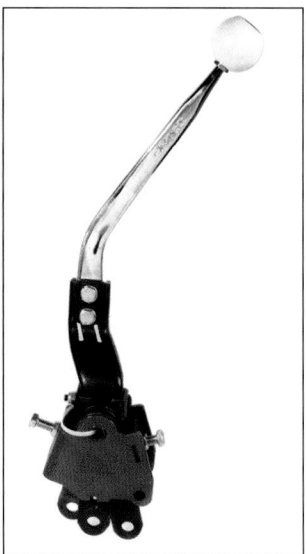

**Left:** A performance drivetrain starts with a performance transmission, like this GM automatic prepped by Bowler Transmission. Heavy-duty clutches and a reworked valve body will provide firmer, crisper, quicker shifts that both improve performance and lengthen transmission life. *Bowler Transmission photo*

**Middle:** While some vintage muscle cars had true performance shifters (Hurst Olds 4-4-2s and certain Pontiacs with the "His-&-Hers" Hurst shifter, for example), most could benefit from an aftermarket shifter like this Hurst ProMatic 2 for automatics, which provides short, positive, ratcheted shifting to prevent overshifting. *Hurst photo*

**Right:** On the manual-shifting side, 40+ years of experience have kept Hurst's Competition Plus line at the top of the heap. They still provide short, crisp shifts and are available for a wide variety of transmissions, including modern five- and six-speed manual boxes that are often retrofitted to older vehicles. *Hurst photo*

rebuilding the tranny to ensure all the gears, synchros, bushings, and other parts are up to snuff. Depending on the transmission, there may be replacement gears available in different ratios than the transmission originally came with. Borg-Warner T-10 and Super T-10 four-speeds, in particular, were used in a number of vehicles from different makers. Several companies offer replacement parts for them, mainly because they're still popular transmissions with racers.

Every transmission needs a good shifter. Some production cars were shipped with high-quality Hurst shifters, but most relied on factory-designed linkages that had long, sloppy throws that contributed to many a missed shift. There are a handful of other performance shifters available, but Hursts are the standard. They've got the mystique, the performance, and even a reasonable price.

Another practical upgrade is to replace your manual transmission's conventional oil for a synthetic lubricant that will greatly reduce friction. Tests in a 1970 Hemi Charger with a "Heavy Duty" Hemi four-speed showed a 0.1-second drop in quarter-mile ET and a gain of nearly 2 miles per hour at the traps simply from changing the transmission fluid. Synthetic fluid also withstands heat better and better protects your transmission.

**Shifting Gears to Something Better**

Swapping your factory transmission for a newer factory or aftermarket box is a worthwhile way to improve performance.

If your vehicle had a three-speed manual or even an automatic transmission, you may want to replace it with one of the four-speed manual gearboxes that were available when the car was new. It's fairly straightforward to replace a three-speed manual with a four-speed manual. The only snags you'll likely hit are the driveshaft length (since different transmissions are sometimes different lengths), the need for a different shifter, and possibly a different rear mount. But these are relatively minor differences.

Swapping a four-speed in place of an automatic is more complex. You need to get all the necessary clutch linkage, including the clutch and brake pedals. You'll also need a bell housing and clutch assembly, a flywheel (to replace the automatic's flexplate), a pilot bushing for the crankshaft, a shifter, and you'll have to cut a hole in the floor for the shifter. If your car has a console between the front seats, the odds are pretty good that it's not going to work with the manual shifter (at least not without some modifications). You'll probably need either a new, longer driveshaft, or have your current one shortened. Few transmission mounts (or crossmembers, for that matter) are the same between automatics and manuals, so that will probably need to be changed.

You might also find that you simply want to swap a close-ratio transmission for a wide-ratio version of the same transmission. This is generally the easiest, though there can still be differences in the number of splines on the input and output shafts.

Newer manual transmissions, such as Borg-Warner's T5 five-speed and T56 six-speed are a great way to add an overdrive transmission to improve fuel economy and extend engine life by reducing engine rpm when cruising. Likewise, the ZF six-speed used in many fourth-generation Corvettes was a sturdy tranny that survived well behind even race-prepared ZR-1 engines (which, at their peak, were good for 425 *net* horses from the factory). Swapping these transmissions in place of your old-world box is hardly a simple remove-and-replace operation, however. Modern transmissions are rather large; they have to be to fit those extra gears in them. They generally use a rail-style shifter, which has its shift linkage inside the transmission. Depending on the location of the shifter, it may dictate changes to your floor pan, or perhaps a nonstock setback of your engine in the engine compartment. There are often differences related to clutch systems (the new transmissions use hydraulic clutches, whereas vintage vehicles use mechanical linkage clutches), and even speedometer drives complicate such swaps.

Several companies, including Richmond, Tremec, Jerico, and others, manufacture manual transmissions for high-performance or racing use. These transmissions are somewhat easier to swap into an older vehicle because you can customize the transmission with longer or shorter tail sections or different shifter locations to match your vehicle's floor pan and other factors. Such transmissions also offer performance advantages in the form of a vast assortment of gear ratios and other repair and maintenance parts.

Naturally, you could swap out your existing manual transmission and replace it with an automatic—including a late model unit—with relative simplicity and still reap the benefits of an overdrive ratio, but without all the hassles of clutch linkages, shifter locations, and other problems.

## Clutches, Flywheels, and Bell Housings

There is nothing wrong with the clutches of most vintage vehicles, other than the fact that heavy-duty clutches featured high pedal pressures. Most stock-type clutches will even endure some abuse. But if you've modified your engine in any way, it's likely that the clamping force of a stock, replacement-type clutch won't get the job done now, and certainly not during racing-style blasts when engine speeds—and torque—are soaring.

Thanks to decades of gradual improvements in clutch linings and pressure plate designs, aftermarket performance clutches provide far superior clamping forces *without* the high pedal efforts. Some performance clutches actually increase clamping forces relative to engine speeds, so when extra clamping force is most needed, the clutch continues to hold firmly.

Depending on your application (whether you're racing or driving on the street, for example), consider replacing the stock flywheel with a lighter one, which allows the engine to accelerate faster, but gives up some flexibility in around-town use. In any event, when changing clutches, it's wise to have your flywheel magnaflux inspected for cracks and resurfaced to ensure a smooth, flat friction surface for the clutch disc to grab.

### CLOSE RATIO VERSUS WIDE RATIO

Ads from the muscle car era frequently pointed out when a vehicle had a close-ratio manual transmission available, typically a four-speed unit. They rarely mentioned that if you didn't get a close-ratio gearbox, you ended up with a wide-ratio transmission, and that was sometimes the better equipment.

The terms *close ratio* and *wide ratio* refer to the spread between gears in the transmission. A close-ratio transmission's gearing results in a smaller drop in engine rpm than a wide-ratio transmission, because the gears are similar in size. For example, the two transmissions might have the following ratios:

| Gear | Close | Wide |
|---|---|---|
| 1st | 2.20:1 | 2.50:1 |
| 2nd | 1.9:1 | 2.1:1 |
| 3rd | 1.5:1 | 1.5:1 |
| 4th | 1:1 | 1:1 |

Note that while the wide-ratio box drops 0.4:1 from first to second, the close-ratio box drops only 0.3. Likewise, the drop from second to third is 0.6 in our theoretical wide-ratio tranny, but only 0.4 in our close ratio.

The actual ratios used by the different manufacturers differed, but the result was always the same. The close-ratio box was geared to keep the engine working closer to its peak power, while the wide-ratio box might result in a drop of several hundred more rpm between gears—possibly to a point where the engine made less power.

Wide-ratio boxes multiplied torque better, however, and made it easier to get rolling from a stop. They gave you a better choice of gears around town.

When installing a flywheel or replacing a clutch, it's a good idea to replace the bolts that secure them with aftermarket racing-grade bolts. It's also comforting to install locking bolt assemblies, like those from Stage 8 Fasteners, which ensure that you won't have a flywheel or clutch problem related to a bolt coming loose.

Finally, it may be possible to replace a stock-style solid pilot bushing with a roller bearing for reduced friction and wear and smoother clutch and transmission operation. Roller pilot bearings are available from the manufacturer of your engine. General Motors, for example, installed roller pilot bearings on a number of production vehicles, and those bearings are direct replacements for old-style solid bushings used on nearly any GM vehicle with a manual transmission.

## Automatic Transmissions

As with manual transmissions, your automatic-equipped vintage car or truck can have its transmission upgraded in a number of ways, including improving your current transmission or replacing it with something better.

### Improving Automatic Transmissions

Depending on your transmission, you may have a number of upgrades that you can make. One of the first things you should do is have your automatic transmission rebuilt, even if it doesn't have many miles on it, because things tend to break down after 30 or so years.

While the transmission is being overhauled, you might opt to make certain modifications, such as performance clutch packs or other changes. Aftermarket transmissions, like those from TCI, Art Carr, or other rebuilders, do exactly that—they take a stock transmission and rebuild it with high-performance internals and various (sometimes proprietary) modifications to increase its durability, change shift patterns, and more.

Shift kits are popular upgrades that can either be incorporated at the time the transmission is being rebuilt, or afterward, if you feel you need changes to your vehicle's shift patterns.

Speaking of shift patterns, you may be able to replace your automatic's valve body with one that provides a reversed

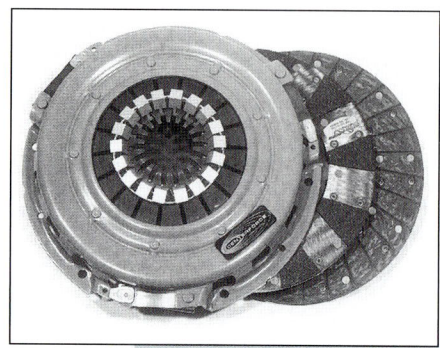

shifting pattern (P-R-N-1-2-3 instead of P-R-N-3-2-1) or even one that converts your automatic into a clutchless manual, requiring you to shift gears. (There are even ways to add a clutch to an automatic, but they're for specialized applications and not common now.)

One of the smartest upgrades you can make is to incorporate an aftermarket transmission fluid cooler into your vehicle. Factory automatics nearly always used a transmission oil cooler, which usually consisted of cooling lines running from the transmission to the radiator. A line that ran inside one of the radiator tanks transferred heat from the transmission fluid to the coolant in the radiator. Aftermarket coolers can either be plumbed in series with the stock cooler or used in place of it. The rule of thumb is that for every 10 degrees you drop the transmission fluid temperature, you double the life of your transmission. It is possible to lower your transmission fluid temperature too much. This can cause accelerated wear, so be sure to select a cooler that is appropriate to your application.

Some easier, and very beneficial changes, are to swap your stock transmission pan for a deeper pan. Running a deeper pan will increase the fluid volume, which lowers transmission fluid temperatures and extends transmission life. The deeper pan also hangs down into the airstream beneath the vehicle, which further cools the transmission fluid. Finned aluminum pans also dissipate heat because the aluminum conducts heat well and the fins increase surface area. Some sheetmetal pans are available with cooling tubes that run front to rear through the bottom of the pan. The effect is the same as ribs: increased surface area for air to contact and thus remove heat.

**Left:** A high-performance flywheel is a must to replace heavy, crack-prone stock units. *Hays photo*

**Right:** Clutch technology has come a long way in 40 years. Even optional "heavy-duty" clutches from the 1960s just don't compare to modern clutches like this Hays setup. More clamping force means less slippage behind high-output engines, yet most feature lighter pedal effort for easier use. *Hays photo*

Adding a deep-sump oil pan to your automatic transmission will increase oil capacity, which in turn allows the oil to remain cooler, so that it performs better. This pan, from Summit Racing Equipment, is constructed of aluminum which further helps shed heat, plus stiffens the transmission. *Summit Racing Equipment photo*

A good quality shifter helps, though it may be difficult to incorporate into a stock console. If you are more concerned with performance than keeping a stock shifter, you will want a shifter with positive detents, and some mechanism that prevents you from upshifting more than one gear at a time when banging the shifter forward. A reverse-lock-out feature is common on almost all aftermarket shifters and prevents you from accidentally popping your transmission into reverse when flying along. This can cause immediate catastrophic failure of the transmission (picture lots of oil and debris spurting from beneath your vehicle at speed).

There are many reasons to change your torque converter. These are covered later in this chapter.

Last, change your transmission fluid regularly. Switching to a synthetic automatic transmission fluid can extend the life of your transmission and improve performance because of its ability to stand up to heat better than conventional oils.

### Retrofitting Modern Automatics

Early automatic transmissions, like Ford's C6, GM's TH400, and Chrysler's A727, were pretty darn tough. They had to live behind engines like the 428 Cobra Jet, Ram Air IV 400, and the 440 Magnum of the 1960s and 1970s. But they had one major drawback—they lacked an overdrive gear to allow an engine to turn slower when cruising, which greatly extends engine life. As great as these transmissions are, there's always room for improvement.

Modern transmissions have the overdrive gear, but few are suitable for use behind high-performance powerplants, either because they can't handle the power, or because they don't have the right characteristics for racing or high-performance use. Several aftermarket transmission rebuilders offer high-performance versions of modern transmissions that can handle the power and driving conditions of high-performance vehicles.

It is possible to have your local transmission shop rebuild a late-model transmission to your specifications, but since performance transmission builders convert these transmissions for high-performance use far more frequently, you should strongly consider having them do the work. A performance transmission rebuilder will know the tricks of the trade that can make the difference between your transmission staying together or possibly puking its fluid.

Newer transmissions tend to be longer than older ones, and may require a shorter driveshaft and an altered or relocated crossmember. In some cases, older shifters can be retained and upgraded for use with the new shift pattern (remember, the shifter is designed for three forward gears, but the newer transmission has four).

Beyond that, the same sorts of upgrades apply to replacement transmissions as to upgraded stock ones: a shift kit (which will likely be included in the performance rebuild) and a transmission cooler plus a deeper transmission oil pan.

## Torque Converters and Flexplates

Torque converters are mysterious devices to many auto enthusiasts, but essentially they serve the same function for an automatic transmission as a clutch does for a manual transmission. Torque converters transmit power from the engine's crankshaft to the transmission's input shaft. At the same time, they provide a means for the input shaft to stop (when the vehicle stops) without causing the engine to stop in the process.

While the operation of a clutch is easily understood (when engaged, the pressure plate presses the disc against the flywheel, causing the input shaft to spin in a one-to-one relationship to the crank), torque converters are a little more difficult to explain and understand.

**Left:** High-performance torque converters feature superior construction plus optimized design to allow your engine to get into its powerband quicker for improved acceleration.

**Right:** A heavy-duty flex plate, like this one from Hays, will provide maximum strength at minimal weight.

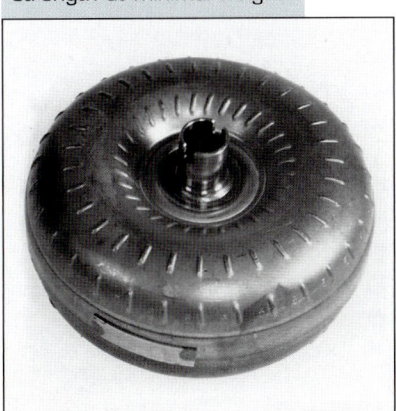
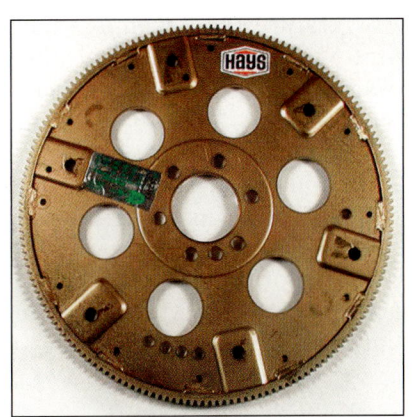

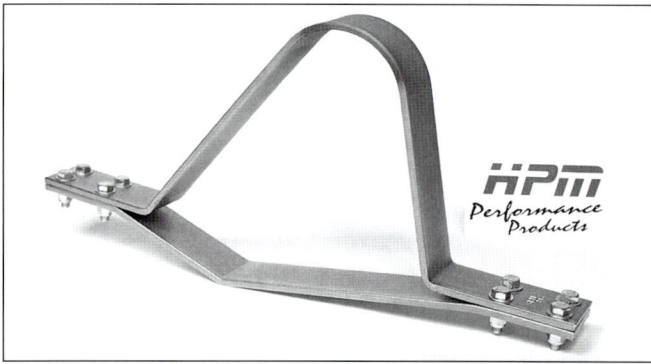

The shell of the converter is connected to the crankshaft, via the flexplate (or flywheel). As the converter spins, impellers inside cause transmission fluid in the converter to spin a corresponding set of impellers that are connected to the transmission's input shaft, forming what is known as a viscous coupling. Newer torque converters have a lock-up feature that provides a mechanical link between the drive and driven impellers, but otherwise there is no mechanical connection between the two sides, only the fluid connects them.

The beauty of the fluid coupling is that at low engine speeds, it's easy for the driven impeller to resist turning (such as when the brakes are applied, holding the vehicle at a stop), even though the drive impeller is free to spin. But when engine rpm increases, the flow of the fluid becomes hard to resist, so the driven impeller begins to spin. The rpm at which the driven impeller will begin to spin is known as the converter's stall speed.

Stall speed is an important concept to grasp. A higher stall speed allows drag racers to rev their engine into their peak operating range, while they hold the car still with the brakes. When they release the brakes, it allows the converter's driven impeller to start spinning even though the rpms may be below the stall speed.

For street use, however, torque converter stall speed isn't necessarily a good thing to alter, because it affects drivability, and it raises transmission fluid temperature, which can shorten transmission life. Ultimately, however, your torque converter choice will depend on your engine's power curve; an engine that produces little low-end torque will generally need a higher stall speed converter that allows the engine to reach the rpm where it produces enough torque to move the vehicle efficiently. In general, smaller diameter torque converters have higher stall speeds than larger, stock-sized converters.

## Driveshafts

Stock steel driveshafts connect the transmission's output shaft to the pinion gear of the rear-axle assembly, and they do this exceptionally well in stock vehicles that are driven on the street. But they're not high-performance pieces, and that can become painfully clear on racetracks where they endure sustained high-rpm use and extreme torsional (twisting) forces during acceleration.

Because balancing imperfections increase exponentially in relation to rpm, even the slightest imbalance will become a serious strain at high rpm. Since steel driveshafts weigh more to start with, imbalances weigh more, too, so the risk of the driveshaft warping becomes very real at high rpm. That weight takes its toll on acceleration, since it adds to the weight the engine must overcome in order to rotate.

Aftermarket companies manufacture aluminum and even composite driveshafts that weigh much less than a steel unit. They're also balanced to more exacting specifications than factory units, which allows them to withstand much higher rpm.

Of course, any driveshaft needs good universal joints to function properly, and aftermarket companies are the best places to turn for them. With large, heavy-duty needle bearings and heavy-duty construction throughout, performance U-joints are cheap insurance against driveshaft failure.

**Left:** Whether or not you believe the urban legend of the car that flipped over when its driveshaft broke, dropped, and dug into the ground, there's no good excuse for not running a driveshaft safety loop. A broken driveshaft can easily rip right through a flimsy floor, severely injuring you or your passengers. *HPM Performance Products*

**Right:** Power travels rearward from the transmission through a driveshaft. Muscle cars relied on standard steel tube driveshafts. Today's high-tech composite driveshafts, like this one from Inland Empire Driveline Systems, can sustain higher torque, higher rpm, and harder launches, plus they reduce weight. *Inland Empire Driveline Systems photo*

Heavy-duty universal joints are better able to handle increased torque from your higher-output, high-performance engine. These units from Lakewood are roughly comparable in price to stock replacements, but far superior. *Lakewood photo*

# Drivetrain 137

In addition to further multiplying torque, your car's rear-axle assembly performs the crucial function of funneling the rotating force of the driveshaft into forces that cause the tires to turn. When you're talking about muscle car engines, you're talking about a lot of torque, so only the strongest rear-axle assemblies will suffice. This is a racing-prepared AFCO rear-axle assembly, complete with disc brakes and a Ford 9-inch-style center section. *AFCO photo*

Speaking of driveshaft failures, you should protect yourself in case your driveshaft or U-joints break. A driveshaft safety loop is inexpensive insurance against a costly—and potentially life-threatening—driveshaft failure. If a rear U-joint breaks, the rear of the driveshaft will drop to the ground, possibly ruining the driveshaft. It's also probable that the driveshaft will be pulled from the transmission once it hits the ground, allowing transmission fluid to flow out of the transmission, potentially causing an accident by dousing your rear tires with oil. Believe it or not, that's a *good* scenario. If a front U-joint were to break during hard acceleration (such as on a drag strip), the front of the driveshaft could drop and dig into the ground. Then it will either bend itself into a pretzel (and possibly poke through the floor into your passenger compartment), or it could lift the rear of the car off the ground and cause a horrendous accident. Driveshaft safety loops prevent that; if either U-joint were to break, the driveshaft would drop an inch or so, but the safety loop would catch it and prevent it from hitting the ground.

## Rear-Axle Assemblies

Rear-axle assemblies from the 1950s, 1960s, and 1970s are generally considered to be the strongest rear ends to come off an automotive production line. In fact, Ford's 9-inch rear end is so tough that it is still the rear end of choice for many motorsports.

Modern rear ends, by comparison, are generally too weak for high-performance engines and offer no other advantages that would make them worth considering, unless you're considering grafting an independent rear suspension system underneath your car or truck.

Cars from the muscle car era are popular and have been regular staples in drag racing for years. Because of this, a staggering assortment of performance parts are available for the more popular rear-axle assemblies, such as the Ford 9-inch, Chevy's 10- and 12-bolt assemblies, and Chrysler's 8¾-inch and Dana 60 setups.

When it comes to tackling your rear-axle assembly during a high-performance restoration, there are a number of steps you can take to improve it.

### Bulletproofing Your Rear

When you increase your engine's power, you need to increase the rear end's strength to ensure reliability. Unfortunately, depending on the rear end that you're working on, upgrades may or may not be a straightforward process. It depends on whether replacement parts are readily available and how complicated installation is.

Although—or perhaps *because*—there were so many different rear ends used under so many different vehicles from the 1950s through the 1970s, few of them are blessed with an abundance of aftermarket parts. Sadly, that situation worsens every day as the need for parts for the less popular rear ends diminishes. Aftermarket companies understandably focus on the rear ends that are popular. As a result, you can get pretty much anything you want for a Ford 9-inch, but finding parts for an Oldsmobile 12-bolt (which has almost nothing in common with a Chevy 12-bolt other than their names) is nearly an exercise in futility.

You should ensure that your rear end is in proper working condition, which means inspecting the gears for wear and proper adjustment, replacing the carrier and axle bearings, replacing the axle and pinion seals, changing the fluid, and installing a new gasket. Naturally, any damaged or worn parts should be repaired.

Beyond simple maintenance is the possibility for improvements. You can make your rear-axle assembly stronger, more efficient, and, of course, set it up to improve performance. The more common upgrades involve

replacement gears, stronger limited slip units, stronger axles, and other miscellaneous changes.

## Getting in Gear

One of the most common desires among high-performance enthusiasts is to change the gearing in their rear end, usually for a ring-and-pinion set that will yield higher torque multiplication for quicker acceleration or easier towing. If your vehicle already has a low (high-numerically) gear set, such as 4.33:1 or 4.56:1, you may want to install a set of gears that will be more suitable for cruising, such as 3.55:1 or even 3.27:1 or higher (lower numerically).

Assuming gears are available for your rear end, you'll need to determine the gear ratio you need, which is based on your engine's power curve, transmission gearing, tire sizes, and how your vehicle will be driven. Gear selection is far more critical for race cars than for street cars, but improper gearing can result in disappointing performance. Take your time when making a decision, and get the advice of professionals, like the folks from Precision Gear or Richmond.

Although this is hardly a recommendation, most street vehicles work well with a gear ratio somewhere between 3.27:1 and 3.73:1, which provides good acceleration but reasonable engine speeds when cruising on the highway, especially when used with an overdrive transmission.

Speaking of transmissions, most automatics have a lower first gear than manuals (even wide-ratio boxes), so they tend to favor a slightly higher (lower numerically) rear-axle ratio. For instance, while a 3.42:1 ratio may be perfect for a manual transmission, the same vehicle with an automatic transmission would have more balanced performance with a 3.27:1 ratio.

## Limited-Slip Units

Limited-slip differentials—popularly known as Posi units, which is actually a short version of GM's Positraction brand of limited-slip units—were quite common on vehicles of the 1950s, 1960s, and 1970s. They greatly improved traction by transmitting power to both rear wheels, rather than just one, as with open rear ends. More traction meant quicker acceleration times, plus the car was more controllable and predictable during high-performance driving.

There are a number of different designs for limited-slip units. Most factory limited-slip systems used spring-loaded clutch packs to keep the two axles turning. Ford also used what it called the Detroit Locker, which consisted of beefy ratchet-like gears that disengaged during cornering. Both systems work quite well, though the Detroit Locker is generally credited with being the stronger system. The clutch-style systems generally provided quieter, smoother cornering than the Locker systems, which tended to cause jerky cornering as the gears locked and released repeatedly. The Locker was called the Dapco No-Spin by its manufacturer; it was also available in some Mopar and GM rears, but the units aren't interchangeable.

Today we have other alternatives, including an on-demand limited-slip system that relies on air pressure to engage two halves when full traction is needed. During normal cruising, the system can be left disengaged, allowing one axle to freewheel for quiet, smooth cornering.

**Left:** Your car's rear-axle assembly houses the ring and pinion gear set; as the pinion rotates, it engages the teeth of the ring gear, causing it to rotate in turn. By varying the ratio of turns of the pinion needed to turn the ring gear once, you can improve acceleration or top speed, or pick something in between for decent all-around performance.

**Middle:** If you happen to be prepping a 9-inch-style rear-axle assembly for your muscle car, a Detroit Locker CTR 9-inch differential is an excellent upgrade that will minimize slip during all but the sharpest of corners. *Detroit Locker photo*

**Right:** The ubiquitous Ford 9-inch rear-axle assembly, as installed in a Cobra kit car tube frame chassis. Note the easily removable center section. That plus the 9-inch's reliability behind even the most powerful engines makes it a favorite with drag racers, road racers, and even NASCAR's Nextel Cup teams.

If you are building a race-only vehicle, then you may be interested in replacing your differential assembly with a spool, which permanently locks both rear wheels together. Spools provide excellent straight-line traction, but they present problems while cornering, especially for right corners like those typically encountered during street driving.

### Axles

Anyone who has ever broken an axle knows what a hair-raising experience it can be. If you have a rear end with a design that retains the ends of the axle even if the axle snaps, then you'll probably get off relatively easy. A loud noise, a momentary loss of control as the remaining powered wheel gets a sudden power boost, then a trailer ride back to the pits where you can change your shorts. If your rear end doesn't retain your axles, things get considerably more dangerous and expensive. When the axle snaps, the body drops down on the wheel (causing considerable body damage), then the wheel will likely spring out from under the car, allowing the vehicle to drop to the ground (causing more damage). Meanwhile, you'll have little control over the vehicle, and—as a result of the momentary surge of power through the remaining driven wheel—you're probably headed off-road or into a guardrail (either of which will likely cause more damage). There's a good chance your rear-axle housing will be destroyed in the process too.

Aftermarket high-performance or racing axles can prevent such scary circumstances, but they aren't available for every rear-axle design. Aftermarket axles are generally manufactured from superior materials with precise forging and machining processes. Some aftermarket axles may address shortcomings of your original axles. For instance, tapers may be eliminated, shaft diameters may be increased, or other changes may be made.

### Miscellaneous Upgrades

If, as with most GM rear-axle designs, your axles are not positively retained, it may be possible to modify your rear end to add this feature. For GM vehicles, this

## LIMITED SLIP AND WHY IT'S NEEDED

Standard rear-axle differential assemblies don't power both of your rear wheels. You already know this because when a vehicle with a standard, low-performance rear axle does a "burn out," only one wheel turns. The other one (the left one) just rolls along as the car moves.

From a performance standpoint, "open" differentials aren't the hot setup, since you have to rely on only one wheel to propel you forward. Obviously, sending all of your engine's torque through one tire is more likely to cause that tire to spin than if you were able to split that power between two tires.

Spools are the opposite of an open differential. Instead of sending power to just one tire, a spool locks both axles together and always powers both rear wheels. Now that might sound like a great and simple system, but there's one big problem with running spools on the street: corners.

You see, when your car turns a corner, whichever wheel is on the "inside" of the corner rolls a short distance; but the wheel on the "outside" of the corner must roll farther to go around the same corner. The radius of the turn it must make is much larger. This means that your wheels have to travel at different speeds around the corner (slower for the inside wheel than the outside).

To accomplish this, engineers came up with "limited-slip" differentials, which are commonly known as "Posi" units, though that term technically only refers to General Motors' brand name for its limited-slip systems, Positraction.

Limited-slip units transmit power to both wheels under straight-line traveling, which provides excellent traction, and therefore excellent acceleration under performance-driving conditions. When it comes to turning corners, the systems "disengage" one of the axles, allowing it to turn at a different rate than the other so that the tires don't hop, chirp, and skip their way around a corner (which, by the way, isn't very good for tire wear, let alone driving comfort).

For the street, the hottest setup you should ever think about using is a limited-slip unit, but for the drag strip, feel free to go with a spool—if you don't mind horrible cornering abilities.

frequently means installing a C-clip eliminator kit, which retains axles at the axle-bearing assembly.

An area that many enthusiasts overlook is the importance of high-quality wheel studs. If your wheel studs are old or in any way questionable, they should be replaced, preferably with high-performance aftermarket studs and nuts. Weak wheel studs could break, allowing the wheel to come off unexpectedly. This could cause a life-threatening accident by causing you to lose control. At the very least, losing a wheel is a great way to damage your vehicle's body as it drops down on the wheel and tire.

When upgrading your wheel studs, you may be able to use larger diameter studs, which provides increased strength. In addition, race sanctioning body rules may dictate that you run longer wheel studs, which ensure that the wheel is secured by all the threads of the lug nut and therefore securely fastened.

Although not all rear ends use a separate rear cover, those that do may benefit from a replacement cover that acts as a girdle, strengthening the carrier bearing caps. In addition, a finned aluminum cover can cool the oil in the rear-axle assembly. Auxiliary differential coolers are available, but are generally only useful for vehicles in road racing or stock car racing competition, which endure long hours at high speeds. The value of an aluminum differential cover wasn't lost on Oldsmobile, which offered one under RPO W27 for 4-4-2 buyers in 1970. The unit did its job well but looked good, too, thanks in part to a design that resembled a quick-change, racing-style rear end.

Finally, replacing your rear-axle assembly's thick lubricant with a synthetic lube will reduce friction and extend the life of bearings and gears because it will not break down when subjected to heat.

## Replacement Rear-Axle Assemblies

Sometimes replacing your stock rear-axle assembly with something better is the way to go. One good reason might be that there aren't many (or any!) performance parts available for your rear end. You might also lack the skills, desire, or time to rebuild your rear end.

If you decide to simply swap your rear end for something different, you've got the option of either using a design that may have been optional when your vehicle was new, or replacing it with an aftermarket rear-end assembly. (Most late-model rear-axle assemblies aren't worth upgrading to, unless you're looking for an independent rear suspension.)

Upgrading to a stronger, optional rear end is a great plan for vintage vehicles that may have started life as low-performance machines. A six-cylinder Camaro would have been equipped with a light-duty, 10-bolt rear end. If that car now has a big block, the six-cylinder rear won't handle the power. Upgrading to a factory 12 bolt—especially one that's been rebuilt with better axles, a fresh Posi unit, and other bulletproofing changes—would add a certain degree of comfort, because there would be little fear of breaking the rear end.

But you need not stick with originally available rear-axle assemblies. With

Breaking an axle at the track is a sure-fire way to ruin your day…or worse. Replacement axles from companies like Summers Brothers are used in all forms of racing behind the most powerful engines available. *Summers Brothers photo*

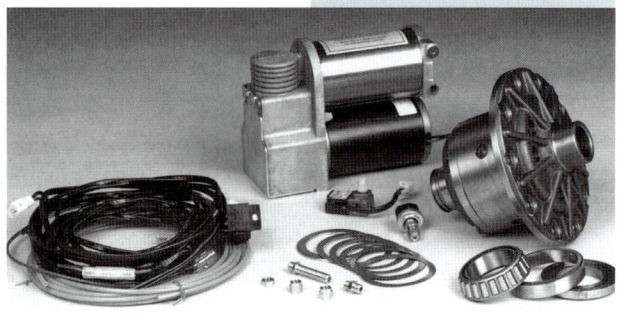

**Left:** Of course, today, higher-tech solutions exist that provide full lock-up when needed, but full slippage for improved routine driving. Detroit Locker's Electrac is electrically operated for touch-of-a-button convenience. *Detroit Locker photo*

**Right:** Air Locker's system uses an air pump to lock the differential for performance use. *Air Locker Systems photo*

# Drivetrain

**Below:** Detroit Locker's EZ Locker is a good upgrade over stock, but at a lower cost than the full Detroit Locker. It provides automatic lock-up under demanding conditions and superior strength over stock. *Detroit Locker photo*

**Bottom:** The traditional Detroit Locker differential uses gears instead of clutch discs to prevent slippage during straight-line acceleration and deceleration. The Detroit Locker has been around for decades but the new versions feature superior materials and construction for exceptional durability. *Detroit Locker photo*

the right flange-to-flange width, suspension mounts, and other changes, you can adapt nearly any rear-axle assembly to almost any vehicle. And when it comes to installing nonstock rear ends, there's none more popular than the Ford 9-inch.

Aftermarket companies produce a staggering assortment of performance parts for improving the 9-inch, from gears to axles to entire housings set up to fit nearly any car or truck.

In addition to the strength of the famous Ford third member, the 9-inch also features a removable center section (usually referred to as a pig or sometimes the chunk or pumpkin) that contains the ring and pinion. The design makes it easy to change gearing for different applications within minutes. Simply slide the axles out a couple of inches, remove the center section, install a new center section with different gearing, reinsert the axles and gear lube, and you're on your way. If you ever get the chance to see a NASCAR team change the gearing of their race car (a common occurrence during practice or before happy hour), that's what they're doing, because they use 9-inch Ford rear ends (yes, even under the Chevys and Pontiacs).

## Differential Types

It's a common misconception to think of an entire rear end as a differential. The differential is the device that transfers power to one or more of the axle shafts within the rear-axle assembly. The whole idea behind a differential is to enhance a car's cornering abilities, because while cornering, the wheel at the inside of the corner must travel a shorter distance than the wheel at the outside of the corner. Obviously, the wheels shouldn't spin in a one-to-one relationship.

Three basic types of differentials are available. Open differentials that power only one wheel at a time and are well-suited to low-speed cornering. Limited-slip differentials, like GM's Positraction units, turn both wheels when traveling straight but allow the inner wheel to slip somewhat while cornering. Spools permanently spin both wheels equally and consequently make turning more difficult.

All production vehicles (perhaps with a few early exceptions) rely on either an open or limited-slip differential. Spools have never been used as production pieces because they can be dangerous when turning corners and cause premature tire wear on the street.

There are advantages to each type of differential, however, depending on your particular application. If your vehicle is solely driven on the street, and you rarely attempt to race anyone (thus ultimate traction is not a high priority), an open differential will provide the best driving experience and longer tire life.

For most performance enthusiasts, a limited-slip differential will be a better choice because it provides full, two-wheeled traction under straight-line acceleration. It still allows some differentiation between the two wheels while cornering, however, so the vehicle doesn't hop and skip in a turn and won't dramatically increase tire wear.

Spools are strictly for racing use and should never be used on the street. On the track, however, they will provide the ultimate in traction because both wheels will always provide full traction—except when the inside wheel hops during cornering.

A new type of differential worth discussing is the so-called Air Locker, which is a special differential design that operates like an open differential under normal conditions. By pressurizing components within the differential with an electric air pump, the differential is converted to the equivalent of a spool, doing away with any slip for maximum straight-line acceleration. These systems should be especially attractive to weekend racers because they really provide a best-of-both-worlds system without a lot of fuss. It should be noted that air locker–type systems are fairly complex to install. Still, the designs are simple, most units have proven reliable under normal use, and they are easy to operate.

# Chapter 9
# Chassis, Suspension, and Steering

**M**uscle cars are incredibly adaptable to a variety of driving disciplines. Basic cruising, drag strip action and even road-course work are all possible—with the right suspension preparation.

The undercarriages of vintage vehicles can best be described as diamonds in the rough. The cars have as much potential to be comfortable, well-handling vehicles as today's cars, but when they were made, technology hadn't advanced enough to tap into that potential.

Three decades later, we know a great deal more about the dynamics of vehicles as they roll down the street, turn corners, hit bumps, and more. Applying a little modern thinking to your car or truck can work wonders for its demeanor on the street, strip, or even on twisting, turning road courses, if that happens to be your passion.

When it comes to your car's handling abilities—which includes its launch capabilities for you straight-line jockeys—there are three areas that you need to concern yourself with: the chassis structure, the suspension system, and the steering system. Each interrelates and has a dramatic effect on the final outcome —how your car *feels* while driving.

## Chassis Structure

The chassis structure is the foundation your vehicle is built on. It's important for your vehicle's structure to be as sturdy as possible, because your suspension, steering, engine, and drivetrain can't function properly and predictably if the structure is bending and flexing.

There are three basic types of chassis structures, one of which describes your vehicle.

Vehicles with a body on frame design use a frame that is manufactured separate from the body. The two are connected by bolting them together, and rubber bushings are used to cushion the installation and provide a (it is hoped) rattle-free assembly. Frames are generally one of two types. A ladder-style frame uses two parallel rails with multiple crossmembers to tie the rails together at various points. A perimeter-style frame is similar to a ladder frame but is wider where it sweeps outward at the rocker panels, between the front and rear wheelwells (thus, it's said to trace the perimeter of the vehicle). Ladder-style frames are most commonly used for truck chassis, while perimeter-style frames were frequently used for intermediate and full-sized cars.

Most modern vehicles and a number of vintage ones are built with a unibody chassis structure. With a unibody vehicle, there is no separate frame; the body structure incorporates frame-like rails that are inseparable from the body. The biggest benefits of unibody construction are reduced manufacturing costs and reduced weight. Unfortunately, unibody structures are rarely as strong as body-on-frame designs and are prone to twisting, bending, and flexing over uneven road surfaces. Mustangs, most Mopars, and a host of small GM cars are examples of unibody vehicles.

Semi-unitized structures are a blend of the two previous categories: The majority of the vehicle—usually everything from the firewall rearward—is a unibody construction, but from the firewall forward the vehicle uses a bolt-on frame section to which the front suspension, steering components, and engine are secured. Semi-unitized construction, like that used for GM's Camaro/Firebird F-bodies, kept manufacturing costs down, yet provided the big car ride that buyers during the 1960s and 1970s had come to expect.

### Structural Enhancements

Each structure has its pros and cons, but it's pointless to debate which design is best, because short of completely re-engineering your vehicle, you're stuck with the structure your vehicle was manufactured with. It does make sense to focus your attention on improving your vehicle's chassis structure to best suit the

Whether your muscle car was originally intended for drag racing duty or corner carving, it's a fair bet that modern suspension technology can make it better at either. Or both, like this Shelby GT-500 that's equally at home during a quarter-mile blast as when turning sizzling lap times on a road course.

Just how bad were vintage muscle car suspension systems? This '69 Chevelle clearly shows body lean was excessive, which resulted in dramatic camber changes that hampered the tires' grip on the road.

The same Chevelle after treating it to a host of H-O Racing suspension upgrades, including super-sized front and rear anti-roll bars. It corners flat and stable, and with modern performance tires that provide shorter, stiffer sidewalls and wider tread, the handling is amazing.

use your vehicle will see. Regardless of what type of chassis structure your vehicle has, it's likely that the same methods that can be used to strengthen one type of structure will work on the others.

### Subframe Connectors

Vehicles with a unibody or semi-unitized structure usually have frame-like rails for the front and rear portions of the vehicle; however, the middle of the vehicle—beneath the passenger compartment—is generally just the stamped sheetmetal floor pan. Because of this, the middle of the vehicle is relatively weak and can easily twist, bend, and flex. The condition is much worse on convertible models, which lack the metal structure of a roof.

The most common method of overcoming this is installing a set of subframe connectors. For some vehicles, usually newer models, subframe connectors are readily available, but for most vintage vehicles, you may need to fabricate the connectors. Fortunately, subframe connectors need only be fairly simple lengths of steel tubing, with the necessary bends to connect to both the front and rear frame rails. For the strongest subframe connectors, you should fabricate them from heavy-gauge, round steel tubing, and the bars should be welded to the frame rails over an area at least six inches long.

Unfortunately, it's not possible to conceal subframe connectors on your vehicle. Luckily, few people will bend over far enough to see them, and by painting them to match your undercarriage (which is probably just black, if you drive your vehicle on the street), they'll blend in.

### Le Mans Braces

Another common improvement for unibody vehicles is a Le Mans brace, also known as a shock tower brace because it spans across the engine compartment from one shock tower to the other or from the shock towers to the cowl. Better braces will connect the shock towers to the center of the firewall and each other, resulting in a triangular brace. Such braces prevent the front end of a vehicle from twisting during cornering or over uneven roads, by tying the front end together. Again, such braces are commonly available for newer vehicles but will likely need to be fabricated for vintage vehicles. They are typically made of heavy-gauge, round steel tubing of approximately 1-inch outside drag. Welding the braces in place would make a stronger assembly, but because they need to be removed if the engine needs to be pulled or worked on, it's best to bolt the brace to the vehicle.

As with subframe connectors, it's not really possible to hide a Le Mans brace. It's a pretty obvious change, but only when your hood is open. When you open your hood for others to inspect, the brace shouldn't call attention to itself if you finish it to match your engine compartment. That means that for vehicles with chrome dress-up packages you might want to chrome the brace, but for vehicles with little chrome, you might make it black or body color.

### Convertible Braces and Frames

You can strengthen any type of chassis structure by doing what the factories did with their convertible models: reinforce them. By adding bracing to the vehicle's structure in specific locations, you can increase the vehicle's strength. When you get right down to it, that's really what subframe connectors and Le Mans braces are.

First-generation Mustang convertibles are well-known for their extra bracing, as are many other vehicles. Vehicles with a body-on-frame structure had sections of their frames boxed by welding steel to the open portion of the normally C-shaped frame rails, and police vehicles often have factory bolt-on triangulated braces on their frames. Any extra bracing will increase weight, but if added in moderation, the structural integrity gains should outweigh any weight penalty.

The specifics of what the braces should look like and where they should go vary based on the vehicle, and if you're going to use Le Mans braces and subframe connectors—both of which are strongly recommended for performance vehicles—the need for additional bracing should be negligible.

As far as making these look like they're factory pieces, the job is generally pretty simple, since they often *are* factory pieces. Painting them to match your chassis structure after installation is more than enough to conceal them unless someone knows to look for them.

### Reinforcement Plates

Late-model (1997 and newer) Corvettes employ a fairly simple yet radical structural aid, in addition to their incredibly stiff hydro-formed frame. Because vehicles have transmission tunnels, the floorpan is inherently prone to bending since each side of the floorpan acts almost as an independent component. The C5 Corvette still has a transmission tunnel but uses a large, thick steel plate that measures about 2 feet long and 18 inches wide to tie the two sides of the floorpan together. The plate is secured by 36 bolts—18 per side! Granted, the C5 Corvette was designed for such a plate, and its driveshaft doesn't need to have any vertical travel like a normal vehicle. But a sizable plate could be fabricated to begin beneath the rear of the transmission and extend rearward roughly 2 feet, where driveshaft travel would be minimal, even with the rear end at full droop. You would have to customize the length and shape of such a plate to your vehicle, and you should consider using a piece of steel on each side inside the vehicle to serve as a brace for all the bolts.

There isn't any great way to hide a reinforcement plate if someone looks under your vehicle. But, as with subframe connectors, take some comfort in the fact that few people will look under your car, and painting it to match your undercarriage will help conceal its presence.

### Crossmembers

Finally, depending on your vehicle and whether you're changing engines or transmissions, you may need to change the engine and transmission crossmembers too. Mopar fans are probably more familiar with the term *K-frame*, which describes the shape of the engine crossmember in those vehicles. Engine crossmembers are often specific to both a particular engine family and a particular vehicle model. For instance, 340 and 360 Mopar small blocks use the same K-frame in a given Barracuda (and its twin, the Challenger); however, a 440 Barracuda would use a different K-frame, as would a 360 Imperial. Likewise, different transmissions often require different crossmembers due to different mounting locations, transmission tailshaft configurations, bolt patterns, and so on.

## Suspension

Your vehicle's suspension has two basic jobs: to maximize the contact between your tires and the ground, and to provide the desired degree of comfort for you and your passengers.

In the old days, suspension setups were largely a tradeoff: You couldn't have great handling without a harsh ride, but a soft ride meant sloppy handling. Thanks to 30-some suspension system breakthroughs, though, it's now possible to have exceptional handling *and* a comfortable ride. The

How well your car handles will ultimately boil down to how well you prep its chassis and suspension. This Cobra kit car chassis features a tubular steel frame, a short/long-arm front suspension and a typical leaf spring, suspended, 9-inch rear-axle assembly.

One of the easiest and cheapest upgrades is to replace your tires. Reproduction Goodyear Polyglas GT—in F60-15 size, here on this '69 Boss 302—were high tech in their day. But their day has gone. Use 'em for shows and maybe cruise night. But if you're doing any performance driving, you'll want performance tires.

# Chassis, Suspension, and Steering

## NAME-BRAND TIRES, NAME-BRAND VALUES

Few people give much thought to the impact the purchase of new tires has on the value of their vehicle. To some people, tires are tires, and when they compare name-brand tires to "no-name" tires, they don't see any point in spending twice as much for the name-brand tires; after all, either one's going to put more tread under the car, right?

Regardless of whether the no-name tire really does have better treadwear and ride comfort characteristics than the name-brand tire (like the salesman probably claimed), no-name tires are a bad investment if you have any thoughts of selling your vehicle.

Buyers trust name-brand tires, such as Goodyear, BF Goodrich, and Firestone, so they will perceive them as a valuable asset. No-name tires, on the other hand, won't be trusted, so a buyer will expect to have to replace them (most likely with name-brand tires), and thus will reduce their perceived value of your vehicle by at least the cost of the new tires. So while the no-name tires may ride well and last a long time, they aren't necessarily a good value.

On the street, something like Goodyear's Eagle F-1 GS is about as high tech as you can get. They're great on dry roads or wet, plus its tread and sidewalls are designed to provide excellent handling with a reasonable ride quality. *Goodyear photo*

The particular suspension setup—the components you run and how you tune and adjust them—to use on your vehicle depends on how and where you will be using it, as well as your own driving preferences. Obviously, a drag car needs a different suspension system than one that might enter sports car–style road racing. While there are no magical suspension setups that will work perfectly for every car, every condition, or every driver, certain configurations will usually get you in the ballpark. From there you change and adjust parts to fine-tune the handling of your vehicle.

The easiest way to get your car or truck's handling act together in a hurry is to install a suspension upgrade kit, which usually consists of shocks, springs, stabilizer bars, bushings, and possibly stronger or altered control arms or modified spindles. The beauty of the kit approach is that suspension component manufacturers have designed and selected components that complement one another and should provide satisfactory results.

Some kits, like those available from Air Ride Technologies, use high-tech air-springs (or airbags) to provide the spring function of the system, while replacing stock leaf springs with a far more effective four-link setup that provides more accurate positioning of the axle assembly, and smoother, more predictable motion.

Of course, sometimes there's just no getting around the piece-meal approach, and you'll find yourself having to mix Company A's shocks, Company B's springs, and Company C's stabilizer bars and hoping for the best. Although this makes the process a bit more difficult, the results can be phenomenal if you hit on the right combination of parts. To better your odds, make sure you get recommendations from the shock manufacturers as to what spring rates work well with the shocks you're getting.

To simplify the process of upgrading your vehicle's suspension system, we'll look at the two most likely uses you will have for your vehicle and explore some basic setups that should get you headed in the right direction.

## High-Performance Street Driving

Street driving is actually one of the hardest applications to design a satisfactory suspension system for because it needs to work under a broad spectrum of operating and road conditions. One moment, the car may be cruising along on the highway, lazily soaking up cracks or seams in the road surface, and the next you're swerving to avoid an accident.

Most public streets are rarely as well maintained as racetracks, so you'll want some compliance in your street vehicle's suspension to deal with cracked pavement, potholes, small rocks, and so on. This is especially important if you spend any time in your vehicle, because a stiff race car–like suspension system will pound you in the same way a boxer pounds on an opponent's body to wear him out.

### Tires and Wheels

Working from the road surface toward you, the driver, the first components of your vehicle's suspension system are its tires. Tires provide traction for acceleration, cornering, and braking, but—through their flexible sidewalls—they also act as springs to soften the ride.

The right tires for your high-performance vehicle will depend on how you use (or intend to use) it. No matter what tires you use, it is critical that you tune them by adjusting air pressure, and by using alignment settings to provide the biggest tire contact patch without unnecessary drag.

Most tires on production vehicles during the 1950s through the 1970s equate to a modern tire with a 70-series aspect ratio, which means that the sidewall is roughly 70 percent as tall as the tread section is wide. In those days, 14-inch wheels were the norm, even for most high-performance handling packages.

Making what is termed a Plus 1 upgrade would involve switching to 15-inch (14 inches *plus one*) wheels with 60-series tires. The larger wheel and shorter sidewall will reduce the likelihood of the tire rolling under the wheel during hard cornering maneuvers. But because most vintage vehicles are softly sprung, this won't result in an uncomfortable ride. For those reasons, many buyers find that 60-series tires are an excellent choice for their muscle car truck. It helps that many original wheels were produced in both 14- and 15-inch sizes, so you can usually upgrade the wheel size without any noticeable change in appearance.

Depending on other suspension components, you may wish to run extreme wheels and tires, such as 20- to 22-inch wheels with correspondingly ultra-low profile tires, to maintain the proper overall size. Such massive upgrades will typically degrade ride comfort noticeably, and few stock-looking wheel designs are available in those sizes. Still, they are easy enough to swap on or off and can make an excellent high-performance restoration upgrade if greatly increased cornering is your goal.

Specialty tires, such as street-legal drag-racing tires, are available from a number of tire manufacturers. Of particular interest is BF Goodrich's Drag Radial, which is the only drag-racing tire that can safely be run at the track with modern radial tires on the front of your vehicle. You should never run a mixture of radials and nonradials on a car at the same time, because they can cause unstable handling that could result in a dangerous accident (as opposed to an accident that's simply expensive).

If you show your vehicle in restored classes, you can always purchase a set of reproduction tires, such as vintage-looking Goodyear Polyglas or Firestone Wide-Oval tires. Mounting them on restored wheels of the proper size will make it easy to swap the wheels and tires for show events.

As for wheels, you've got more choices than you can possibly imagine. Aside from choosing diameters and widths, you also need to be concerned about the offset (also called backspacing) of the wheel, its bolt pattern, its appearance, and even the material the wheels are made of.

Many people opt to upgrade to wheels that were optional for their vehicle, or were installed on production vehicles during later model years. Production wheels are typically made of stamped steel. Unfortunately, they aren't well-suited to performance use since they can bend or flex under high cornering forces. Steel wheels are also susceptible to rust, plus they're rather hefty and that increases unsprung weight, which makes your suspension work harder to control wheel movements.

**Left:** M+H Racemasters are another great tire for the quarter mile. They feature a soft, sticky compound, huge contact patch, and soft enough sidewall to allow for good weight transfer.
*M+H Tires photo*

**Above:** For drag racing, something like BF Goodrich's drag radial is ideal—but make sure you only run them along with radials on the front wheels, too.
*BF Goodrich photo*

No tire will perform well if it isn't properly inflated, and that "proper" inflation will vary depending on what type of driving you're doing. Road racing will often want more air pressure, while drag racing will typically go toward the lower end of the pressure gauge's readout.

## SELECTING WHEELS WITH EASY CARE IN MIND

Cleaning wheels can be a pain in the neck (and back, and arms, and ... ). Complex wheel designs, like basket-weave patterns or ones with numerous drilled holes, simulated rivets, or whatever, can be tiresome and difficult to clean. Simple designs with only a few large spokes, or even solid wheels, are the easiest to clean. If you're at all like most people, the harder a wheel is to clean, the less you'll want to clean it, so they'll look grungy, which will make your car look grungy, and you'll inevitably be less happy with the wheels, and maybe even the entire car.

The finish applied to a wheel has a lot to do with the wheel's appearance and the maintenance you need to do. Most aluminum wheels are treated to some form of clear-coat protective finish to help preserve the wheel. These sorts of finishes will usually keep the wheels looking good for several years, but be aware that some coatings can become easily scratched, chipped, "fogged," or may flake off, which can make the wheels look uglier than if they had no protective finish at all.

Aftermarket wheels—including vintage-style wheels, like American Racing Equipment's Torque Thrust wheels—are typically made of aluminum, which makes them considerably lighter. Plus, aftermarket wheels are available in a broader range of sizes and styles.

The only big trick to buying oversized wheels is making sure they'll fit your vehicle properly and look good in the process. Typically, increased diameter won't cause problems. If anything, it creates additional clearance between the wheel and brake or steering hardware. Width can create big problems, however, because the wheel could be so wide that it interferes with steering or suspension components, which would obviously be a bad thing. Last is offset or backspacing, which is the distance from the rear edge of the rim to the mounting surface, when bolted to the vehicle. You should try to preserve the factory front-to-back spacing ratio, because it will preserve steering and suspension geometry. For example, if your car originally came with 6-inch wheels that had 4 inches of backspacing, if you upgrade to 9-inch-wide wheels, they should have a backspacing measurement of 6 inches (two-thirds the total wheel width).

You should *always* check the fit of new wheels to make sure they have sufficient clearance throughout lock-to-lock turns and the full range of suspension travel. If your wheel contacts part of your vehicle in either test, it may be possible to install a rubber or polyurethane stop to prevent the steering linkage from turning farther than is safe, or to prevent the suspension from contacting the wheel. Remember that the rubber bumper should *not* contact the wheel directly, but rather a non-rotating part.

### Bushings

Suspension bushings, such as control arm bushings, absorb small road imperfections so that your vehicle doesn't shake and vibrate relentlessly every time you hit a bump.

Since the late 1980s, many enthusiasts have upgraded to stiffer polyurethane and even solid bushings that have less compliance, and thus make for a more precise suspension. While this makes sense from an all-out performance standpoint, for the road, hard bushings often result in a harsh ride.

Stock rubber bushings, on the other hand, are excellent for street use, because they absorb the minor bumps and jolts instead of transmitting them to the rest of the vehicle. The one area where it does pay to use polyurethane bushings is for your stabilizer bar mounts and end links. Poly bushings for your stabilizer bars will eliminate some body roll while cornering, but will be barely noticeable compared to rubber bushings on the street.

Today, you can buy reproductions of the legendary muscle car wheels, like this Pontiac Rally II wheel. The reproductions often improve on the originals with superior construction, finishes, and even additional sizes that let you retain the stock look but improve performance with higher performance tires. *Wheel Vintiques photo*

Rubber bushings are generally only available in black, so they'll look stock right out of the box. If you go with polyurethane bushings, some vendors sell them in a rainbow of colors, in addition to black. From a restoration standpoint, the black poly bushings are best, despite the fact they are somewhat shinier than rubber bushings.

**Control Arms**

Nearly all vehicles built in the 1950s, 1960s, and 1970s feature stamped-steel upper and lower control arms for their front suspension system. Vehicles with rear coil springs, such as the GM A-bodies, use stamped-steel upper and lower control arms to secure the rear-axle assembly as well.

For mundane driving applications, stock control arms are usually suitable as is. For high-performance driving, you should consider reinforcing or replacing your stock arms to increase strength. The inexpensive (but more difficult) process of reinforcing the control arms involves welding reinforcing gussets of similar gauge steel to the open sections of the arm (usually the underside) as well as any high-load areas, such as the sides of the arms and the shock and stabilizer bar mounts.

Tubular or boxed steel replacement arms are available from aftermarket manufacturers for a number of vintage vehicles and are significantly stronger and somewhat lighter. Depending on your vehicle's suspension, aftermarket front, lower control arms may be available with recessed spring pockets, which effectively lower the vehicle's ride height. This lowers the center of gravity and roll center for better handling. Note, however, that deeper spring pockets reduce ground clearance at the control arms.

While tubular steel control arms won't look stock, you can do your best to minimize them by painting them or other modified arms to resemble stock units. Typically, this will mean painting them with a semiflat black paint.

**Springs and Torsion Bars**

Whether your vehicle uses coil springs, leaf springs, torsion bars, or a combination of the three, each has the same job—to keep your vehicle from sitting on its bump stops by controlling compression.

Most vintage springs were relatively weak (rated in pounds per inch), so the suspension compressed easily, and the ride was soft— even on the vehicles with the high-performance or heavy-duty suspensions.

New production springs are a pretty good starting place for your street suspension system. If complemented with better stabilizer bars and shocks, the production rate springs should help your vehicle retain its comfortable ride, while the other parts improve the handling.

Aftermarket springs are available for nearly every vintage vehicle and are typically higher rate (stiffer) springs, but are rarely rock hard (though some are available that way if you *really* want them). Conversely, if you want a super-soft ride, you can replace your stock-rate springs with lower-rate production springs. For example, springs for a big-block-powered car with a heavy-duty suspension package would be stiffer than the base six-cylinder model with no special suspension systems. In fact, springs for six-cylinder models are common upgrades for drag cars because they allow faster weight transfer.

Many Mopar models used torsion bar front suspensions that need to be indexed, or preloaded, which gives the bar its spring tension. By increasing the preload slightly you can increase the spring rate; decreasing the preload has

One of the most obvious wheel upgrades would be to bolt on a set of whatever the best optional wheels were for your vehicle. These are the legendary Corvette "knock-off" wheels that were lighter than steel wheels, wider than standard steel wheels, and, of course, featured the racing-inspired spinner that could be "knocked off" with a rubber mallet to quickly remove the wheel. Be careful when buying used wheels, however, to ensure they're round, true, and in otherwise good condition.

**Left:** Modern wheels are available in all designs and sizes, as well as a variety of materials and finishes. *Enkei photo*

**Right:** When selecting wheels, make sure you get the right backspacing for your vehicle. Backspacing is the distance from the center of the wheel, where it mates to the hub, out to the edge of the wheel.

# Chassis, Suspension, and Steering 151

Don't forget to upgrade your spare tire, too—especially if you've installed oversize brakes that require large-diameter wheels to clear them. You don't want to be out on the road, get a flat, and find out that your spare doesn't fit over your big-inch brakes.

the opposite effect. This tune-ability allows you to make subtle refinements to a Mopar's front suspension without replacing the torsion bars. The changes will alter ride height, however, so if you are searching for considerably stiffer or softer spring rates, you will need to locate replacement torsion bars with the desired tension.

A modification that used to be common on vehicles with leaf springs was adding an extended shackle kit to jack up the rear of the car. While such a change would give your car that as-it-used-to-be look, there are safety concerns. First, jacking up the rear of a vehicle makes it much more likely that its gas tank will be struck in a rear-end collision, because other cars will likely dive under your jacked-up rear end. Any time a gas tank is struck in an accident, the possibility for fire is greatly increased. The second reason the rear of your vehicle shouldn't be jacked up is that it alters front-end steering and suspension geometry, which can lead to erratic handling.

Conversely, many enthusiasts have removed sections of coils from coil springs to lower a vehicle's ride height.

## WHEELS: TRY BEFORE YOU BUY

Appearances are personal matters, so you've naturally got to decide what you like the looks of. Of course, few people can afford to order wheels, bolt them on, then decide whether or not they like them.

There are a couple of methods that you can use to get some idea of whether you like a particular wheel on your car. The first is to see the wheels on another vehicle like yours, such as at a car show. Color differences aside, if the wheels look good (to you) on another model like yours, they'll probably look good on yours too.

Of course, if you've got a buddy with the wheels you like, you should be able to "borrow" two so you can see what they look like mounted on the same side of your vehicle.

If you can't find another car like yours with the wheels you're interested in, and you don't know anyone with a set of the wheels you like, you can get a pretty good idea of how things will look as long as you have access to a computer with a photograph scanner. Scan in a picture of your

You can use your PC to shop for wheels. American Racing Equipment's website features an interactive wheel selector that lets you choose your make and model, select a similar color to your car, then choose the wheels that fit. You can do the same thing by taking a digital picture of your car and copying and pasting images of different wheels onto it.

vehicle that shows the side (profile) of the car. Then scan in photos of the wheels you like and place those "virtual" wheels on the digital picture of your car. It's a great way to quickly get an idea of how things will look.

American Racing Equipment's website also features a handy Wheel Visualization tool that lets you select your vehicle, then click to try out different wheels, in different sizes. You can customize the color of the vehicle (to approximate yours) and even lower or raise the vehicle ride height to closely simulate your own vehicle (or the one you want).

Although such a modification may be possible on some springs for some vehicles, many coil springs do not feature linear rates but rather have one (usually softer) rate for the first inch or so of travel, then the rate gets progressively stiffer. By removing material from a progressive spring, you may alter the vehicle's handling characteristics—and not necessarily for the better.

As with most other suspension components, making sure that your replacement springs have a stock-like finish is usually ample camouflage. A few minutes with a can of spray paint ought to do it, then stick on some reproduction spring tags or identification/inspection paint marks.

### Shock Absorbers

Shock absorbers don't really absorb bumps, they dampen the movements that result from encountering a bump. Valves inside the shock absorber control how quickly the shock rod can extend (rebound) and compress within the shock body. This, in turn, controls how quickly the spring can extend and compress, so the shock effectively acts as a timer, delaying the spring's reaction to a bump.

Shocks can be of three basic types: hydraulic twin-tube; gas-charged hydraulic twin-tube; and high-pressure, gas-charged monotube. Of the three, a gas-charged twin tube will typically provide a more compliant and comfortable ride. Monotubes, because of their large pistons, react quickly and noticeably to even the slightest inputs, but that generally makes for a more responsive, performance-oriented feel. Different shocks use different valving to achieve different compression and rebound characteristics.

Consider adjustable shocks that allow you to dial in more or less compression and rebound damping to tune the ride to the needs of the moment. Keep the shocks set soft for street driving, then at the races crank them up for a firmer, higher-performance ride. Some shocks are rebound-adjustable only, while only a few offer adjustments for both rebound *and* compression strokes. A few companies offer some shock units with an electronic adjustment mechanism that allows you to change the damping characteristics from within the car while you're driving.

Since most shocks are simply tall, skinny cylinders, applying a coat of paint that approximates what was used on your vehicle's original shocks should be good enough for all but the closest of inspections.

### Stabilizer Bars

Most older vehicles excelled at pillowy-soft rides, but fell short in cornering abilities. Older cars and trucks often had stabilizer bars that were too small, if they had any at all. With weak or no stabilizer bars at both ends of the vehicle, a car leans to the outside of the corner. A stabilizer bar spans from one control arm to the other in front or from one frame rail to the other in back. As the weight of the body transfers toward one side of the car during a corner, the suspension for that side of the car begins to compress, twisting the stabilizer bar. Meanwhile, the suspension on the other side of the car is attempting to extend, attempting to twist the stabilizer bar, but in the opposite direction. As the bar resists twisting and tries to remain flat, it pushes the outer wheel back down while pulling the inner wheel back up, effectively leveling the body.

Fortunately, moderate-sized stabilizer bars have little or no effect on a suspension's ability to soak

> ### NAILING DOWN YOUR BUSHING UPGRADES
>
> If you're interested in increasing the stiffness of your suspension bushings, but don't really want to go to the trouble and expense of replacing them with polyurethane or other solid bushings, there's an old trick that can help.
>
> By driving common nails into your rubber bushings, you can effectively increase their durometer (hardness). Just choose nails that are close in length to the width of your bushings, then pound them in (evenly spaced around the bushing). Grind or cut off any excess length to make sure that the nails do not protrude from the bushings anywhere.

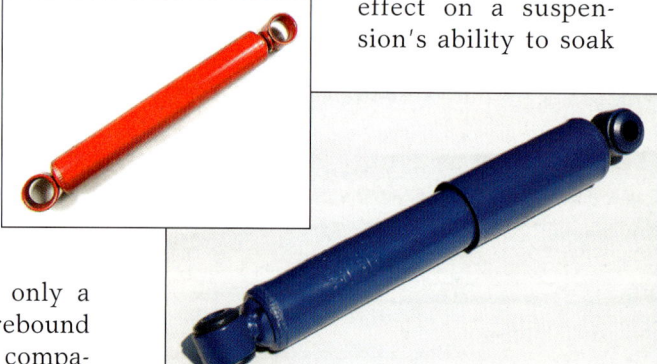

**Far left:** Not all shocks are created equally. In fact, some are created specifically for certain kinds of driving, like these Lakewood drag shocks. They're designed to promote weight transfer to help plant your rear wheels upon take-off. *Lakewood photo*

**Left:** One of the easiest suspension mods to make is to replace your stock (and probably worn-out) shocks with new gas-charged shocks. Shocks are responsible for controlling the upward and downward motions of your car in response to steering or road inputs with the goal providing stable, predictable handling under all conditions.

# Chassis, Suspension, and Steering    153

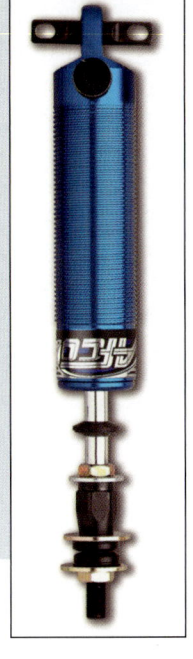

**Right:** AFCO makes a variety of race-ready shocks for circle and road racing, including these adjustable shocks with a high-tech, anodized aluminum body. Adjustable shocks allow you to tune the shock's performance to best meet your needs and preferences. *AFCO photo*

**Far right:** Coil-over shocks take adjustability to an extreme. You can quickly, easily adjust the spring rate or replace the spring entirely, plus you can adjust the shock's valving. *AFCO photo*

Moving beyond the shocks, new springs are a next logical step for suspension upgrades. The basic function of the springs is to keep your car up in the air (i.e., *suspended*) so that it can float over bumps rather than smashing through them. Shocks have to be matched to springs in order to properly counteract the spring's rebound action. *AFCO photo*

up bumps, because if both front or both rear wheels compress or extend the same amount, the bar simply pivots in its mounts, which are attached to the body structure. Large-diameter bars do tend to make a vehicle feel as though it has higher spring rates, so you don't want to get too carried away with the size of your stabilizer bars.

In most cases, however, adding stabilizer bars to both ends of your vehicle can greatly improve its cornering abilities without significantly diminishing ride comfort. To hide the bars, give them a stock-like finish. For most vehicles, stabilizer bars either had a natural cast-iron finish or were painted semigloss black. Adding a couple of paint marks to duplicate those that identified the part to assembly line workers or showed it had been inspected is a subtle touch that will throw almost anyone off the track, including knowledgeable enthusiasts.

### Traction Devices

First, ensure that all of the rotational forces of your axles are being translated to turning the tires. While you might assume that's what happens anyway, it's often not. In vehicles with leaf spring rear suspensions, when your axles try to turn the wheels, the tires will resist turning (by gripping the pavement), causing the rear-axle housing to rotate around the axles. While that, in itself, is a problem, what happens next causes a bigger problem: The springs, which are now bent into a subtle S shape, will rapidly and uncontrollably unwrap. This causes the rear-axle housing to flip back to its original position, and in the process, the tires generally bounce off the road surface. You might know this as wheel hop or axle hop.

There are a number of ways to minimize axle hop and increase traction. Chevrolet installed what it called a rear-axle radius rod on early Camaros, which was really an upper control arm that prevented the housing from rotating. Chevy also switched to a staggered shock layout, where the left shock was mounted behind the axle housing, while the right shock was mounted in front of the housing, so the shocks resisted the rotating forces. Chrysler employed pinion snubbers, which mounted to the front of the rear-axle housing and contacted the chassis structure to prevent rotating. All three manufacturers installed stronger springs (or more springs in each spring pack), which resisted the bending forces in the first place. Unfortunately, the heavy-duty springs also hampered ride quality.

Aftermarket options include traction bars that bolt to your leaf springs and use a snubber to prevent the springs from winding up; ladder bar suspension systems, which are intended for vehicles that don't use leaf springs; no-hop adapters for air bags; and spring spacers and spring wedges, which are all ways of changing your spring rates to varying degrees.

## Drag Racing

In drag racing, the name of the game is planting those back tires as firmly as possible to maximize traction. Since you don't have to concern yourself with widely varying road terrain and conditions, the job of upgrading a suspension to work well at a drag strip is much more, well, straightforward.

### Tires and Wheels

When it comes to selecting wheels and tires for a drag car, the classic big 'n' little combination still works. Narrow front tires will reduce rolling resistance, while wide rear tires (keeping within class rules, of course) provide the traction.

It doesn't make sense to hamper your efforts by sticking with street tires for a race car, so decide between a traditional bias-ply slick and the DOT-approved BF Goodrich Drag Radial, which has a minimal tread. Slicks, because they have such weak sidewalls, are never to be used on the street; plus, since mixing bias-ply slicks with radials is a known recipe for disaster, it's just not a wise thing to do.

Selecting wheels for drag racing is fairly straightforward. They need to be lightweight, yet strong enough to withstand the forces they'll endure at the track. Steel wheels are fine, but aluminum usually weighs less, which gives it an edge.

From an appearance standpoint, there's no real reason you need to keep things looking original on a drag car. After all, drag cars aren't street cars. But if you want to retain a stock appearance, running plain steel wheels will help you do that, or you could always run some aftermarket wheels that resemble wheels available when your car was new, like Cragar S/S or American Racing Equipment Torque Thrust wheels.

### Bushings

Bushings deserve some immediate attention. Soft, stock rubber bushings allow too much axle housing movement, but polyurethane bushings may bind up, which can cause other problems. Heim joints and solid bushings will eliminate the slop and are a good route to go if the car is solely used for drag racing. Another option, Del-A-Lum bushings from Global West Suspension, is a good choice for dual-purpose street/strip use because they're more forgiving than solid bushings, but they won't bind like polyurethane bushings.

### Control Arms

For racing, your control arms should be as strong as possible, otherwise you'll have inaccurate suspension geometry, which

---

### WEEKEND WARRIOR SUSPENSION TIPS

Suspension setups for street driving and racing are often very different, so it's hard to make your car exceptional in both arenas. But if you only race occasionally, there are a few quick changes you can make on race day to improve performance at the track, yet can be easily undone at the end of the day to restore street-worthy handling traits.

One of the easiest things to do is to unbolt your vehicle's stabilizer bar end links, which will allow the suspension to compress or rebound more quickly, which allows faster weight transfer.

In most vintage vehicles, changing the shocks is at most a 30-minute job. Many cars can have four new dampers on in as little as 15 minutes, once you've got the routine down. This makes it possible to install drag-racing shocks that will also allow for faster weight transfer to the rear wheels, for better traction.

Vehicles with rear coil springs, such as the GM A-body intermediates (GTO/Le Mans, Chevelle, Olds 4-4-2/Cutlass, Buick GS), can often have their rear springs changed in a matter of moments, making it possible to swap your firmer street springs for softer drag springs.

Last, don't forget to swap your street tires for some soft and sticky drag tires, which will increase traction considerably. The job is obviously easier if each set of tires is mounted on its own set of wheels. If you run radials for the street (and will be leaving those on the front of the vehicle at the track), you should run BF Goodrich's Drag Radial; mixing and matching radials with nonradial drag tires makes your vehicle's handling very unstable, which can cause a potentially serious accident.

---

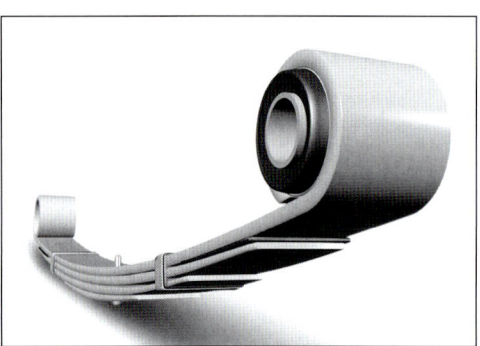

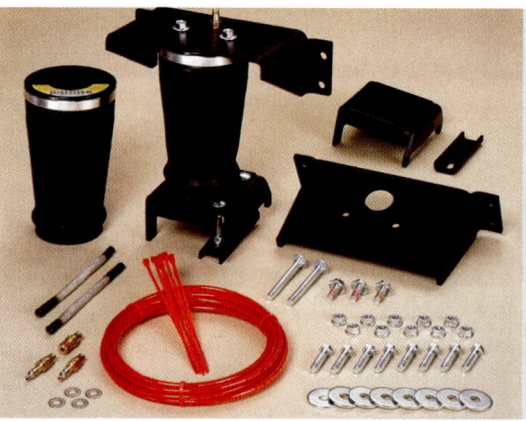

**Far left:** Leaf springs, like coils, fatigue over time and lose their ability to support your vehicle and rebound after encountering a bump. *AFCO photo*

**Left:** Air bags have been used for years to enhance drag strip performance. Now, air bags systems can be used to replace springs entirely. *Firestone photo*

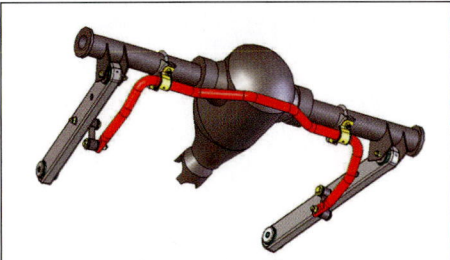

This Hotchkis animation helps explain how anti-roll bars work: as the suspension on one side of the car compresses (as the car leans), it has to bend the anti-roll bar, which resists, acting like a helper spring, and keeps the car flatter and thus the tires in better contact with the road. *Hotchkis image*

will make your car unstable and difficult to dial in.

As with street-bound vehicles, you can brace your stock control arms, or you can replace them with aftermarket pieces. Aftermarket control arms are usually stronger and weigh less than modified stock arms, so they're probably a wiser choice. But if you're on a budget, boxing your own control arms will get the job done for next to nothing.

Not that their appearance is likely to be your highest concern, but painting them with a stock-like color will camouflage them and will help them last longer by preventing corrosion.

### Springs

For most vehicles, softer front springs help unload the front suspension at the launch and transfer weight to the rear wheels, which helps plant them better. It used to be common to run springs from a six-cylinder version of your vehicle. Purpose-engineered aftermarket springs are usually the same price or less, as well as more effective.

In back, you'll have to try different spring combinations, starting with stock and determining whether you need more or less spring tension. You'll often find that your right rear wheel will need additional support, which for leaf-spring cars usually means a different spring pack with a couple of extra leafs. For coil-spring cars, a stronger coil can be used on that side, or you can install an air bag inside the coil and adjust the pressure—or you can do both.

Again, painting the springs to look like stock is a simple enough matter. A factory-style paper spring tag is a terrific touch to throw people off track.

### Shocks

Since gas-charged shocks effectively increase spring rates (by further damping the spring oscillations), you'll want to stick to straight hydraulic-only shocks. Aftermarket parts are available for this, including adjustable drag shocks that provide tuning flexibility. *Do not* use worn-out shocks on any vehicle, whether they provide the desired degree of weight transfer or not. Doing so is as good as begging for an accident.

You may be able to install a set of adjustable coil-over shocks and springs on your vehicle, and that may be an excellent way to go, given their tune-ability. They're too expensive for most hobbyists, however, and too difficult to adapt to their vehicle.

It's also wise to get a set of four drag shocks from the same company, which would normally have engineered their front shocks to complement their rears. And if an original appearance is high on your list, spray painting the new shocks to resemble old ones is a simple job. Reproduction ID decals are available and can really complete the look.

### Stabilizer Bars

Up front, start by removing the stabilizer bar, or at least disconnecting it from the lower control arms when racing (reconnect it for street driving), otherwise it may limit weight transfer. Removing the bar will reduce vehicle weight somewhat and may be worthwhile, since shaving pounds can help you go quicker and faster.

A rear stabilizer bar may or may not prove helpful, depending on your vehicle's powertrain, the track conditions, and even your driving style. Try a few *cautious* runs with and without the bar and let the time slips and feel of the car dictate what to do. On some vehicles, the stabilizer bar may

**Right:** Aftermarket control arms, like this AFCO lower A-arm, offer improved strength and geometry for better handling. *AFCO photo*

**Far right:** For a restoration, you can rebuild and refinish your stock suspension control arms. The Eastwood Company has easy-to-apply paints that give a near-perfect stock finish for all your chassis parts. *The Eastwood Company photo*

### MAXIMUM TIRE TRACTION, MAXIMUM TIRE LIFE

Let's face it: performance tires are expensive. Unless you've got deep pockets that are lined with more than just lint (like mine), then it's in your own best interest to maximize your tire's tread life. It just so happens that most things necessary to make a tire last a good long life also improve traction under most normal driving conditions.

The most important steps you can take to get the most from your tires are to keep the tire pressure properly adjusted, rotate the tires periodically to even out wear, keep them properly balanced, and keep the front end properly aligned.

**Tire Pressure**—The pressure indicated on the sidewall of your tire is a *maximum* pressure the tire is designed to withstand. While there may be times when you'll want to run your tires at that value—during autocross or road-racing types of competition, or for better fuel economy on a long trip—more often than not your tires will last longer and work better at a pressure somewhat lower than that maximum. Instead of running your tires at their maximum 32-psi rating (or whatever the actual rating is on your tires), you may find yourself running them at 30 or even 28 psi. Also note that you may need to run different pressures in your front tires than your rears because most V-8-powered cars and trucks have much less weight over their rear wheels than their fronts, so the rear tires require less air pressure than the fronts to provide optimal wear.

Overinflating your tires will cause the center of the tread section to wear rapidly, while underinflating them will cause the sides of the tread to wear, but not the middle. There are two ways to determine the optimal pressure for your tires: (1) monitor treadwear and adjust accordingly for even wear across the face of the tread; and (2) take a long, straight drive (several miles on a highway, for example) then pull over and immediately take three to five temperature readings across the face of the tread. Temperatures should be the same. If the center readings are hotter, the tire is overinflated. If both sides of the tread are hotter than the center, the tire is underflated. If only one side of the tread is hotter than the rest, the camber alignment setting is improperly adjusted.

**Tire Rotation**—Rotating tires from one corner of the vehicle to another gives each tire a chance to experience a variety of road and handling conditions. A good example would be moving the rear tires forward to subject them to steering forces that they wouldn't experience on the rear of the car.

Tires should be rotated every 6,000 miles. There are two commonly used methods of rotating tires: fronts move straight back, while the rears cross to the opposite side when brought forward; rears move straight forward, but the fronts cross while moving back. If you have a full-sized spare, you should incorporate that into the rotation as well. The actual rotation "pattern" that you use—which tire goes where—isn't vitally important, so long as every tire gets its turn at each corner of the car (and possibly the trunk), and that you use the same pattern every time you rotate the tires.

**True balance**—A tire that's out of balance will wear unevenly, as the tire wobbles its way down the road. The "heavy" spot on the tire will thrust itself outward, causing it to wear more quickly than the surrounding tread. There are a number of ways to balance a tire, including a static "bubble balance," and various methods of dynamic spin balancing. Because spin-balancing most closely approximates the conditions the tire will be subjected to on your vehicle, it is the best method to use for balancing purposes.

---

be beneficial because it will keep the rear of the car flatter, thus delivering equal power to each rear wheel.

### Traction Devices

While the same sort of bolt-on traction devices that work on the street will work at the track—traction bars, pinion snubbers, and so on—if you're competing for point or prize money, you would be wise to consider a real ladder bar suspension, or a four-link setup with adjustable coil-over shocks.

## Steering

Your vehicle's steering system is one of two vital safety systems (the other is the brake system), so you need to take extreme care that any modifications you make or parts that you replace are 100 percent safe. If you have any doubt about whether a change will work or whether it will be safe, don't take the chance. If your steering fails at high speeds—whether on a racetrack or a highway—you could find yourself

Control arms and slapper bars use snubbers to prevent metal-to-metal contact under full compression. Old snubbers degrade and need to be replaced. *Lakewood photo*

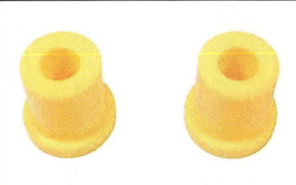

Stock rubber bushings compress and deflect, which makes for a comfortable ride, but does so at the expense of accurate suspension movement. Polyurethane bushings will keep your suspension responding predictably and will allow for more precise suspension movement. But poly bushings do transmit more vibrations to the chassis, which is a bit less comfortable. *Lakewood photo*

**Left:** Here, you can see the difference between stock, stamped-steel lower rear control arms and tubular steel arms from Global West Suspension. The stock arms flex and deflect, especially when subjected to side loads while cornering. The Global West arms prevent that and therefore keep your rear axle properly positioned under the vehicle and help it respond predictably.

**Right:** Some classic mods still make sense: Lakewood's legendary traction (or "slapper") bars help prevent rear axle wind-up under hard acceleration. This unit is for a typical leaf-spring rear suspension. *Lakewood photo*

heading for a tree, a ditch, or a guardrail far faster than your brakes will stop you.

For the same reasons, even if you aren't making changes, you should make sure that it is in perfect working order and that nothing is old or worn and potentially dangerous. Rag joints (steering shaft couplers), the various steering linkage components, and your tires all need careful inspection. Any questionable parts should be replaced.

## Steering Wheels

From your perspective in the driver seat, your steering system begins with the steering wheel. For most older vehicles, the steering wheels were large-diameter, thin rims of hard, slippery plastic. Not exactly ideal performance equipment.

Many people think of their steering wheel only in terms of its appearance and its comfort. But your steering wheel can dramatically affect how your vehicle feels while driving it.

A large-diameter wheel gives you more leverage to turn the wheels, so the steering effort is reduced, possibly to the point of being too light. Replacing the wheel with a smaller-diameter one will increase the steering effort you need to apply. The opposite change will have the opposite effect: steering that feels too heavy can be lightened up by switching to a steering wheel with a larger diameter. Of course, production steering wheels were already pretty large, so it may be rough to find a larger wheel that will still fit in your vehicle without looking ridiculous.

You should also consider the rim of the wheel and how it affects your steering experience. A thin, plastic wheel, like a stock one, can easily slip through your hand at the wrong moment, possibly leading to an accident. But a wheel with a thick rim of soft vinyl or leather will provide much better grip, so you won't have to hold on as tightly to get a good grip. In fact, many racers use rubber-covered steering wheels because of their exceptional grip and vibration isolation.

Many later-model vehicles have thick-rimmed, small-diameter steering wheels that can easily be retrofitted to vintage vehicles, or there are many excellent aftermarket wheels available that may also look right at home.

## Steering Columns

Your steering wheel is connected to a shaft that runs through your steering column, and while you are right in thinking that your steering column doesn't do anything to alter the steering effort, it still affects performance.

While most steering columns of the 1950s through the 1970s were fixed-length, fixed-angle assemblies, columns with tilt and telescoping features can enhance the car's ergonomics by allowing you to better position the steering wheel to suit your preferences. The tilt feature is helpful because its column lets a driver get closer to his or her ideal setup, so the driver is more comfortable and can concentrate on the road.

Telescoping steering columns are rare but were commonly installed in Corvettes from the mid-1960s on. The telescoping feature lets you extend the steering column by several inches, to bring the steering wheel closer to you. This is an invaluable aid when the seating design of your vehicle leaves you too far from the wheel when your feet hit the pedals right, but too close to the pedals when you're the right distance from the steering wheel.

In some cases, you may be able to swap a later-model tilt-wheel steering column into your vehicle, but be prepared

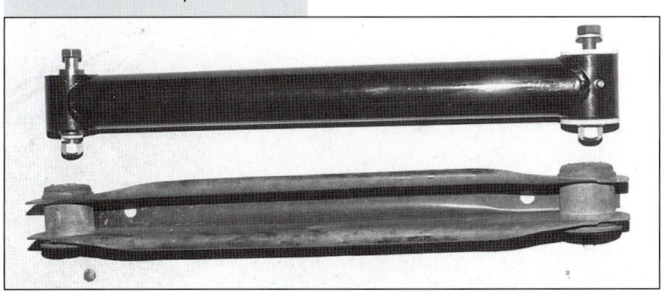

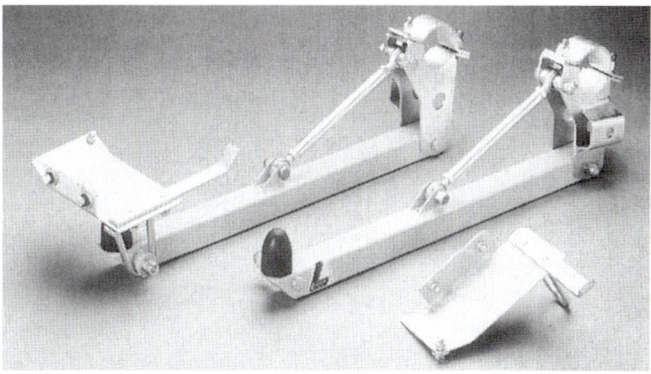

to possibly spend a bit of extra time adapting its wiring to your vehicle's harnesses. Several aftermarket companies can custom build a tilt or tilt-tele column to fit your vehicle. Steering columns can be painted to complement your interior, which could make the switch virtually undetectable.

## Steering Box

From the steering column, steering inputs pass through a flexible steering coupler (commonly known as a rag joint) to a steering box.

Most vintage vehicles rely on a traditional steering box design that uses either a recirculating ball or a worm-and-sector steering mechanism to translate the rotary steering wheel inputs to linear movements that turn the front wheels. The systems are effective, but require a bulky, heavy, and complex assembly of steering linkages.

While it may be possible to retrofit a modern rack-and-pinion steering system to an older vehicle, it would take considerable effort and an extensive knowledge of steering geometry. A more reasonable approach would be to retrofit a later-model steering box with a faster steering ratio than what was available when your vehicle was new.

If no later-model steering boxes will bolt in, you should consider upgrading to the fastest-ratio steering box that was available for your vehicle, if your vehicle isn't already equipped with it.

Only steering boxes that look similar tend to be interchangeable, so the odds are good that whatever you do to upgrade your steering box, it will likely look original as is. A couple coats of paint (either of the appropriate color or simply clear) would protect its finish for years.

If you plan to run power steering, and there's no reason you shouldn't if you want to, consider a few modifications that will extend the life of the system and increase the steering effort.

First, to extend the life of your power steering system, install a power steering fluid cooler, as described in Chapter 6. Another device that may be desirable is a power-steering pump flow restrictor to decrease the amount of assist that the power-steering pump provides. The restrictor is a valve that you plumb into the supply line going to the steering box or slave cylinder. By closing the valve orifice slightly, you decrease flow to the pump or slave cylinder, which decreases the assist and thus increases steering effort. Most hardware or plumbing supply stores will have valves sized for your pressure lines, and the job shouldn't take more than an hour or so to complete. This may not be as easy as it sounds in a high-pressure line. Heidt's Hot Rods offers a kit with a valve with an adjustment knob for dialing in the steering effort.

## Pitman Arm

The Pitman arm connects to the output shaft of the steering box and translates that rotary motion into a linear movement of the center link. Pitman arms typically have no moving parts, no grease fittings, and no possible modifications, other than possibly installing different-length Pitman arms. Different length Pitman arms would alter the steering leverage applied to the steering linkage.

## Center/Drag Link

The center link is a steel bar approximately 2 feet long that connects to the Pitman arm, and to which the left- and right-side inner tie-rod ends connect. As the Pitman arm swings, it moves the center link, which moves both inner tie-rod ends. The center link is supported on the right side of the vehicle by an idler arm. Center

The best way to test for proper tire inflation in high-performance driving scenarios is to test tire temps across the tire tread. Here, we're using a thermal-sensing infrared gun to read the temp of the outside tread blocks.

The center of the tread shows a five-degree difference.

# Chassis, Suspension, and Steering 159

The inside tread area is slightly up from the middle, but still four degrees below the outside. Since the inside and middle temps are so close, the pressure is probably about right, but the high outside temp indicates the camber may be off, causing the car to ride on the outside tread more.

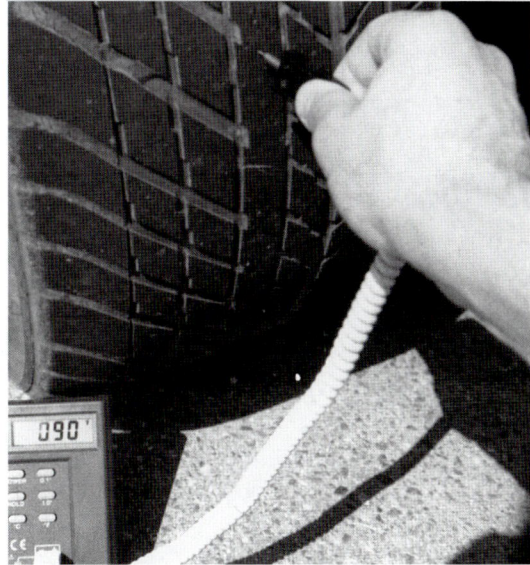

Professional race teams often use a probe-type tire temp gauge, because it allows them to get a measurement of the tire's internal temp, not just its surface temp, which changes quickly—especially in cooler air.

links often have no moving parts and don't normally require service or replacement, unless they become damaged in an accident.

### Idler Arm

The idler arm is a small, L-shaped arm that supports the right-side end of the center link. Because it has a built-in pivot, it will eventually wear out and need replacement, even if you regularly grease it. There are no worthwhile upgrades for idler arms, beyond replacement, when necessary.

### Tie-Rod Adjustment Sleeves

Tie-rod adjustment sleeves work like turn buckles, bringing the tie-rod ends closer together or moving them farther apart to adjust front wheel toe settings. Stock tie-rod adjustment sleeves are made of stamped steel and were originally designed to work with 14-inch wheels and relatively narrow tires that were prevalent during the 1950s, 1960s, and 1970s. Larger diameter wheels, plus wide, sticky tires, place more stress on the tie-rod adjustment sleeves and cause them to flex or even bend, either of which will change the toe and make steering unpredictable. The stock adjustment sleeves can be strengthened by welding bracing material around the sleeves; however, the sleeves can't be fully reinforced because the stock sleeves are retained by constricting clamps that require the sleeves to be flexible in the clamped area. Heavy-duty aftermarket sleeves are available for some vehicles, or you could make your own by drilling and tapping (remember: one side needs to use counterclockwise threads, while the other uses clockwise) a piece of either round or square metal stock.

### Tie-rod Ends

Tie-rod ends transmit steering actions from the center link to the steering knuckles. Stock tie-rod ends are made of cast iron and have a ball-and-socket joint that allows the arm to flex as the suspension moves, relative to the center link or steering rack. Stock tie-rod ends are usually acceptable for high-performance use, though for racing it would be wise to have them magnaflux inspected to detect any cracks. It is also possible to replace the stock tie-rod ends with Heim joints for more precise steering in competition.

### Steering Knuckles

Steering knuckles are the last link in the steering system before the tires. They connect the outer tie-rod end to the spindle. In most cases, the steering knuckle will be made of cast iron, and there's little that can be done to improve it. The only upgrade that you may be able to perform is finding different steering knuckles that would yield a different degree of leverage.

### Steering Stops

If you are installing oversized wheels and tires on your vintage vehicle, inspect for any possible contact between the new wheels and tires and any chassis, suspension, or steering components, while cycling the front wheels from lock to lock and through the full range of suspension travel. If the wheels or tires contact the vehicle, you may be able to install a thicker steering stop to prevent the steering knuckle from turning far enough to let the wheel or tire rub. Your stops may either be bolted or welded on.

### Alignment Settings and Tips

All of the best shocks, springs, stabilizer bars, and performance tires won't make your car feel good driving down the road if the front-end alignment isn't optimized for the kind of driving that you do.

The three settings that determine overall front-end alignment for each wheel are toe, caster, and camber.

**Far left:** Likewise, tubular upper A-arms strengthen your suspension for more predictable action, while geometry is optimized to keep wheels and tires in proper contact with the road surface. *AFCO photo*

**Left:** Car's like GM's A-bodies (Chevelle, GTO, 4-4-2/Cutlass, GS) can really benefit from aftermarket control arms, like these Edelbrock upper arms, to replace the flimsy, stamped-steel arms. *Edelbrock photo*

*Toe* expresses the direction of the front of the front wheels. It is expressed as toe-in if the wheels point inward, toward the center of the car. Conversely, it is called toe-out if the tires point away from the center of the car. Toe is generally what people are referring to when they say their car needs an alignment because it is pulling to one side or the other. If one wheel is adjusted with more toe-in than the other, the effect is similar to turning the steering wheel (i.e., both wheels are, more or less, pointed in the same direction, but not straight ahead), and either the front or rear edges of individual tread blocks will display feathered edges. Toe is often set differently for the front wheels to counter the tendency for crowned roads (where the center of the road is raised higher than the sides to promote water runoff) to cause the car to turn off the road.

*Caster* is the angle of the wheel's steering axis, described as viewed from the side of the vehicle, and generally affects the overall stability of the car, and the steering wheel's tendency to self-center (i.e., return to straight-ahead from a turn). If the top of the steering axis tilts rearward, the wheel has positive caster, but if it tilts forward, it has negative caster. Positive caster makes the car much more stable at high speed, but increases steering effort, while negative caster has the opposite effect.

Finally, *camber* describes the tilt of the top of the front wheels, as viewed from ahead of or behind the wheels. If the top of the wheels tilt inward, toward the center of the vehicle, the wheel has *negative* camber, whereas positive camber would be tilting the top of the wheel outward, away from the center of the car. Camber directly affects the tire's contact patch, by altering what part of the tread, and how much of it, from side-to-side contacts the ground. For autocross and road-racing competition, a certain degree of

**Far left:** Muscle car steering boxes tended to err on the light side for easier drivability. Aftermarket steering boxes—including later-model OEM boxes—feature a quicker ratio and better feel for performance driving.

**Left:** When upgrading your power steering system, don't forget to replace the hoses with high-performance hose. Stock hose can flex and expand when subjected to rapid steering inputs, causing your power steering to respond lazily. High performance hose also features a higher burst rating for improved reliability. *Earl's photo*

# Chassis, Suspension, and Steering

## ALIGNMENT SETTINGS EXPLAINED

All of the best shocks, springs, stabilizer bars, and performance tires won't make your car feel good driving down the road if the front-end alignment isn't optimized for the kind of driving that you do.

The three settings that determine overall front-end alignment for each wheel are toe, caster, and camber. If your vehicle happens to have an independent rear suspension, like a Corvette, the rear wheels have the same sorts of settings.

**Toe** expresses the direction of the front of the front wheels. It is expressed as "toe-in" if the wheels point inward, toward the center of the car. Conversely, it is called "toe-out" if the tires point away from the center of the car. Toe is generally what people are referring to when they say their car needs an alignment because it is "pulling" to one side or the other. If one wheel is adjusted with more toe-in than the other, the effect is similar to turning the steering wheel (that is, both wheels are, more or less, pointed in the same direction but not straight ahead), and either the front or rear edges of individual tread blocks will display feathered edges. Toe is often set differently for the front wheels to counter the tendency for "crowned" roads (where the center of the road is raised higher than the sides to promote water runoff) to cause the car to turn off the road.

**Caster** is the angle of the wheel's steering axis, described as viewed from the side of the vehicle, and generally affects the overall stability of the car and the steering wheel's tendency to self-center (return to straight ahead from a turn). If the top of the steering axis tilts rearward, the wheel has positive caster; but if it tilts forward, it has negative caster. Positive caster makes the car much more stable at high speed, but increases steering effort, while negative caster has the opposite effect.

Finally, **camber** describes the tilt of the top of the front wheels, as viewed from ahead of or behind the wheels. If the top of the wheels tilt inward, toward the center of the vehicle, the wheel has negative camber, whereas positive camber would be tilting the top of the wheel outward, away from the center of the car.

negative camber is preferred because it maximizes tire contact during hard cornering, when the angle of the vehicle (and thus the angle of the wheel) would normally tend to lift the inside of the tire and roll the tire onto its outer sidewall. Improper camber settings will wear the inside (too much negative camber) or outside (too much positive camber) of the tread abnormally. Camber settings have a lot to do with whether a car oversteers (the back end tends to swing around) or understeers (the front end keeps going straight) through corners.

Unfortunately, most vehicles are so different (even within the same make) that it's pointless to try to give any further advice beyond the notion that wheels should have only a slight toe-in condition, and have a fair amount of negative camber and positive caster.

An old racer's trick for autocrossing or road racing is to add shoe polish in three or four spots around the tire, making sure it's applied to the tread and about an inch onto the sidewall. Then go run a lap or two and check out the wear pattern.

# Chapter 10
# Better Brakes

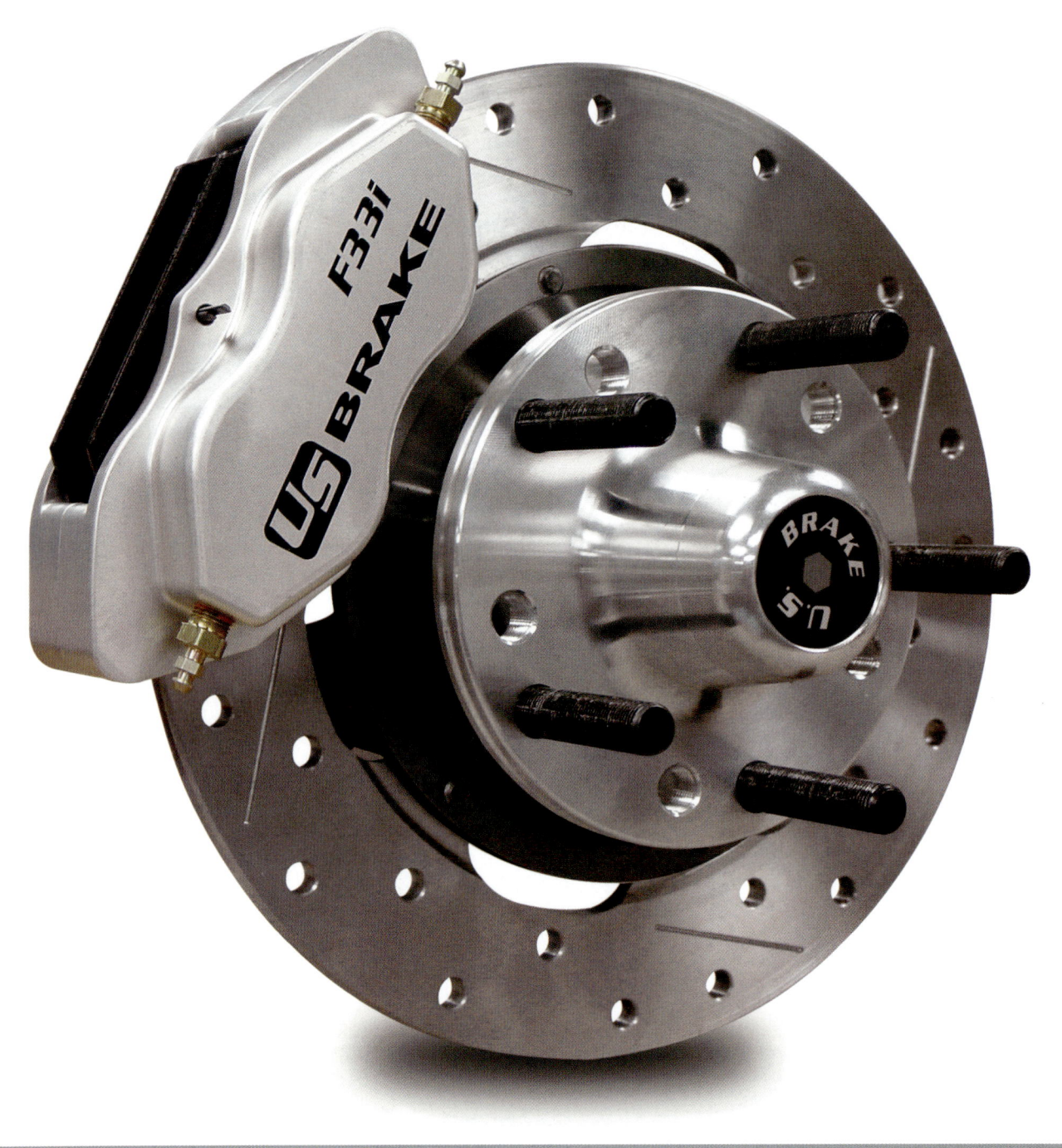

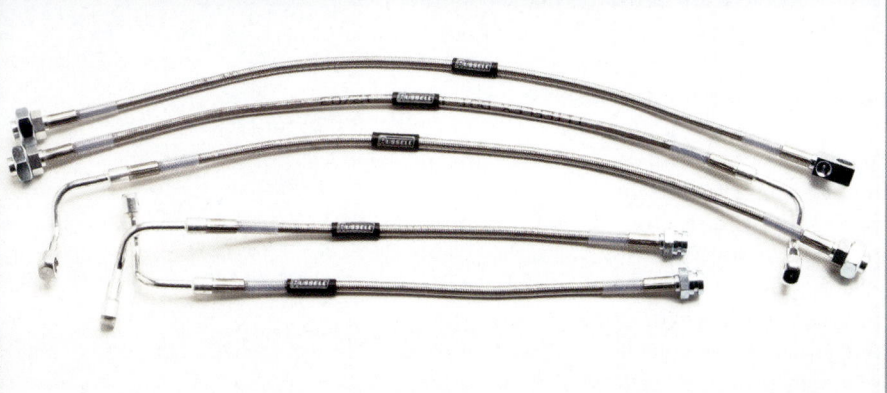

**M**any muscle car enthusiasts feel that "brakes only slow you down." True as this may be, there really is no such thing as too much capacity in your braking system. Being proactive here will save you a lot of grief—especially if you drive your car hard!

Your muscle car's brake system is actually its most critical system. Proper function of any other system is largely optional, from a safety standpoint. If the engine doesn't work, the car's no fun, but it's probably not going to kill anyone. And if your steering or suspension systems fail, as long as you have your brakes to stop you, damage and injury can be minimized. But if your brakes don't work ... well, the best that you can do is hope you hit something soft and inexpensive.

When thinking about your brakes, you might be tempted to simply leave well enough alone when restoring the vehicle. After all, if your brakes are working properly, why change them? Of course, if that's the way you thought, you would have little use for this book.

There are several very good reasons to upgrade your brake system: to improve safety, reliability, performance, and appearance. While modern brake systems rarely suffer complete failures, older brake systems—perhaps like the one on your vintage vehicle—weren't as reliable.

By injecting your aging brake system with some modern technology and components, you can easily improve your vehicle's braking.

## The Trouble with Older Brakes

While your engine and drivetrain are responsible for moving your car, your brake system has the opposite function—stopping it. As powerful as your engine is, your brakes actually need to be more powerful to slow your vehicle safely. This is an especially important concept to grasp, because as you increase your engine's power (and thus your car's potential speed) the need for improved brakes becomes even greater.

While most production-stock braking systems on vintage cars and trucks are fine for stopping stock vehicles, they are often grossly inadequate on vehicles with elevated performance. With some careful forethought, you can upgrade your vintage brake system to overcome its weaknesses.

One of the most common shortcomings of early brake systems is their almost exclusive reliance on drum brakes. It wasn't until around the mid-1970s that manufacturers started including disc brakes as standard equipment on a number of their models. Prior to that, disc brakes were typically optional, even on many high-performance models. A few rare cars—like the 1965 and later Corvettes and the ultra-scarce 1969 Camaros with RPO JL8—featured four-wheel disc brakes, but even those systems weren't ideal.

Countless vehicles relied on drum brakes at all four corners, but drum brakes were (and are) notorious for their poor operation in wet weather, as well as their inability to withstand high temperatures generated by hard stops at even modest speeds. Hit the brakes in rain or at speeds above 50 miles per hour and you would have done almost as well to drag your feet on the ground Fred Flintstone-style.

Even if early drum brakes did their job properly, it often didn't take much to suffer a complete brake system failure, given that most systems prior to the mid-1960s used a single-reservoir master cylinder. Because each of the four wheel cylinders were fed from that single fluid reservoir, a puncture in a line or hose anywhere on the vehicle would cause the fluid to drain from the master cylinder. This made it impossible to generate any pressure within the system to operate any of the four wheel cylinders. Dual-reservoir systems, which

Upgrading your muscle car's braking system is one of the smartest—and safest—changes you should make to your car. Companies like Master Power Brakes make it easy and economical to add some serious whoapower to your muscle car, with kits like this four-wheel Corvette disc system installed on a GM A-body.

manufacturers migrated to in the latter part of the 1960s, had one reservoir for the front brakes and another for the rear, so a puncture in the rear line would still allow your front brakes to work, or vice versa.

Couple these questionable brake systems to a car equipped with a high-powered engine—as manufacturers of so many 1960s muscle cars did—and you had the makings of a car that could easily out-accelerate its ability to slow down. As if that wasn't bad enough, the cars were often heavy (by today's standards), which gave them more momentum, making the brake system's job that much harder.

A well-thought-out brake system needs to correct for each of these deficiencies and others; it must function properly *every* time it is used. Safety is the top concern, so any modifications should always err on the side of caution. Any changes that you're not 100 percent confident in should be avoided.

## The Basics of Brake Systems and Their Problems

Before you start tearing into things, replacing parts left and right, it's worthwhile to know as much as you can about your car's brake system, so that you can understand its shortcomings and how to address them.

If you are not already familiar with the operation of your vehicle's brake system, do yourself a favor and pick up a shop manual. It will explain how it works, how everything fits together, and it clearly identifies the components so you can use the right terminology when ordering parts. But for the sake of simplicity (and to make sure we're all on the same page), we'll consider the common components and general principles at work on a typical brake system.

All but the earliest cars feature hydraulic brake systems. Brake fluid in the system is pressurized when you step on the brake pedal. Because the fluid isn't compressible (at least, it's not supposed to be compressible), the pressure in the system forces the brake pads (in disc systems) or the brake shoes (in drum systems) against the rotor or drum, respectively, which creates friction, which slows the vehicle.

Those of you with even a vague recollection of high school physics will recognize this as that old law that says energy is neither created nor lost, but merely converted. In this case, it's converted from momentum (the vehicle's velocity times its weight) into heat generated by the friction. This is important to keep in mind, because any upgrades should be aimed at increasing the heat your brake system can generate *and* withstand without failing.

That's actually one of the failings of drum brakes: They can actually generate loads of heat, but they have trouble dissipating it, so the shoes quickly overheat and begin to melt (a process referred to as glazing over), leaving them unable to generate sufficient friction to slow the turning drum. Drum brakes also have difficulties in wet weather. Because they are a closed design, with the shoes and linkage contained within the drum, any water that gets inside has difficulty draining out. That water causes two problems: First, the water acts as a lubricant, minimizing the friction between the shoes and the drum; second, it acts as a coolant by carrying off the heat, preventing the shoes and drums from converting the car's momentum into heat.

Disc brake systems, on the other hand, feature an open-air design that allows them to dissipate heat quickly, and it allows them to easily shed water.

Production disc brake assemblies have their own problems, however. Early disc brake rotors are frequently undersized for performance use, their calipers cause uneven pad wear, the pads tend to fade quickly under high-performance use, and front-to-rear braking bias is rarely well balanced.

Leaks in a brake system create problems. First, it helps to understand why brake systems are closed hydraulic systems, why no air or moisture is supposed to get into or out of the system—ever.

In the old days, disc brakes were rare and expensive. The first performance brake options from the factory consisted of ways to improve drum brakes in the hope of preventing them from overheating and glazing over. This is an early Corvette vented-drum system.

Leaks reduce the effectiveness of the system in several ways. One, leaks allow fluid loss, so the volume of fluid is less than the volumetric capacity of the system. The lost fluid is replaced by air that is allowed into the system. Each time you step on the brake pedal, more fluid is forced out through the leak, which further reduces the total volume of the fluid in the system, further reducing pressure. That lost fluid is replaced by air, as you let up on the brake pedal, causing air to be sucked into the system. Eventually, there will be so much air in the system that you won't be able to build any pressure, because pressing the pedal will simply compress the air in the system and won't generate any pressure to force the friction pads or shoes against the rotor or drum surfaces—you won't have any brakes.

Another problem that production brake systems (drum and disc alike) are prone to is that of moisture getting into the system. While the moisture can enter through any puncture in the system, a more common method is that the moisture forms within the brake system following periods when the brake fluid overheats. How does that happen? Well, hard, sudden stops, such as those that occur in a panic situation to avoid an accident, cause the brakes to generate lots of heat very quickly. If the fluid overheats, it can begin to boil within the brake caliper, wheel cylinder, or lines. But if you remain stopped after the panic stop, that heat doesn't have the benefit of flowing air (from the car rolling along) to cool things off, so the heat is trapped in the system until it eventually dissipates. As the overheated fluid cools, condensation forms inside the system, introducing moisture.

Stock-type brake fluids absorb a certain degree of moisture before performance degrades appreciably. Silicone-based brake fluids, however, do not absorb or mix with moisture. The water remains as water droplets within the lines.

The good news is that moisture in the system isn't compressible, so it doesn't immediately diminish your brake system's performance. The bad news is that when that moisture is subjected to heat, it boils and turns to steam, which *is* compressible. And brake systems generate *lots* of heat.

Since the steam is compressible, when you step on the brake pedal, some of the pedal travel is used up compressing the steam, rather than moving the caliper or wheel cylinder pistons. The steam also gives the brake pedal a spongy feel, too, which makes it relatively easy to diagnose air in the system.

Slightly less basic is the concept of brake bias, or balance of pressure between the front and rear brake channels, to minimize premature lockup of either set of wheels. Since weight transfers forward during braking, the back end of a vehicle becomes lighter, and it takes less brake pressure to make the rear wheels lock up. If both the front and rear channels were given equal brake pressure, the rear wheels would lock up much earlier than the front wheels during braking. Vehicle manufacturers do two things to adjust brake bias: they reduce the pressure for the rear brakes from within the master cylinder, and smaller passages are used in the master cylinder for the rear brake channel. In addition, manufacturers often employ a proportioning valve to fine-tune the pressure bias.

Antilock braking systems are hardly basic equipment, and in all honesty, they're not likely to be easily adapted to vehicles that weren't originally designed for them. But because they are so prevalent on modern vehicles, it's worth devoting a few words to giving you a basic understanding of them. Essentially, sensors monitor the speed of the individual wheels (actually, less costly systems monitor the rear wheels together but each of the front wheels individually, while high-end systems monitor each of the four wheels independently). A computer determines whether one wheel is moving slower than the rest, which might indicate that it is locked up, so the system reduces brake pressure to that wheel (or wheels) momentarily, allowing it to spin.

If your budget won't allow for a four-wheel disc system, Master Power offers a rear drum upgrade option for many cars. It uses oversize drums and bigger shoes to increase swept area and it's pretty effective. *Master Power Brakes photo*

The actual measurements are straightforward, using either optical or magnetic monitoring sensors. The comparison of the data is pretty complex, however, because it isn't as simple as comparing each wheel to every other, given that wheels on opposite sides of a vehicle necessarily turn at different speeds while cornering. Thus, the antilock braking systems need to determine whether the vehicle is merely turning or whether the wheels are indeed locked up.

In addition to your primary brake system, your car also has a parking or emergency brake. Unlike the primary system, parking brakes are almost always mechanical, operated by cables and linkages, rather than hydraulics. Mechanical systems provide a good backup for the primary hydraulic system: even if a brake line ruptures and all the hydraulic brake fluid is lost, the mechanical parking/emergency brake system won't be compromised because it doesn't rely on the fluid. In addition, the mechanical systems are well-suited to prolonged use because they do not strain the entire system in order to merely hold the vehicle in place. So whether your car sits parked with the brake on for a few days or even a few months, the brake system shouldn't suffer any adverse effects.

Those are the basics of brake systems, and they pretty much operate the same in cars from AMC to Volkswagen. In real life, of course, there are differences between specific systems. But if you know the basics of how brakes operate, you can start diagnosing problems and correcting them and begin to map out some upgrades.

## What Kind of Upgrades Do I Need?

The brake system upgrades you should consider depend on how your vehicle will be used. For a street-bound vehicle, your needs will be much less than those of a vehicle that will see frequent competition on a drag strip, which in turn has different needs than a car that will be used for road racing. And show vehicles have still different needs. Assessing how your vehicle will be used will go a long way toward answering the question of what modifications need to be made.

## Show Cars

If a vehicle is being built for show-only duty, the appearance of the brake system is of greater importance than its operation, though, of course, it should always be operational and safe if the vehicle is driven.

For vehicles that will be shown in restored classes, you want to ensure the system appears stock. In particular, you will want to ensure the parts are of the correct design and have a stock-appearing finish. Of course, we're talking about high-performance restorations, so you'll want to make sure the finishes on the brake components are actually much more durable than the original finishes, which were typically just bare metal. Metal parts, such as calipers, brackets, the master cylinder, brake drums, and the centers (or hats) of rotors can be bead blasted to restore their original appearance, then cleaned to remove any dust. Typically you will want to protect their finish by applying several thin layers of an appropriately colored spray paint. Restoration supply companies often carry paints that closely match natural cast iron or aluminum, as well as machined metal surface and clear paints. Since cars that are used only for show generally won't be driven, it's not absolutely necessary to concern yourself with using high-temperature paints and coatings, since the parts won't ever generate enough heat to discolor standard spray paints. It's still good practice to use high-temp finishes if you or a subsequent owner puts the car on the road. In particular, you'll want the calipers and non-swept surfaces of your drums and rotors to be painted with high-temp coatings.

Flexible brake hoses, which have rubber sheaths and metal ends, should be protected from the elements. The metal surfaces can be painted with a clear spray paint, while the rubber hose can be coated with spray silicon or even a light application of petroleum jelly to keep it from drying out.

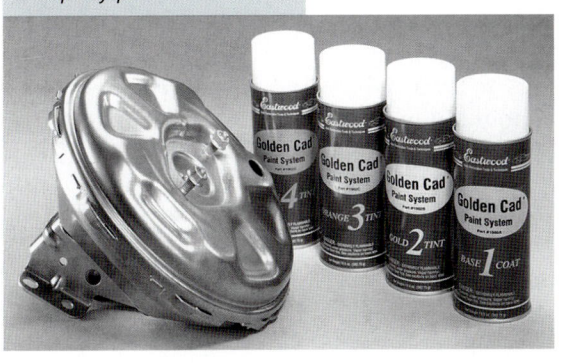
While replacement power brake boosters are available, if yours functions fine, you may be able to restore its appearance with the Eastwood Company's Golden Cad paint system for a whole lot less money. *The Eastwood Company photo*

Brake lines typically had a natural metal finish or had varying degrees of overspray, depending on the vehicle. Natural finishes call for either an appropriate color paint or a thorough cleaning (such as with a relatively coarse steel wool pad to remove any surface rust) followed by the application of several light coats of clear paint to prevent rust.

For vehicles competing in modified classes, you should consider some modifications that will add visual appeal to the brake system.

Oversized rotors that are either cross-drilled or slotted have a racy look; however, to get the full effect, you will need wheels that show the brake rotors. Protecting surfaces (such as the rotor hat area) with vibrant colors that match or contrast the primary vehicle color not only wards off rust and corrosion, but helps draw attention to the normally unseen components.

Installing aftermarket calipers is another excellent upgrade. Many calipers are either made of cast aluminum or machined from billet aluminum, which gives them a high-tech look. If the calipers don't already have an attractive finish, such as anodizing, polishing, powder coating, or paint, you can have a finish applied or do it yourself. Again, wheels that permit a good view of the caliper will maximize visual impact.

Braided steel flex hoses are an inexpensive upgrade that conveys a racy appearance, which makes them well-suited to modified cars. Braided lines aren't always visible, however, unless a wheel is removed for display. The braided lines should get a few light layers of clear paint to help prevent them from corroding, or it may be possible to have the hoses treated to a colorful coating if you really want them to stand out.

As with the flex lines, applying a colorful—but tasteful—finish to your steel brake lines will both protect them from the elements and dress up your chassis and engine compartment.

Installing an adjustable brake proportioning valve will give you the ability to tune your brake system balance and will also add another custom performance touch to the engine compartment. As with most other parts, the valve can be given a brilliant, durable finish to improve both its appearance and longevity.

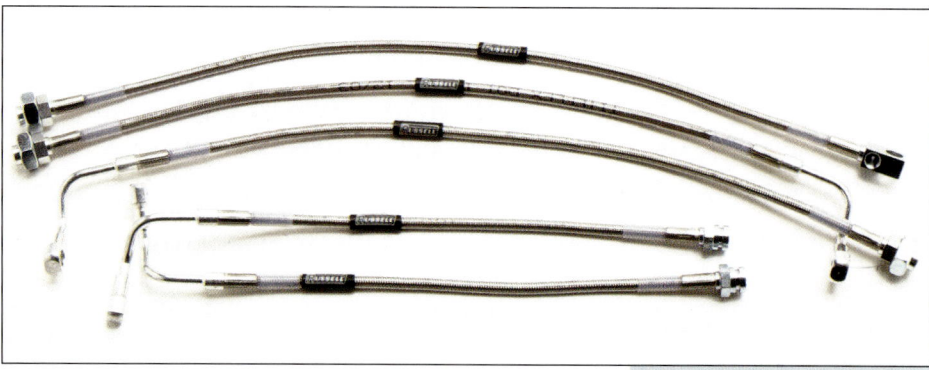

Stainless-steel brake hoses are available for most vehicles and are an excellent upgrade for spongy rubber stock hoses. Don't forget to replace old brake lines, too. *Russell Performance photo*

## Street Driving

Street driving, which is the primary focus of this book, presents relatively modest demands on a braking system: even highway speeds (assuming, of course, that you obey the law) are much lower than those encountered during most forms of competition. Also, stops are far less frequent and can often be accomplished with far less pedal pressure, since prudent street driving dictates gradual stops.

**Proper Maintenance**

Given those conditions, one of the most important improvements you can make to your brake system is to simply give it the regular maintenance it should already be getting. For street cars, you should plan on changing your brake fluid at least once per year. If the car isn't driven much, you may be able to stretch that frequency, as long as the system isn't exhibiting any leaks, which would allow moisture to contaminate the brake fluid. When you do change the fluid, use only high-quality, new fluid from sealed containers. Brake fluid acts like a sponge, attracting and absorbing moisture that lowers the brake fluid's boiling point, destroying the fluid's ability to do its job. Note, however, that you should only use DOT 3 or DOT 4 fluid and not DOT 5 silicone-based brake fluid, which is incapable of absorbing moisture, should some enter the system. With silicone-based fluid, moisture pools in the lines and calipers and can quickly boil, creating a large air pocket in the system that is highly compressible, so braking effectiveness may be considerably diminished or even eliminated.

And while you're changing the fluid, swap out those sad and sorry flexible rubber hoses for braided lines, or at least for new rubber ones, if yours are at least three years old. Many braided brake lines are not DOT approved and are for off-road use only.

## Brake Pads and Shoes

Beyond the fluid, street-bound braking systems benefit from mild upgrades to specific areas that improve all-around braking. The most dramatic improvement will come from installing new, high-performance brake pads (or shoes, for drum-equipped cars), which are also cost-effective.

## Drum Brake Upgrades

Next up in terms of cost and complexity are upgrades to the brake drum and disc assemblies.

In addition to high-performance brake shoes, drum brake systems can benefit from modifications that increase cooling and promote drainage of any contaminants—especially moisture—that may enter the system. Old, nonfinned brake drums can usually be upgraded to finned drums (from a different model offered by the same manufacturer). The fins increase surface area and increase heat dissipation. Some vehicles may even be able to take advantage of finned aluminum brake drums found on the rear brakes of many modern vehicles. The lightweight drums shave precious pounds and dissipate heat better, and as a bonus, they don't rust either!

If you can't find replacement drums for your drum brake system, you may be able to swap a *larger* set of drum brakes. Full-size station wagons and police models often had larger brakes than regular sedans. The larger brakes offer increased swept area (total surface area contacted by the friction material during one revolution of the drum or disc) within the drum, which improves heat dissipation. You need to make sure that larger brake cylinders are compatible with the master cylinder's volume.

It's also possible to increase the cooling efficiency of drum brakes by directing brake cooling hoses toward the backing plates (preferably with one or two vent holes drilled in them to get the cool air inside the brakes, where it will do the most good). Corvettes of the late-1950s and early-1960s were available with a system that used large scoops attached to the backing plates, rather than hoses. Although they are more difficult to route, hoses funnel more cool air to the brakes than simple scoops.

Many high-performance vehicles had a front disc–rear drum combination during the 1960s and 1970s. Interestingly enough, rear disc brakes aren't necessary for street driving. Although rear disc systems do provide some worthwhile benefits—easier maintenance, better wet-weather operation, improved cooling, to name a few—your rear brakes provide only a fraction of your vehicle's overall braking ability, and production drum brakes provide that stopping power for less money. If your vehicle is modified for quicker acceleration, either top speed or handling performance (which includes simply replacing the tires with wider, stickier rubber), stock drum brakes may no longer provide enough stopping force.

## Disc Brake Upgrades

Of course, unless you have some reason to stick with the original drum brakes, the logical upgrade is to simply replace them with disc brakes. If disc brakes were optionally available for your vehicle, you might want to hunt down a donor vehicle that is so equipped or purchase all the parts needed to make a swap. Not all models were blessed with a disc brake option. In those cases, you can usually turn to the aftermarket. Manufacturers offer disc brake swap kits that usually include everything you need to replace your drums with discs. Depending on your vehicle, the systems may be based on production disc brake systems with specific modifications for your vehicle, or they may be completely custom systems that offer significantly higher performance than any stock systems.

If you already have disc brakes, you face similar options: Upgrade the current equipment, or replace it with high-performance or racing-type equipment.

Another Corvette brake upgrade added large scoops to funnel air to the drums, plus an impeller inside the drum to circulate the air.

A common upgrade involves replacing stock, solid-faced disc brake rotors with aftermarket cross-drilled or slotted rotors that are better able to shed heat. Some aftermarket companies also offer replacement rotors that are larger in diameter than the stock units they replace. Larger rotors increase the swept area of the disc brake assembly, which provides more material to disperse heat during use, so the rotors run cooler. Note that oversized rotors may necessitate relocating the brake caliper, or possibly even new calipers of a different design.

In addition to new rotors, you may be able to improve the appearance and performance of your brake system by upgrading the calipers to newer production units or aftermarket models. Of course, nonstock caliper designs typically have different mounting requirements, which may require you to purchase aftermarket mounting brackets or fabricate your own.

You may be able to upgrade your stock discs with newer, better production equipment. A good example of this is the installation of slightly modified 1970s GM F-body (Camaro/Firebird) front disc brakes on 1964–1972 GM A-body vehicles (Chevy Chevelle, Olds 4-4-2, Pontiac GTO, Buick GS). The F-body brakes offer larger, 11-inch rotors and heavier duty calipers than the stock components that were optionally available on the midsize models; however, note that such swaps are rarely direct bolt-on replacements. They often require modifications to spindles, control arms, steering linkage, or other parts.

If you're changing the size, compound, or even just construction (bias ply or radial, for example) of your tires, you should consider adding an adjustable brake proportioning valve. This will allow you to re-establish proper pressure distribution between the front and rear brakes.

You may also have reasons to change your master cylinder. If your vehicle has manual (nonpower-assisted) brakes, you can upgrade to power brakes, which is fairly easy, since power brakes are a common option. If you already have power brakes, but have made engine modifications that decreased engine vacuum, vacuum-operated brake boosters may not function properly. In such cases, you have two options: vacuum canisters, which essentially store vacuum, or hydraulic brake boosters, which were often used on large, heavy-duty trucks, motorhomes, and diesel-powered passenger cars.

Finally, consider upgrading how you drive. If your braking skills aren't well-suited to high-performance driving, you will warp rotors, burn up pads, and boil fluid. Under those conditions, your brakes can't possibly perform well. Nor can they endure such punishment for long. See the sidebar on high-performance braking for advice on how to use your brakes better without using them up in the process.

## Drag Racing

Two factors make drag racing particularly hard on brakes: high speeds and short deceleration zones. Fortunately, several other factors offset these challenges and minimize the need for exotic brake system components for all but the quickest cars. Brakes on a drag car are only used for a few seconds per run, and usually have ample time to cool off before the next pass.

### Proper Maintenance (Again)

First, make sure that every component of the braking system on a drag car is in perfect working order. That includes changing the fluid to minimize any moisture and air pockets within the system.

Given the significant speeds—and more important, the heat that will be generated when stopping quickly from those speeds—it's vitally important that disc brake rotors and brake drums be of sufficient thickness to prevent cracking under the harsh conditions.

### Drum/Disc Upgrades

Aftermarket rotors are available with oversized cooling vents between the rotor faces. Some rotors even offer directional cooling fins within the vents, which further maximize cooling, but such equipment is rarely necessary for

*If you are running a stock-type vacuum brake booster, but your engine doesn't make enough vacuum to create the necessary vacuum, a vacuum canister can store vacuum to keep your brakes operating properly. Competition Cams photo*

# Better Brakes 171

Another option is to replace your vacuum-powered booster with a hydro-boost unit. Late-model, heavy-duty trucks often feature them, like this one on a 1-ton Chevy used for towing.

nonprofessional levels of competition. Many cars that are slower than 10 seconds in the quarter-mile will typically do fine without the exotic parts.

Calipers, of course, are an option for upgrading drag car brakes as well. While aftermarket performance calipers can deliver superior stopping power, they are rarely a necessity.

## Pads and Shoes

Pad selection is one area where it does pay to make some improvements, and fortunately it doesn't cost much to get vastly superior brake pads and shoes. Standard organic compound pads and shoes will overheat because of the high pedal pressures, short distances, and high speeds from which drag racers do their braking after a run. Once the pads overheat, they glaze over and allow the rotor or drum to slip through their grasp. Semimetallic pads are much more suited to demanding, high-temperature environments.

When selecting a pad compound for the street, be careful that you don't select one that's too hard. This will result in poor braking under most street conditions because the pads will never heat up to the point where they are most effective.

## Power-Assist Methods

Because race engines often have radical camshafts that are designed to breathe well at high rpm, they lack sufficient vacuum to operate traditional factory-style power brake boosters.

If that describes the boat you're in (or expect to be in), you have three options: revert to manual brakes, install a vacuum reserve can, or use an alternative power brake booster.

Manual drum brakes have the beauty of simplicity on their side, but that's about it. Manual brakes typically require excessive pedal pressures to stop a vehicle, and if you're running disc brakes (especially with semimetallic pads), pedal pressures would be exorbitantly high. This is hardly desirable, and since there are ways to retain power assists, there is little reason to resort to manual brakes.

Depending on the severity of your vacuum deficiency, you may be able to simply add a vacuum reserve canister. Vacuum cans simply store a vacuum that can be used by your brake booster when necessary. The devices are available from a number of aftermarket suppliers, including most camshaft manufacturers (since it's the cam that essentially determines vacuum characteristics of your engine).

If your camshaft has lots of overlap, or you don't like the idea of using a vacuum canister, you might install a hydraulic power brake booster. Popular on heavy-duty trucks and motorhomes, hydraulic brake boosters typically operated on power steering fluid from the power steering system. (You wouldn't necessarily need to run power steering, but you would need the power steering pump, so you might as well run power steering too.) The system worked in much the same way as power steering: the pressurized power steering fluid amplifies movements of the piston in the brake system master cylinder.

### Roll Control Devices

Drag racers need to keep their vehicle steady while they do a burnout to heat the tires, and again when they're staged awaiting the green light. The best way to keep the vehicle still while allowing the rear wheels to spin freely is to install a roll control device. Sometimes called a line rock, this device allows the front brakes to remain locked up without applying any pressure to the rear wheels.

Roll control devices are electrically operated solenoid valves that trap pressure within the front brake lines. To use the system, simply step on the brake pedal firmly enough to lock the front wheels, press the roll control activation button (usually mounted on the shifter), then release the brake pedal. The front wheels will remain locked as long as the button is pressed. When you want the vehicle to move forward, just release the button. They're simple devices that work exceptionally well for drag racing.

Roll control devices really have no use on the street, though there have been some enthusiasts who have modified the systems to serve as antitheft devices. By using a button that can lock in the engaged position (a simple rocker switch will do the trick), you can engage the roll control after parking your vehicle, making it difficult to steal. Note, however, that the roll control solenoid will require power to hold the pressure, which could drain your battery if left for an extended period of time.

## Antitheft Devices

Perhaps inspired by the use of a roll control device, aftermarket brake locks perform the same function as a roll control device, but without the electronics, and they generally hold pressure to all four wheels.

As with a roll control, you step on the brake to apply pressure in the system. Then you turn a mechanical valve in the brake lock device to lock the pressure in the system. A key is required to activate and deactivate the device. The brake lock is usually installed under your vehicle's instrument panel.

## Brake System Components

Whatever upgrades you need, they will typically involve removing, replacing, or installing certain brake system components. Naturally, it makes sense for you to know what the various parts of a typical brake system are, how they work, and what upgrades are possible.

In this section, we'll go through the brake system in some detail, starting with how you interact with it—the brake pedal—and eventually winding up with the tires, where the rubber literally meets the road.

### Brake Pedal

The brake pedal is fairly simple: It's a lever that lets you create a high pressure within the brake lines from little pressure applied to the pedal. Brake pedal arms are typically steel with either a narrow pedal pad (for vehicles with a manual transmission) or a wide pedal pad (for vehicles with an automatic).

The pedal arm is suspended from the firewall on a pivot rod through a hole in the arm. Many older vehicles, notably those from General Motors, have multiple pivot rod holes, which can vary the leverage ratio so that one pedal arm assembly could be used regardless of whether a vehicle was equipped with manual or power brakes. (Less effort is required with power brakes, so those systems could use the lower pivot hole, which also decreased pedal travel.) A pushrod typically attaches to the pedal arm below the pivot point and extends into a seat in the master cylinder (or power booster assembly) through the firewall.

While it may seem that there's little that can or should be done to improve your brake pedal, there are a couple things worth considering: First, you could consider better pedals themselves. Stock pedals usually featured a rubber pedal pad. Through the years, that pad has likely become harder and more slippery, making it more likely that your foot will slide off it—which is never a good thing, since it will lengthen your stops, perhaps allowing an accident to occur. Aftermarket pedals are available that not only look great, but usually feature grippy surfaces to make sure your foot stays on the pedal when it should.

Second, take a look at how the pedal is positioned, relative to the other pedals, and get a feel for how that

# Better Brakes

Racing parts, like this US Brakes caliper and vented rotor, can make for great performance, especially if you plan to race your car. *AFCO/US Brake photo*

positioning will either aide or hinder your use of the pedal. Many Mopars have a high-riding brake pedal, which requires you to raise your leg noticeably to be able to step on the pedal. If your vehicle is like that, you may be able to modify or adjust the pedal to a more natural height. Just make sure you don't prevent the pedal from reaching full compression before hitting the floor—you still need all of its travel, you just don't want it to start quite so high.

## Master Cylinder Assembly

The master cylinder has two basic functions: First, it's a reservoir that stores fluid for the system. Second, it creates the pressure (with input from you and the brake pedal) on which the system operates.

When you step on the brake pedal, the pushrod forces a plunger into the master cylinder assembly. The movement of the plunger reduces the internal volume of the master cylinder and forces fluid out of the master cylinder into the brake lines.

Most master cylinders have two internal channels, one for the front wheels and another for the rear. There are two channels because your front brakes have different pressure requirements than your rear brakes. An added bonus is it's also a safety feature, so a leak will only affect half the brakes. During braking, weight transfers forward, causing your front brakes to provide the bulk of the stopping power. By contrast, the rear of the car becomes lighter during braking, which makes it easier for the rear wheels to lock up. Manufacturers compensate for this by reducing the size of the master cylinder's internal orifices that feed the rear brake channel. The smaller passage reduces the volume of fluid that's sent from the master cylinder into the brake line, and thus results in a lower line pressure, compared to the unrestricted front brake channel. The reduced pressure minimizes the chance that the rear wheels will lock up during braking maneuvers, which could otherwise cause the car to become uncontrollable.

The pressure difference varies depending on the car's weight and weight distribution, tire sizes, brake equipment (front discs with rear drums versus four-wheel drums versus four-wheel discs), and even the size of the braking components and specific pad selection.

## Proportioning Valves

While pressures are altered somewhat within the master cylinder, a proportioning valve is used to fine-tune the brake pressure for a specific vehicle, based on its front and rear brake system specifications, front-to-rear weight bias, wheelbase, and even wheel and tire combinations.

Manufacturers typically had a variety of proportioning valves, based on the vehicle's particular combination of standard and optional equipment. For instance, cars with manual drum brakes received one proportioning valve, but cars with front discs and rear drums used a different proportioning valve.

While you could attempt to locate and install a factory proportioning valve that may deliver the proper brake pressure balance between the front and rear halves of your brake system, it's easier to use an adjustable proportioning valve like those used in race cars. By turning a knob, you can reduce the brake pressure to the rear wheels to prevent them from locking up before the front wheels. (To prevent the front wheels from locking up, you simply reduce how much pressure you exert on the brake pedal.)

## Rotors

If your disc brake rotors are warped (the pedal pulses when you apply the brakes), or simply worn, you should consider replacing them with cross-drilled or slotted versions, or at least new stock replacements if you're on a budget. Don't waste your time or money turning warped rotors, though, because that's only a temporary fix. They'll warp again, but sooner and more severely, because they'll have less material through which to disperse and dissipate heat.

When replacing your rotors, apply some form of coating to any surfaces that will not come in contact with the brake pads. High-temperature paints will work, as will powder coating for an even more durable finish. Nyalic can also be applied if you're happy with the stock, as cast (or machined) look.

**Drums**

In the "Street Driving" section earlier in this chapter, we covered a number of possible upgrades for drum brakes, including replacing them with aluminum drums (if available), swapping them for larger drum brakes, such as those off of a police car, or swapping them for disc brakes.

Performance-wise, your rear brakes don't bring an awful lot to the party, because vehicle weight transfers forward under braking, requiring the rear brakes to operate at relatively light pressure to avoid lockup. Thus, improvements really aren't necessary.

If you do wish to improve your drum brakes, however, there are a few things you can do. First, ensure the drums are crack free, of sufficient thickness, and actually round (inside). If the drums check out, make sure they are rust free and clean, because rust, dirt, and other debris minimize the cooling efficiency of the drums. Apply a coating of some sort to prevent the drums from rusting in the future, then make sure you keep them clean.

Finally, you can consider drilling small holes in the face of the drums to both reduce their weight and improve their cooling efficiency. Be aware, however, that any holes drilled in the drums will weaken them and could make them unsafe. Holes will also allow moisture inside. If you do drill holes in the drums, take the time to bevel the edges of the holes to reduce the likelihood of cracks forming. In the end, this is a modification best handled by and reserved for professionals.

## Flex Hoses

Your vintage vehicle originally came with flexible rubber brake hoses to connect the hard steel brake lines of the chassis to the brake hardware at your wheels. The rubber hoses allow the suspension and steering to move. While the rubber lines work well enough (after all, they're still used on new vehicles today, which says something about their reliability), they aren't well-suited to high-performance applications, because they swell when subjected to high line pressures.

Replacing the rubber lines with Teflon-lined braided steel hoses will reward you with more accurate braking and a greatly reduced risk of a hose failure. Again, pay attention to DOT requirements, as many of these lines are not DOT-approved for highway use.

If you want your brake hoses to appear stock, you can camouflage the braided hoses by gutting rubber hoses and slipping them over the braided hoses, then securing them in place.

## Steel lines

OEM brake lines are generally made from steel tubing. Over time, the steel will rust, which both weakens the tubing and makes it look pretty darn ugly. That's the bad news.

The good news is that there really aren't any performance benefits to be derived from different brake lines, other than the improved appearance. Stainless-steel brake lines are available, which are much more resistant to rust and corrosion, or you can paint your brake lines to protect them against the elements. Stainless lines are difficult to work with and require special flares (and flaring tools) and need AN fittings, not regular ones.

## Calipers

Brake calipers on most vintage vehicles were generally made of cast iron, which meant that they rusted if left unprotected, as the factories typically left them. Applying a high-temperature coating to the caliper can keep it looking great for a long, long time.

When you start changing your brakes, it's likely you'll need to adjust the pressure modulation between the front and rear wheels. An adjustable pressure regulator, like this one from Kelsey-Hayes, makes adjustments a breeze.

Depending on the design of your brake calipers and the availability of aftermarket parts and services for them, you may be able to upgrade your brake calipers to increase their durability and performance.

The 1965–1982 Corvette calipers—including those used on 1967 and 1968 Camaros, Chevelles, and other GM vehicles, plus 1969 JL8-equipped Camaros, can be repaired with new caliper pistons and seals, plus the piston bores can be repaired with stainless-steel sleeves to cure pitting problems and aid in better sealing.

## Wheel Cylinders

Unfortunately, there's really not much you can do to wheel cylinders (which spread the brake shoes in drum brake systems) beyond repairing or replacing them when they wear out or simply preserving their appearance with a high-temperature coating.

## Pads and Shoes

Aftermarket pads and shoes are available with performance friction compounds to improve braking efficiency. In general, semimetallic compounds will work best, though you should base your selection on the specific combination of parts that make up your brake system, as well as your driving conditions and requirements.

In terms of preserving a reasonable finish, you should apply high-temperature coatings (paint, powder coating, and so on) to the metallic areas of the shoes or pads.

## Power Brake Boosters

Power brake boosters typically operate off the vacuum generated by your engine. However, if your engine has been modified with a lumpier performance camshaft, your engine may not generate enough vacuum to properly operate the booster, which could diminish your car's braking performance and could lead to dangerous situations.

There are a couple ways of dealing with this problem. The cheapest, easiest method is to use a vacuum reservoir can, available from companies like Moroso. These cans store vacuum, theoretically ensuring that your brake booster will then have enough to operate properly when needed. But vacuum cans have their limitations. Specifically, if you use your brakes hard, repeatedly in a short span of time, there won't be enough time to recharge the system, because the engine may not be making enough vacuum.

If that's your case, you may want to consider a fluid-based brake booster instead, such as those employed on many heavy-duty pickup trucks by the manufacturers. These systems use an engine-driven pulley to pump fluid through a special booster system to augment pressure in the system. You may be able to source one from a junkyard or just order a new one from your dealer.

It's also possible to install an electric vacuum pump to power your brake booster. Or you could simply choose to switch to manual brakes, as are used on most race vehicles because of simplicity and reliability.

Whether you run discs or drums, you need performance brake pads and shoes. Semi-metallic linings stand up to heat better than organic linings so your brakes won't fade as much under heavy use. *Performance Friction photo*

## Chapter 11
# Electrical System

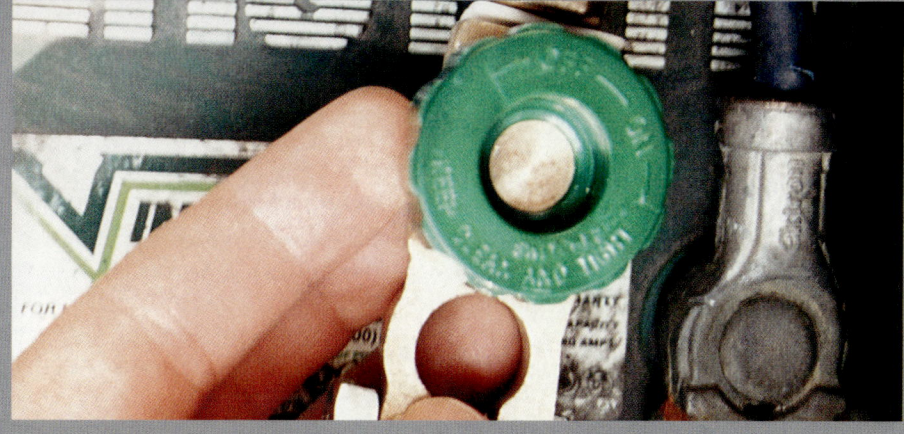

**F**ew things are as frustrating as electrical gremlins in your muscle car. The additional load created by high-powered stereos and other electronics can wreak havoc on an already marginal electrical system. Planning ahead here can save you many headaches in the future.

Your vehicle's electrical system supplies the electricity for your engine's ignition system, lights, windshield wipers, audio system, and a number of other accessories.

While factory electrical systems were generally adequate for low-performance use, under high-rpm, high-performance driving conditions your stock electrical system may not be adequate. It will also be heavily taxed if you have installed power-hungry equipment.

In addition to improving your vehicle's ability to generate and distribute electricity, various electrical components and accessories on vintage vehicles can be improved to provide better performance and a longer service life.

The information that follows steps through the various parts of your car's or truck's electrical system, describing what they do and methods of enhancing them. As with the other chapters of this book, it is unlikely that anyone will employ each and every one of these upgrades, because certain changes only make sense for certain situations. But read through the various sections and determine whether they make sense for your vehicle.

## Battery

Your vehicle's electrical system starts with the same thing that starts your vehicle—its battery.

Batteries have the seemingly simple job of storing enough electricity to start your vehicle when it's not running. While that may sound simple, it's actually a demanding job. Not only does the battery have to supply power to the starter motor, but it must also power the ignition system. On high-compression, high-performance engines, both of these tasks can be tough on a battery, because the high compression requires a lot of torque to crank the engine over, as well as additional ignition power to ignite and completely burn the air/fuel mixture in the cylinders.

The energy stored in a battery is provided by the alternator (or generator) while the engine is running, and it's the alternator (or generator) that provides the electricity that your vehicle needs while it's running.

The power that a battery can store is rated in Cold Cranking Amps (CCA), and better 12-volt batteries will have 600 CCA or more. Note that as batteries get cold, the electrons inside them slow down, which effectively diminishes the battery's power. Hence the reason for a cold cranking rating, indicating the power it delivers in cold weather. Cold weather delivers a double whammy to a battery, because not only is it not putting out its peak power, but the engine requires additional torque to start, because the oil is thick, which resists cranking.

There's really nothing you can do to improve the battery that you have beyond basic maintenance, and if you need a stock-appearing battery, you're stuck with the reproduction batteries available from restoration parts suppliers.

If you're willing to forsake an original appearance in favor of better performance, you can upgrade to a modern battery that will provide more cranking power in a smaller, lighter weight package.

When it comes to your car's electrical system, it's just not any good without some electricity. Today's batteries produce far more cold-cranking amps than original equipment batteries, which makes for faster cranking speeds when starting. *Optima Batteries photo*

# Electrical System    179

For high-rpm, high-performance engines, the factory often fitted an alternator with an oversize underdrive pulley to slow the alternator speed. This move saved the alternator bearings plus prevented the alternator from making too much electricity, which could burn out wiring or electronics equipment.

If you need the ultimate in cranking power, you could take a hint from heavy-duty truck electrical systems and hook up two batteries to provide twice the cranking amps. If doing so, you must hook the batteries up in parallel to avoid overloading your electrical devices. If connected in series, you would supply 25.2 volts to your starter and other equipment, which would quickly burn out nearly everything in the electrical system—wires, lights, electrical components, everything.

Batteries are heavy, so it's fortunate that two of them are rarely needed (they are nice on tow vehicles, motor homes, or if you live in extremely cold climates).

Of course, for racers, even a single battery is too much weight, especially to be mounted on the front end of a vehicle. But the weight of the battery can be put to good use, if it is relocated to the trunk and positioned over or behind the right rear wheel. Aftermarket companies like Moroso Performance have the necessary extra-long, heavy-gauge cabling for the job. Most racers mount the battery in a marine-style battery case, bolted to the trunk floor.

A final modification for the battery is to install a quick-disconnect battery terminal clamp. Such a clamp is useful when storing a vehicle, because it provides a simple way of preventing continually running accessories like clocks or any minor shorts from draining the battery. Some systems make for a good, low-cost antitheft device, because you can remove the knob that normally completes the circuit, thus preventing the vehicle from starting. Some racing classes may also require an externally accessible battery cut-off switch as well.

## Alternators and Generators

As we covered in the battery section earlier, your vehicle's alternator or generator provides both the energy your vehicle needs to operate, as well as the electricity to recharge your battery.

Generators were common during the 1950s and early 1960s, when alternators became popular because of their smaller size, lighter weight, and higher efficiency.

Because stock electrical systems and components were fairly basic during the 1950s through the 1970s, factory alternators and generators were rather low powered. Most created between 60 and 80 amps and about 14.2 volts at a 2,000-rpm engine speed. The shaft speed of the alternator (or generator) is determined by the pulley system that drives it. Stock pulleys spin the alternator faster than the crankshaft to ensure the alternator or generator produces sufficient power, even at idle. If your vehicle is operated at sustained high engine speeds, however, the alternator's bearings may overheat. In such cases, underdrive pulleys can slow the shaft speed of the alternator. This can be accomplished with either a smaller crankshaft pulley, a larger alternator pulley, or both.

Aftermarket alternators are available that produce higher amperage, which can be handy if you load up your car with power-robbing accessories like a killer audio system, power windows and door locks, auxiliary lights and more. MSD's Advanced Power System alternator is built to cope with high-rpm use and has a super-flexible mounting system. *MSD Ignition photo*

While underdrive pulleys are especially popular modifications for late-model vehicles, slowing the alternator can result in insufficient power at idle or slow cruising speeds. This may result in a gradual discharge of your battery, because the system may not be able to replace the battery power used to start the vehicle. Most alternators need to produce between 14 and 15 volts of electricity to provide a reliable electrical system operation—12 to 13 volts to operate your vehicle on, plus a couple of volts to recharge your battery. This is especially important if the driving you do consists of mostly short trips at low engine speeds (such as around-town driving).

A great upgrade is to replace an older alternator or generator with a modern unit that creates more amperage, which is necessary to run all the electronic gear that modern vehicles have. Trucks tend to have the strongest alternators and typically put out 100 amps or more, a significant improvement over a stock unit. Some modern alternators use different mounting systems than vintage alternators, so you may need to make or modify brackets.

## Wiring Harness

Your alternator or generator makes the electricity, but the job of getting that power to the components is up to the wiring harness (or harnesses).

There's nothing inherently wrong with original factory wiring harnesses, other than they're about 30 years old. Age can be a problem because wires break down over time, increasing resistance. Eventually, the resistance in the wire will degrade the performance of the device it's connected to.

Wire insulation becomes brittle with age and can crack and split, which allows electricity to jump to a ground source. Old wire insulation can also lead to cross-talk between two or more wires in a harness, inducing a charge into a wire that shouldn't have one. This leads to elusive and odd electrical problems.

It makes sense to either replace your wiring harness (reproduction harnesses are readily available), or rebuild it yourself, one wire at a time. A third option is available. Wiring kits and component panels are very common in the street rod market. They often have extra circuits for late-model accessories such as EFI, power accessories, AC, and stereos and are easy to install.

Original starters weren't well-suited for turning over mega-inch, high-compression engines, so starting was often a lackadaisical affair. High-torque aftermarket starters, like this one from MSD, will spin your engine faster for quicker starts and won't suffer from the heat like OEM starters. *MSD Ignition photo*

Installing a reproduction harness is a considerably easier move; simply buy it, and swap it for the old one. However, rebuilding your old harness allows you to improve it by upgrading the original factory connectors with late-model-style WeatherPac connectors that seal out moisture and contaminants for a more reliable connection.

When rebuilding your harness, solder the wires to the connectors to ensure an efficient and reliable connection, then protect those connections with a waterproof insulation or electrical tape.

## Lighting System

Perhaps the most visible portion of your electrical system is your vehicle's lighting system, including its headlights, taillights, marker lights, turn signal indicator lamps, and interior, underhood, and trunk lighting. A variety of improvements can be made to your lighting system that will increase your safety and even improve your performance under certain driving conditions.

## General Maintenance

The first step to take is to ensure that your lighting system is in perfect health. Specifically, pay attention to the wires that power your lights, as well as to the connectors at the lamps themselves.

Muscle car lighting is rarely described as anything more than "adequate." Even cars like this Shelby Mustang, which featured Shelby-installed driving lights, were only marginal for night-driving duty.

We've already covered wires, under the "Wiring Harness" section, so we'll dispense with a repetitive discussion here. As for the connectors, three decades is a long time for corrosion to build up, which minimizes current flow through the connector and can result in dim illumination. Corrosion is especially troublesome on ground connections, which are often the fault of dim headlamps on older vehicles.

Once your system is in tip-top condition, you can begin making modifications to improve it.

## Optional Lighting Equipment

One category of improvements—upgrading to optional hidden headlamps—actually falls under the heading of "Body Modifications" and is discussed in Chapter 2. Camaros, GTOs, Chargers, Cougars, and a handful of other vehicles had hide-away headlamps as an option during the 1960s. Although the systems were complex and troublesome, they were also quite attractive.

Besides hidden headlamps, there's other optional lighting to consider for your high-performance restoration. Some vehicles, like the Camaro, featured alternate mounting locations for parking lamps, turn signals, and backup lamps, depending on the options ordered. Chrysler was particularly fond of auxiliary turn signal indicators mounted in the driver's line of sight, hence the small indicators mounted atop the fenders or in hood scoops on many models.

Last, some vehicles—Chevy's 1969 Camaro comes to mind—used headlamp washer systems that sprayed windshield washer fluid from nozzles aimed at the headlamps. The systems weren't particularly effective, but they were an interesting attempt to improve the performance of the car's lighting. Headlamp washers are also available on many modern-day vehicles, and they're simple systems, requiring only a windshield washer pump motor, a button to activate it, some rubber hose, and nozzles.

## Replacement Headlamps

Although vintage headlamp units were state of the art for their day, they literally don't hold a candle (power) to today's standard—halogen headlamps.

Halogen headlamps burn brighter and whiter to provide more light. This allows you to see farther down the roads and to see road hazards sooner and take steps to avoid them without creating a risky situation. Halogen headlamps are a direct plug-in replacement for traditional tungsten headlamps.

But halogen headlamps aren't the leading edge of automotive headlamp

Guide T3 bulbs were common on muscle cars, but today's bulbs are brighter, have a better light pattern, and last longer.

technology. That spot belongs to halon gas headlamps, which burn even brighter and whiter, more closely duplicating daylight. Again, the advantage is earlier warning of possible hazards, and these units are direct replacements.

## Driving Lights

Another way to increase your chances of seeing road hazards before it's too late is to add auxiliary driving lights. Driving lights are hardly a new idea and may be hard to conceal, depending on the design of your vehicle's front end. The basic premise is simple: more lights mean more light on the road and that means better visibility.

## Fog Lights

Fog lights offer a similar advantage to driving lights but are only intended for use in foggy weather and must be properly mounted to be effective. The trick to fog lights is to have them mounted as low as possible to shine beneath any ground fog. Fog lights, even those with clear lenses, should not be mistaken for or treated as driving lights. While driving lights project a long, narrow beam of light, fog lights project a short, diffused beam intended only to illuminate a short distance ahead of the vehicle. Whether you're using fog lights or not, you should always drive with caution, especially in foggy weather when reduced speed (or not driving at all) is your best defense.

## Daytime Running Lamps

Many modern vehicles—including all new GM passenger vehicles—use Daytime Running Lamps (DRLs) not to light their way but to increase the likelihood of other drivers seeing the car with the DRLs.

There are two methods of implementing DRLs in a vehicle: by running your regular headlamps at low power or by running parking lamps at a higher intensity than normal. The former method is more commonly used to upgrade older vehicles, and kits are available at many auto parts stores or GM parts departments to add DRL abilities to almost any vehicle. Running the headlamps at low power has very little effect on the life span of the headlamps. Unless your vehicle uses hidden headlamps, they can be an excellent, easy safety upgrade. Vehicles with hidden headlamps can use a high-intensity parking lamp system, which is similar to having your front turn signals on continually.

## Third Brake Lights

While DRLs may improve your vehicle's visibility from the front, that's not where most people get hit. They get hit from behind, when people fail to notice that the vehicle ahead of them (you) is stopping.

Third brake lights, which are technically known as

Quality auxiliary fog or driving lights can really make a difference when cruising in adverse conditions. This yellow-tinted lamp is a replacement for high-beam units in four-lamp vehicles, but most auxiliary lights can be custom mounted in unobtrusive ways. *Cibie USA photo*

# Electrical System

Installation of an aftermarket security system is a wise investment to prevent your high-performance machine from becoming someone else's high-performance machine. *Electric Life photo*

Center, High-Mounted Stop Lamps, are an effective means of increasing other drivers' awareness of your braking. Aftermarket kits are available to add a third brake light to any vehicle not originally equipped with one. In addition, some aftermarket rear deck lid spoilers offer an integral third brake light, which often makes for a cleaner-looking installation, so long as the wing looks appropriate on your vehicle.

## Power Accessories

As far back as the 1950s, power accessories were beginning to become popular options on vehicles. By the 1960s, power windows were available on nearly any American model car.

Today, there are an abundance of power accessories that you can retrofit to your vehicle to increase convenience and safety.

## Power Windows

Power windows were one of the first power accessories to be available on cars.

But early systems were somewhat crude, rather slow, and proved to be trouble prone. Modern power windows, by comparison, are speedy and reliable. Unfortunately, it can be difficult to adapt modern power window regulators and other parts to your vintage vehicle.

It is possible to install original systems that have been rebuilt for higher reliability, however. Such systems are available for some models through restoration parts companies.

An alternative is to adapt a power window kit intended for use in street rods to your vehicle. Such kits are designed for a wide variety of vehicles.

Or save yourself the hassle and buy one of the many aftermarket power window kits available for a broad range of classic cars and trucks.

## Power Mirrors

Power mirrors are another great convenience, allowing for quick, precise adjustment of either a driver or passenger-side mirror. Older remote mirrors relied upon cables and linkages to tilt and swivel the mirror glass, but modern systems use electric motors, and some even incorporate a heating mechanism to keep the glass from fogging or icing up in cold weather.

The only reasonable method of installing power mirrors is to adapt a late-model mirror assembly to a vintage vehicle. Fortunately, given the wide assortment of power mirror designs used on late-model vehicles, finding a mirror (or set of mirrors) to install on your vehicle shouldn't be exceptionally difficult, and installation should prove quite simple, since only small wires need enter the passenger compartment.

## Power Door Locks

The key advantage of power door locks is the ability to unlock a passenger door without having to lean and stretch across a vehicle. Power door locks take on even greater importance in four-door vehicles since all doors can be unlocked or

If you're having bodywork done, you may want to consider cleaning up your exterior by installing a "shaved door handle" system, which basically consists of remote-activated actuators to release the door latch mechanism plus small springs to gently pop the door open. *Electric Life photo*

locked with a single button, without bending and contorting to reach the door lock buttons.

While it is possible to adapt late-model power door lock mechanisms to work in vintage vehicles, the street rod industry makes universal kits.

## Rear Window Defoggers

Another convenient feature that was rarely installed on vintage vehicles is a rear window defogger.

Some vintage vehicles were available with crude rear window defoggers that used blower motors to direct warm air from inside the vehicle at the inside of the rear window. These systems were generally slow and noisy.

Modern-style rear window defoggers rely on thin wires attached to the glass. When a low voltage is applied to the wires, they heat and warm the glass, which melts ice and snow and, yes, defogs the windows.

Some aftermarket kits are available to add a modern-style system to your vehicle; however, the aftermarket kits rarely look stock, so keep that in mind before installing one on your vintage car or truck.

## Modern Amenities

The whole point of high-performance restorations is to apply modern technologies to older vehicles to improve their performance, and one measure of performance is a vehicle's convenience.

Today there are a number of ways to improve the convenience of your vintage vehicle, most of which are readily adaptable to any vehicle.

If you equip your vehicle with power door locks, you can then consider adding a keyless entry system that allows you to unlock your vehicle's doors by remote control.

Keyless entry systems are fast becoming one of the most popular late-model options, and aftermarket systems are available to add the extremely convenient feature to almost any vehicle

Power windows weren't widely available in the 1960s and 1970s, but thanks to modern-day technology, you can add the convenience to nearly any vehicle. *Electric Life photo*

equipped with power door locks or power windows.

Along the same lines are remote starter systems, which allow you to start your vehicle's engine without getting into the car. The systems work best on vehicles equipped with electronic fuel injection (since those systems do not require any movement of the throttle pedal to start the car), but could be used on vehicles that start reliably.

Antitheft systems are another popular upgrade. Many different antitheft alarm

In many racing classes, a master disconnect switch is required equipment, and its placement may be dictated by sanctioning body rules. *AFCO photo*

# Electrical System

Depending on what electrical equipment you add to your vehicle, you may find yourself in need of high-quality toggle switches. *MSD Ignition photo*

systems can be fitted to any car or truck, plus you may wish to consider additional antitheft systems, such as Jacob's Electronics' Stop Action anti-carjacking system. The system is elegantly simple: it provides a stock-looking, floor-mounted headlamp dimmer–style switch that the driver can inconspicuously activate if confronted by a car jacker. After pressing the switch, the driver can turn over the vehicle to the car jacker; however, the vehicle will only run for approximately one minute, before losing power and stalling. The system prevents the engine from being restarted for a random period of time of several minutes. During this time, the driver can flee, then police can retrieve the vehicle not far from where the carjacking took place.

A third type of antitheft system doesn't do anything to prevent a vehicle from being stolen but does do a lot to help authorities locate it afterward. The LoJack system, and others like it, rely on a small radio transmitter that is easily hidden in a secure location on a vehicle. The transmitter broadcasts a signal to LoJack locator systems, which the company often provides to police departments for free. When a vehicle is stolen, the driver contacts LoJack, which sends a radio signal to the vehicle to activate its homing beacon. Police equipped with the locator systems then follow the beacon to the car. The system has been proven accurate to within a few hundred feet and has led to the breakup of numerous car-theft rings.

Two additional modern conveniences that more and more enthusiasts are finding space—and electricity—for in their vehicles are cellular phones and radar detectors. Thankfully, these devices are simple to install and remove, given that they typically just plug into a cigarette lighter socket. More permanent installations can be hard-wired to the fuse panel, and in the case of remote-mount radar detector systems, can be concealed in anything from ash trays, to glove boxes, to console storage compartments.

**Right:** A battery quick-disconnect can be handy if you store your car for extended periods of time, because it provides for a tools-free battery cutoff. They're even helpful as an extra antitheft measure.

**Far right:** New sending units should be a part of any electrical system overhaul. *AFCO photo*

# Appendix: Sources for Parts, Services, and Supplies

**Body**

Dakota Digital
www.dakotadigital.com
*Instrumentation, antennas, power window systems.*

National Parts Depot
www.nationalpartsdepot.com
*Restoration parts, including seat covers, seat components, headliners, door panels, carpets, trim pieces, etc.*

Original Parts Group
www.originalpartsgroup.com
*Restoration parts, including seat covers, seat components, headliners, door panels, carpets, trim pieces, etc.*

The Paddock
www.paddockparts.com
*Restoration parts, including seat covers, seat components, headliners, door panels, carpets, trim pieces, etc.*

Phoenix Graphics
www.musclecardecals.com
*Decal and stripe kits, stencil kits, etc.*

Sherman & Associates
www.shermanparts.com
*Replacement and performance body panels.*

Stencils & Stripes
www.stencilsandstripes.com
*Decal and stripe kits, stencil kits, etc.*

Unlimited Products
www.unlimitedproducts.com
*Fiberglass body panels and trim components.*

U.S. Body Source
www.usbodysource.com
*Fiberglass body panels and trim components.*

Year One
www.yearone.com
*Restoration parts, including seat covers, seat components, headliners, door panels, carpets, trim pieces, etc.*

**Electrical**

Apple Computer
www.apple.com
*MP3 players.*

Audiovox
www.audiovox.com
*Audio and video systems.*

Blaupunkt
www.blaupunkt.com
*Audio equipment.*

Bose
www.bose.com
*Audio equipment.*

Boston Acoustics
www.bostonacoustics.com
*Audio equipment.*

Jensen
www.audiovox.com
*Audio systems.*

Kenwood
www.kenwood.com
*Audio systems.*

Optima Batteries
www.optimabatteries.com
*Batteries.*

**Engine**

ACCEL
www.accel-ignition.com
*Ignition systems.*

Automotive Racing Products (ARP)
www.arp-bolts.com
*Fasteners.*

Art Carr Performance Parts
www.artcarr.com
*Transmissions and components.*

B&M Racing and Performance Products
www.bmracing.com
*Transmissions and components.*

Be Cool Radiators
www.becool.com
*Radiators and cooling systems.*

Callies
www.callies.com
*Engine blocks, main caps, crankshafts, connecting rods, pistons, etc.*

Crane Cams
www.cranecams.com
*Camshafts and valvetrain components.*

Comp Cams
www.compcams.com
*Camshafts and valvetrain components.*

Dynomax Performance Exhaust
www.dynomax.com
*Exhaust systems.*

Eagle Specialty Products
www.eaglespecialtyproducts.com
*Crankshafts, connecting rods.*

Edelbrock
www.edelbrock.com
*Engine assemblies, induction systems, suspension systems.*

Fel-Pro Gaskets
www.federal-mogul.com/felpro
*Gaskets.*

Flex-a-lite
www.flex-a-lite.com
*Cooling system components including fans and radiators.*

Flowmaster
www.flowmastermufflers.com
*Exhaust systems.*

Fluidampr
www.fluidampr.com
*High performance harmonic vibration dampers.*

Ford Motorsports
www.fordracingparts.com

GM Performance Parts
www.gmgoodwrench.com

Griffin Aluminum Racing Radiators
www.griffinradiator.com
*High performance radiators.*

Hedman Hedders
www.hedman.com
*Exhaust systems.*

Holley Performance
www.holley.com
*Induction systems.*

Hooker Headers
www.holley.com
*Exhaust systems.*

Hurst Shifters
www.hurst-shifters.com
*Shifters, roll-control systems.*

Lunati
www.holley.com
*Crankshafts, camshafts, and valvetrain components.*

Magna Flow Performance Exhaust
www.magnaflow.com
*Exhaust systems.*

Mallory
www.malloryperformance.com
*Ignition systems.*

Milodon
www.milodon.com
*Oil system components, cooling system components, timing chain and gear drives, engine assembly tools.*

Mopar
www.mopar.com
*Chrysler engines, engine components, drivetrain components.*

Moroso
www.moroso.com
*Various racing components.*

Mr. Gasket
www.mrgasket.com
*Powertrain accessories and racing equipment.*

MSD Ignition
www.msdignition.com
*Ignition systems.*

Performance Automotive Warehouse
www.pawengineparts.com
*Engine and drivetrain parts, engine tools, shop equipment, etc.*

Redline Synthetic Oil
www.redlineoil.com

Royal Purple Synthetic Oil
www.royalpurple.com
*Lubricants.*

Summit Racing Equipment
www.summitracing.com
*Engine and drivetrain parts, engine tools, shop equipment, etc.*

TCI Transmissions
www.tciauto.com
*Transmissions, shifters, harmonic dampers, and related components.*

Weiand
www.weiand.com
*Intake manifolds and superchargers.*

**Interior**
Audiovox
www.audiovox.com
*Audio and video systems.*

AutoMeter
www.autometer.com
*Instruments and gauges.*

Corbeau
www.corbeau.com
*High performance seats.*

Custom Autosound
www.customautosound.com
*Audio systems for vintage vehicles.*

Défi
www.defi-shop.com
*Heads-up display systems.*

Dynamat
www.dynamat.com
*Sound deadener.*

Ididit
www.ididit.com
*Steering columns.*

Momo
www.momo.com
*Wheels, steering wheels, high-performance seats, shift knobs, foot pedals, harnesses, etc.*

Original Parts Group
www.originalpartsgroup.com
*Restoration parts, including seat covers, seat components, headliners, door panels, carpets, trim pieces, etc.*

The Paddock
www.paddockparts.com
*Restoration parts, including seat covers, seat components, headliners, door panels, carpets, trim pieces, etc.*

Recaro
www.recaro.com
*High performance seats.*

Sparco
www.sparcousa.com
*High performance seats.*

SportVue
www.sportvue.com
*Heads-up display systems.*

Stewart Warner Performance
www.stewartwarner.com
*Instruments and gauges.*

Vintage Air
www.vintageair.com
*Air conditioning systems.*

Year One
www.yearone.com
*Restoration parts, including seat covers, seat components, headliners, door panels, carpets, trim pieces, etc.*

**Suspension, Wheels & Tires**
AFCO
www.afcoracing.com
*Suspension, brakes, and drivetrain components.*

Air Ride Technologies
www.ridetech.com
*High-performance suspension systems.*

American Racing Equipment
www.americanracing.com
*High-performance wheels.*

Baer Brakes
www.baer.com
*Brake systems.*

Coker Tire
www.coker.com
*Reproduction tires.*

Edelbrock
www.edelbrock.com
*Engines, engine components, suspension systems.*

H.O. Racing
www.horacing.com
*Pontiac suspension systems and components.*

Hotchkis Performance
www.hotchkisperformance.com
*Suspension parts.*

Intro Wheels
www.introwheels.com
*High performance wheels.*

Koni Shocks
www.koni.com
*Shock absorbers.*

KYB Shocks & Struts
www.kybshocks.com
*Shock absorbers.*

Tokico Shocks
www.tokicogasshocks.com
*Shock absorbers.*

Wheel Vintiques
www.wheelvintiques.com
*Wheels.*

**Supplies & Tools**
Eastwood Company
www.eastwoodco.com
*Media blasting equipment, welding equipment, paints, coatings, and other equipment and supplies.*

Performance Automotive Warehouse
www.pawengineparts.com
*Engine and drivetrain parts, engine tools, shop equipment, etc.*

Summit Racing Equipment
www.summitracing.com
*Engine and drivetrain parts, engine tools, shop equipment, etc.*

**Resources**
eBay
www.ebay.com
*Online auction service.*

Hemmings Motor News
www.hemmings.com
*Collector car marketplace.*

# Cost Estimate Worksheet

| Vehicle Year, Make, Model | | | | | |
|---|---|---|---|---|---|
| **Exterior** | Time | Parts (P) | Shipping (S) | Labor (L) | Total (P+S+L) |
| • Body panels | ____ hrs | $ ____ | $ ____ | $ ____ | $ ____ |
| • Paint | ____ | ____ | ____ | ____ | ____ |
| • Vinyl/Convertible Top | ____ | ____ | ____ | ____ | ____ |
| • Trim/Mouldings | ____ | ____ | ____ | ____ | ____ |
| • Emblems/Decals | ____ | ____ | ____ | ____ | ____ |
| • Bumpers | ____ | ____ | ____ | ____ | ____ |
| • Lamps/Lenses | ____ | ____ | ____ | ____ | ____ |
| • Misc. (Handles, mirrors, etc.) | ____ | ____ | ____ | ____ | ____ |
| **Chassis, Suspension, Steering & Brakes** | | | | | |
| • Frame/Subframe | ____ | ____ | ____ | ____ | ____ |
| • Rear underbody | ____ | ____ | ____ | ____ | ____ |
| • Suspension (Springs, shocks, etc.) | ____ | ____ | ____ | ____ | ____ |
| • Steering (Box, linkages, etc.) | ____ | ____ | ____ | ____ | ____ |
| • Brakes (incl. brake lines) | ____ | ____ | ____ | ____ | ____ |
| • Exhaust System | ____ | ____ | ____ | ____ | ____ |
| • Fuel System (incl. tank & lines) | ____ | ____ | ____ | ____ | ____ |
| • Wheels/Wheelcovers/Tires | ____ | ____ | ____ | ____ | ____ |
| • Misc. (Bushings, body mounts, etc.) | ____ | ____ | ____ | ____ | ____ |
| **Engine, Drivetrain & Underhood** | | | | | |
| • Engine (Mechanical) | ____ | ____ | ____ | ____ | ____ |
| • Engine (Cosmetic) | ____ | ____ | ____ | ____ | ____ |
| • Transmission | ____ | ____ | ____ | ____ | ____ |
| • Rear Axle Assembly | ____ | ____ | ____ | ____ | ____ |
| • Engine Cooling System | ____ | ____ | ____ | ____ | ____ |
| • Charging System (Alternator) | ____ | ____ | ____ | ____ | ____ |
| • Windshield Washer/Wiper System | ____ | ____ | ____ | ____ | ____ |
| • Engine Wiring Harness(es) | ____ | ____ | ____ | ____ | ____ |
| • Air Conditioning System | ____ | ____ | ____ | ____ | ____ |
| • Hoses (Fuel, Radiator, Vacuum, etc.) | ____ | ____ | ____ | ____ | ____ |
| • Misc. (Decals, fasteners, etc.) | ____ | ____ | ____ | ____ | ____ |

# Cost Estimate Worksheet

**Electrical & Vacuum Systems**
- Front Wiring Harness(es)
- Instrument Panel Harness(es)
- Passenger Compartment Harness(es)
- Console Harness(es)
- Rear Harness(es)
- Instrument Cluster/Gauges
- Radio, Speakers & Tape Deck
- Power Windows
- Power Top (Convertible)
- Heating, Ventilation & A/C
- Misc. (Battery, misc. switches, etc.)

**Interior & Trunk**
- Seats (Upholstery, trim & tracks)
- Headliner & Package Tray
- Carpet & Floormats
- Door Panels
- Console
- Shifter
- Steering Column & Wheel
- Windows, Glass & Mirrors
- Trim (Handles, knobs, etc.)
- Seals/Weatherstripping
- Trunk Floor
- Jacking Equipment
- Misc. (Seat belts, pedals, etc.)

**Other**
- 
- 
- 
- 

|  | Time | Parts | Shipping | Labor | Total |
|---|---|---|---|---|---|
| Totals | | | | | |
| Estimate Multiplier | x 3 | x 2 | x 2 | x 2 | x 2 |
| Estimate | hrs | $ | $ | $ | $ |

# Index

## A

Air cleaner housings, 90–92
  filtration systems, 91–92
Air conditioning system, 49
Air dams, 35
Air filters, 91–92
Alternators, 179–180
Antenna, 37
Antifreeze, 110–111
Antitheft systems, 184–185
Athanasiades, Len, 6, 7
Audio equipment, 47–49
Automatic transmission, 134–135
  engine-swapping pitfalls, 60
Axles, 139

## B

Battery, 178–179
Bearings, main, rod and cam, 66–67
  function of, 66
  machining, 66–67
  recommended modifications, 72
  selecting, 66
Body building, 24–37
  accessory body components, 34
  base coat/clear coat systems, 26–27
  body shells, 33–34
  brake ducts and scoops, 35
  choosing body/paint shop, 30
  chrome, 28
  color, 27–28
  enamels, 25
  flat look, 30–31
  good, cheap paint job, 28
  Hood tachs, 35
  lacquers, 24–25
  monochromatic, 29–30
  paint, 24
  paint schemes, 28
  primers, 25–26
  replacement panels, 32–33
  roof modifications, 35–36
  spoilers and air dams, 34–35
  super stripes, 29
  trim, 31–32, 37
  two-tone paint, 29
  waterborne paints, 25
  window upgrades, 36–37
Body panels, 32–33
Body shells, 33–34
Bolts, long block assembly, 70–71
Brake duct, 35
Brake lights, 182–183
Brakes, 164–175
  antitheft devices, 172
  basics of brake system and problems of, 165–167
  brake pads and shoes, 169
  brake pedal, 172–173
  calipers, 174–175
  disc brake upgrade, 169–170, 170–171
  drag racing upgrades, 170–172
  drum brakes, 164–165
  drum brake upgrade, 169, 170–171, 174
  flex hoses, 174
  master cylinder assembly, 173
  moisture in system, 166
  pads and shoes, 171, 175
  power-assist methods, 171
  power boosters, 175
  proper maintenance, 168–169, 170
  proportioning valves, 173
  roll control devices, 172
  rotors, 173–174
  show car upgrades, 167–168
  steel line, 174
  street driving upgrades, 168–170
  trouble with older brakes, 164–165
  wheel cylinders, 175
Budget. See Financial considerations
Bumpers, 34
Bushings
  for drag racing, 154
  for high-performance street driving, 149–150

## C

Cam bearings, 66–67, 72
Cam drive sets, 81–82
Camshaft, 77–79
  function of, 55, 77
  recommendations, 78–79
  roller vs. flat-lifter, 78
Carburetion system, 94–101
  aftermarket systems, 98–99
  forced induction, 101
  fuel-injection systems, 99–100
  multipoint fuel injection (MPFI), 100–101
  size of, 95
  stock replacements, 97–98
  throttle-body injection (TBI) systems, 100
  upgrades and modifications, 95–97
Carpets, 44
Catalytic converter, 117–118
Cat-back exhaust pipe/muffler systems, 118
Chassis structure, 144–146
  convertible braces and frames, 145–146
  crossmembers, 146
  Le Mans brace, 145
  reinforcement plates, 146
  subframe connectors, 145
  types of, 144
Chrome, 28
Cold-air induction system, 88–89
Combustion chamber
  cylinder head material, 76
  cylinder head recommendation, 76–77
Connecting rods, 61–63
  function of, 61–63
  inspecting, 62–63
  recommended modifications, 71–72
  selecting, 61–62
Consoles, 46
Control arm
  for drag racing, 154–155
  for high-performance street driving, 150
Convertible braces and frames, 145–146
Cooling system, 108–114
  coolant, 110–111
  fans, 111
  fuel system, 114
  function of, 108
  hoses, 109–110
  induction system, 113–114
  oil system, 112–113
  power steering pump, 114
  radiator, 109
  secondary cooling system, 111–114
  starter, 113–114
  thermostat, 109
  water pump, 108–109
Crankshaft
  function of, 59
  recommended modifications, 71
  selecting, 59, 61
  terminology for, 81
  types of, 59
Crankshaft scrapers, 68
Crate motors, 63
Crossmembers, 146
Cylinder case. See Engine block
Cylinder heads, 115
  function of, 55
  material for, 76
  recommended modifications, 73, 76–77

## D

Dash pads, 44
Daytime running lamps, 182
DexCool, 110–111
Distributors, 102
Door locks, power, 183–184
Door panels, 43
Driveshafts
  length of, and engine-swapping pitfalls, 60
  Le Mans brace, 145
  safety loop, 137
  upgrading, 136–137
Drivetrain, 130–141
  automatic transmission, 134–135
  axles, 139
  close ratio vs. wide ratio, 133
  clutches, flywheels and bell housing, 133–134
  driveshaft, 136–137
  gearing and performance, 130–131
  limited-slip units, 138–139
  manual transmission, 131–133
  miscellaneous upgrades, 139–141
  rear-axle assemblies, 137–138
  torque converters and flex plates, 135–136
  toughest drivetrain, 131
Driving lights, 182
Drum brakes, 164–165

## E

Electrical system, 178–185
  alternators and generators, 179–180
  antitheft systems, 184–185
  battery, 178–179
  lighting system, 180–183
  modern amenities, 184–185
  power accessories, 183–184
  rear window defoggers, 184
  wiring harness, 180
Emblems, 31–32, 37
Enamels, 25
Engine block, 56–59
  aftermarket blocks, 56, 58
  inspecting, 56–57
  recommendations, 57–59
  recommended modifications, 71
  selecting, 56–57
  stock production block, 57–58
  two bolts vs. four, 57
  used blocks, 56
Engine mounts
  engine-swapping pitfalls, 60
Exhaust manifold/headers, 115–117
Exhaust ports
  recommended modifications, 73–74
Exhaust system, 114–119
  catalytic converter, 117–118
  cat-back exhaust pipe/muffler systems, 118
  cylinder head, 115
  exhaust manifold/headers, 115–117
  function of, 114

# Index

improvements, 115
muffler, 118
oxygen sensors, 117
primary exhaust (header) pipes, 117
recommendations for, 119
stock systems, 114-115

## F
Fan, 111
Filters, air, 91-92
Filtration systems, 91-92
Financial considerations
  budgeting long block assembly restoration, 54-55
  cost estimate worksheets, 188-189
  determining budget, 17-19
  planning restoration, 17-19
Flexplates, 135-136
Fog lights, 182
Forced induction
  carburetion system, 101
Fuel system, 92-94
  fuel filters, 93-94
  as secondary cooling system, 114

## G
Gauges, 46-47
Generators, 179-180

## H
Header pipes, 117
Headlamps, 181-182
Headliner, 43-44
Heating system, 49
High-performance restoration
  cardinal sin of, 9
  characteristics of, 6-7
  planning restoration, 15-16
  rules of, 7-9
  safety tips, 10-11
Hoods
  clearance and engine-swapping pitfalls, 60
  replacement panels, 32-33
Hood tachs, 35
Hoses, in cooling system, 109-110

## I
Idler arm, 159
Ignition systems, 101-105
  auxiliary ignition system accessories, 104
  backup systems, 105
  distributors, caps and rotors, 102
  function of, 101
  ignition coil, 102
  ignition wires, 102-103
  multiple-discharge spark system, 104
rev limiters, 105
spark plugs, 103-104
timing retard systems, 105
Induction system, 88-90
  air induction system, 88
  cold-air induction system, 88-89
  function of, 88
  nitrous oxide kit, 122-123
  ram-air induction system, 89-90
  as secondary cooling system, 113-114
  supercharger, 125-127
  turbocharger, 123-125
Instrument panels, 46-47
Intake ports
  recommended modifications, 73-74
Interior, 40-49
  audio equipment, 47-49
  carpets, 44
  changes to, 40
  consoles, 46
  dash pads, 44
  door panels, 43
  headliner, 43-44
  heating, ventilation and air conditioning system, 49
  instrument panels, 46-47
  roll cage, 49
  seatbelts, 43
  seats, 40-43
  sound deadener, 44
  steering column, 45-46
  steering wheel, 44-45
  video equipment, 49

## L
Lacquers, 24-25
Le Mans brace, 145
Lexan, 36
Lifters, 82
Lighting system, 180-183
  daytime running lamps, 182
  driving lights, 182
  fog lights, 182
  general maintenance, 180-181
  optional lighting equipment, 181
  replacement headlamps, 181-182
  third brake lights, 182-183
Limited-slip units, 138-139
Long block assembly, 52-85
  art of deception, 52-53
  camshaft, 77-79
  combustion chambers, 76-77
  connecting rods, 61-63, 71-72
  crankshaft, 59, 61, 71
  crate motors, 63
  cylinder heads, 73
decide what you want, 53-54
determine budget, 54-55
engine block, 56-59, 71
engine-swapping pitfalls, 60
intake and exhaust ports, 73-74
main, rod and cam bearings, 66-67, 72
nuts and bolts, 70-71
oil system, 67-70, 72
parts of, 52
piston rings, 64-66
pistons and wrist pins, 63-64, 72
recommended modifications, 71-85
short-block assembly, 55-56
valves, 74-76
valvetrain, 79-85

## M
Main bearings, 66-67, 72
Manual transmission
  close ratio vs. wide ratio, 133
  engine-swapping pitfalls, 60
  upgrading, 131-133
Master cylinder assembly, 173
Mirrors, power, 183
Molding, 37
Monochromatic, 29-30
Muffler, 118
Multiple-discharge spark system, 104
Multipoint fuel injection (MPFI), 100-101

## N
Nitrous oxide kits, 122-123
Nose cones, 34
Nuts
  long block assembly, 70-71

## O
Oil system, 67-70
  function of, 67
  modifying and preparing, 70
  oil, 69
  oil additives, 69-70
  oil coolers, 68-69, 112
  oil filters, 69
  oil pan and pickup, 67-68
  oil pump, 68
  recommended modifications, 72
  as secondary cooling system, 111-112
  selecting, 70
  windage trays and scrapers, 68
Oxygen sensors, 117

## P
Paint
  base coat/clear coat systems, 26-27
  choosing body/paint shop, 30
  color, 27-28
  enamels, 25
  flat look, 30-31
  good, cheap paint job, 28
  lacquers, 24-25
  monochromatic, 29-30
  paint schemes, 28
  primers, 25-26
  two-tone, 29
  types of, 24-27
  virtual paint job, 26
  waterborne paints, 25
Parts, services and supplies
  sources for, 186-188
Pedestal, 84-85
Piston pins, 63
Piston rings, 64-66
  function of, 64-65
  machining and preparing, 65-66
  recommended modifications, 72
  selecting, 65
Pistons, 63-64
  domed vs. flat-top, 64
  function of, 63
  machining and preparing, 64
  recommended modifications, 72
  selecting, 64
  types of, 63
Pitman arm, 158
Planning restoration, 14-21
  assessing your own skills, 19
  customizing option, 15
  financial considerations, 17-19
  high-performance restorations, 15-16
  how far to go, 16-17
  restoration guides, 14-15
  space for, 20-21
  time considerations, 19-20
Posi units, 138-139
Power door locks, 183-184
Power mirrors, 183
Power steering pump
  cooling system, 114
Power windows, 183
Primary exhaust (header) pipes, 117
Primers, 25-26
Proportioning valves, 173
Pulley system alignment
  engine-swapping pitfalls, 60
Pushrods, 82-83

## R

Radiator, 109
Radio, 47–49
Ram-air induction system, 89–90
Rear-axle assemblies, 137–138
   replacement, 140–141
Rear window defoggers, 184
Reinforcement plates, 146
Rev limiters, 105
Rocker arms, 83–84
Rocker shaft, 84–85
Rocker stud, 84–85
Rod bearings, 66–67, 72
Roll cage, 49
Roof modifications, 35–36
Rotors, 173–174

## S

Safety tips, 10–11
Scoops, 35
Seatbelts, 43
Seats, 40–43
   fix what you have, 40–41
   replace, 41–42
Secondary cooling system, 111–114
Shocks
   for drag racing, 155
   for high-performance street driving, 152
Short-block assembly, 55–56
   function of, 55
Sound deadener, 44
Spark plugs, 103–104
Spoilers, 34–35
Springs
   for drag racing, 155
   for high-performance street driving, 150–152
Stabilizer bar
   for drag racing, 155–156
   for high-performance street driving, 152–153
Starter, cooling system for, 113–114
Steering, 156–161
   alignment settings and tips, 159–161
   camber, 160–161
   caster, 160
   center/drag link, 158–159
   idler arm, 159
   Pitman arm, 158
   steering box, 158
   steering column, 157–158
   steering knuckles, 159
   steering stops, 159
   steering wheel, 157–158
   tie-rod adjustment sleeves, 159
   tie-rod ends, 159
   toe, 160
Steering column, 45–46
   telescoping, 45–46
   tilt, 45
Steering wheel, 44–45
Stripes, 29
Subframe connectors, 145
Superchargers, 125–127
Suspension, 146–156
   bushings, 149–150, 154
   control arm, 150, 154–155
   for drag racing, 153–156
   functions of, 146
   for high-performance street driving, 147–153
   shocks, 152, 155
   springs, 150–152, 155
   stabilizer bar, 152–153, 155–156
   tires and wheels, 147–149, 153–154
   torsion bar, 150–152
   traction device, 153, 156
   weekend warrior tips, 154

## T

Tappets, 82
Thermostat, 109
Throttle-body injection (TBI) systems, 100
Throttle linkage
   engine-swapping pitfalls, 60
Tie-rod adjustment sleeves, 159
Tie-rod ends, 159
Timing retard systems, 105
Tires
   balance, 156
   for drag racing, 153–154
   for high-performance street driving, 147–149
   name-brand, 147
   rotation, 156
   tire pressure, 156
Torque converters, 135–136
Torsion bar
   for high-performance street driving, 150–152
Traction device
   for drag racing, 156
   for high-performance street driving, 153
Transmission
   automatic, 134–135
   close ratio vs. wide ratio, 133
   clutches, flywheels and bell housing, 133–134
   engine-swapping pitfalls, 60
   manual, 131–133
   transmission mounts and engine-swapping pitfalls, 60
Trim, alterations to, 31–32, 37
Turbochargers, 123–125

## V

Valves
   recommended modifications, 74–76
   stock vs. aftermarket, 74–75
   valve guides, 75
   valve liners, 76
Valvetrain, 79–85
   cam drive sets, 81–82
   function of, 55, 79
   planning upgrade, 80
   pushrods, 82–83
   rocker arms, 83–84
   studs, shafts and pedestals, 84–85
   tappets/lifters, 82
   valve keepers, 85
   valve seals, 85
   valve spring retainers, 85
   valve springs, 85
Ventilation system, 49
Video equipment, 49
Vinyl tops, 35–36

## W

Waterborne paints, 25
Water pump, 108–109
Water Wetter, 110–111
Wheels
   for drag racing, 153–154
   for high-performance street driving, 147–149
   selecting for easy care, 149
   try before you buy, 151
Windage trays, 68
Windows
   Lexan, 36–37
   power, 183
   rear window defoggers, 184
   upgrades for, 36–37
Wiring harness, 180
   engine-swapping pitfalls, 60
Wrist pins, 63–64
   function of, 63
   recommended modifications, 72